DATE DUE

MAR 2 0 2003	
MAR 1 3 2003	
OCT 1 2 2004	
OCT 2 8 2004	

GAYLORD   PRINTED IN U.S.A.

The Health of Nations

The Health of Nations

Infectious Disease, Environmental Change, and
Their Effects on National Security and Development

Andrew T. Price-Smith

The MIT Press
Cambridge, Massachusetts
London, England

Set in Sabon by Graphic Composition, Inc., Athens, Georgia.
Printed and bound in the United States of America.

Library of Congress Cataloging-in-Publication Data

Price-Smith, Andrew T.
The health of nations : infectious disease, environmental change, and their effects on national security and development / Andrew T. Price-Smith
p. cm.
Includes bibliographical references and index.
ISBN 0-262-16203-2 (hc. : alk. paper) — ISBN 0-262-66123-3 (pbk. : alk. paper)
1. Communicable diseases. 2. Communicable diseases—Social aspects.
3. Communicable diseases—Political aspects. 4. National security. I. Title.
RA643 .P75 2001
306.4'61—dc21
2001032631

Contents

Acknowledgments

I owe a profound debt to the many teachers, colleagues, family members, and friends who gave me support, comments, and inspiration during the writing of this book. My thesis advisors, David Welch and Janice Gross Stein, allowed me the freedom to pursue an intellectual journey into uncharted waters, while providing a reliable compass to steer a clear course. Their critical insights, support, and encouragement were invaluable during my years at the University of Toronto, and the book is much stronger for their precision and prodding. I would also like to thank Robert Matthews, whose presence on the advisory team encouraged me to think beyond the limits of mainstream approaches and try to integrate findings from the "international relations" and "development" subfields into a greater whole. Additionally, I would like to thank Louis Pauly, Ronald Deibert, and Mark Zacher for their insightful comments and critiques. I would also like to thank Louis Pauly, Janice Stein, and David Welch for investing in the unusual idea of creating the Program on Health and Global Affairs in the Centre for International Studies at the University of Toronto. That program gave me intellectual space, an incentive, and funding to pursue this novel stream of research.

Many others deserve considerable credit for thoughtful discussions, insights, and comments. I am particularly indebted to Marc Levy and Roberta Miller, who made it possible for me to spend a valuable year at CIESIN/Columbia University doing post-doctoral research. I am also grateful to Geoffrey Dabelko of the Environmental Change and Security Project of the Woodrow Wilson Center in the Smithsonian for providing initial funding for my research. I owe a great debt to my colleague and friend Peter Zoutis for his guidance in the realm of statistical inquiry. I would also like to thank everyone at The MIT Press, and my editors Clay Morgan and Paul Bethge in particular.

Sources of generous financial support during my doctoral studies were the Environmental Change and Security Project of the Woodrow Wilson Center, a doctoral research fellowship from the Canadian Institute for Advanced Research, the Alexander Brady-MacGregor Dawson Doctoral Fellowship in political science and an Open Fellowship from the University of Toronto, the Sir Val Duncan travel award, a doctoral fellowship and office space from the Centre for International Studies, a University of Toronto Associates Travel Grant, an award from the Connaught Foundation for a conference on the issue of Health Security, and a doctoral research fellowship at the Boston University School of Public Health.

I want to express my deep gratitude to Cynthia Smith-McLeod and Jack McLeod, and to Richard Price Smith, for their support through all my years of graduate studies, and to the physicians who repeatedly patched me up such that I could actually write this (Dr. Gordon Greenberg in particular).

Finally, I wish to thank my dear grandparents, Margaret MacKay Thomas (dec.), Douglas Cameron (D. C.) Thomas, Marjorie Smith, and Harry Price Smith (dec.), for their constant support and guidance through the years. Their kindness, generosity, wisdom, and commitment have always been the greatest sources of inspiration to me. I dedicate this book to them.

The Health of Nations

Introduction

Ingenuity, knowledge, and organization alter but cannot cancel humanity's vulnerability to invasion by parasitic forms of life. Infectious disease which antedated the emergence of humankind will last as long as humanity itself, and will surely remain, as it has been hitherto, one of the fundamental parameters and determinants of human history.
—William H. McNeill, *Plagues and Peoples* (1976)

In the post-Cold War era, policy-making communities are increasingly confronted with significant new challenges to the security and prosperity of the citizens over which they preside. Policy makers must now address diffuse threats to state interests, particularly scarcity of renewable resources, degradation of the environment, and international migration.[1] Indeed, the rise of "low politics" to the national security agenda of the modern state requires that international relations theorists design new "tools of analysis": models that explain current developments (such as chronic state failure in sub-Saharan Africa) and that foreshadow dangers in order to guide policy. This book develops the idea that increasing levels of emerging and re-emerging infectious diseases (ERIDs) act as stressors on state capacity, undermining national prosperity and governance and in certain cases undermining national security.[2] Arguably, the primary raison d'être of international relations theory is to construct models that will assist in averting the premature loss of human life and productivity as a result of war. Indeed, as Thomas Hobbes claimed in *Leviathan,* it is the central function of the state to guarantee the physical safety of its citizens from both internal and external forms of predation. However, traditional concepts of security have ignored the greatest source of human misery and mortality: the microbial penumbra that surrounds our species. I argue here that it is time to consider the additional form of ecological predation wherein the physical security and prosperity of a state's populace is directly threatened by the worldwide phenomena of emerging and re-emerging infectious disease.[3] Throughout this study, I shall use the following definition:

Emerging infectious diseases are those whose incidence in humans has increased during the last two decades or which threatens to increase in the near future. The term also applies to newly-appearing infectious diseases, or diseases that are spreading to new geographical areas—such as cholera in South America and yellow fever in Kenya. [Re-emerging infections are] diseases that were easily controlled by chemotherapy and antibiotics, but which have developed anti-microbial resistance.[4]

The Scope of the Problem

Throughout recorded history, infectious disease has consistently accounted for the greatest proportion of human morbidity and mortality, surpassing war as the foremost threat to human life and prosperity.[5] Even in the era of modern medicine, states annually suffer much greater mortality and morbidity from infectious disease than from casualties incurred during inter-state and intra-state military conflict. According to the World Bank, of the 49,971,000 deaths recorded in 1990, infectious disease claimed 16,690,000 (34.4 percent), while war[6] killed 322,000 (0.64 percent).[7] This effect is even more pronounced in certain regions, sub-Saharan Africa in particular. According to UNAIDS, premature mortality in Africa from the HIV/AIDS pandemic is now much greater than war: 200,000 Africans died in warfare during 1998, while more than 2 million died of AIDS alone.[8] These statistics demonstrate the relative destruction wrought by disease when compared to deaths from military actions, and in terms of a ratio the deaths resulting from infectious disease compared to war are a significant 52:1 for this year. Infectious disease also accounts for more morbidity and mortality than any other single cause. According to the World Health Organization, of the 51 million worldwide deaths in 1993, ERIDs caused 16,445,000 (32.24 percent). By comparison, "motor and other-road vehicle accidents" accounted for 885,000 deaths (1.7 percent), and "homicide and violence" contributed to 303,000 deaths (0.6 percent).[9]

A recent report issued by the Centers for Disease Control and Prevention (an agency of the US government) warns that "the spectrum of infectious diseases is expanding, and many infectious diseases once thought to be controlled are increasing."[10] Since 1975, at least 33 new pathogens have emerged to compromise the health of the human species. There is no vaccine, therapy, or cure for most of these new diseases, and the ability to anticipate, prevent or control them is extremely limited.[11] The best-known examples of emerging pathogens are the human immunodeficiency virus, the Ebola virus, and the bovine spongiform encephalopathy prion[12]; however, owing to rapid microbial evolution, old scourges such as tuberculosis, cholera, and malaria are becoming increasingly resistant to our anti-microbial armamentarium and are spreading.[13]

It must be understood that infectious disease is one of humanity's oldest and direst enemies. Various diseases have wracked societies from time immemorial, resulting in panic, debilitation, and death. As such we must recognize that we are dealing with a very old adversary here, and it is rather our growing understanding of how pathogens interact with economic, political, and social factors that results in the sense of novelty in regards to the claim that infectious disease represents a threat to human development and security. Indeed, Thucydides, Gibbon, and Hippocrates recognized the enormous negative social and economic impact of infectious diseases on their respective societies. If infectious disease is seen as a "new" threat to political and economic stability it is largely because our species tends to exhibit the affliction of short generational memory.

Before the coming of the "golden age" of antibiotics and vaccines in the 1900s, diseases such as polio, smallpox, and tuberculosis were rampant around the world. These lethal and crippling diseases combined with cholera, malaria and plague to kill and disfigure millions. With the discovery of the cholera vibrio by the Prussian scientist Robert Koch in 1883, humanity began its scientific examination and war against infectious disease. Advances in public health have led to the general eradication of polio in the developed countries,[14] the near eradication of leprosy, and the selective incarceration of the various strains of variola (smallpox) within US and Russian military facilities.[15]

Throughout the twentieth century the human species witnessed successive triumphs over the microbial world, to the extent that prominent experts in medicine frequently spoke about the eradication of infectious disease and the subsequent need to close public health programs and training facilities during the mid 1970s. This hubris led in turn to complacency, and funding for research to control the spread of malaria (and other vector-borne diseases[16]) was cut drastically from the mid 1970s on. Firms and governments subsequently curtailed funding for improved antimicrobial agents and the development of vaccines. In the minds of many, the enemy was vanquished and the medical world turned to focus its wealth of resources on other health scourges such as cancer, heart disease and genetically transmitted infirmities.

The rapid emergence of HIV/AIDS in the early 1980s served as a wake up call to populations in Europe, North America, and Africa. Here was an example of a "new" zoonosis[17] rapidly expanding outward from its animal reservoir in Africa to infect millions around the world by the end of the twentieth century. Similarly, many other viruses began to emerge in the mid 1970s, including pathogens causing hemorrhagic fevers such as the Ebola viruses (subtypes Zaire, Machupo, and Junin) and respiratory viruses such as hanta. New strains of bacteria such as legionella, *Escherichia coli* 0157 H7, and cholera (El Tor) also began to conquer new territory. Adding to the threat is the phenomenon of increasing drug resistance in malaria, tuberculosis, vancomycin-resistant enterococci, and methycillin-resistant *Staphylococcus aureus*. At the start of the new millennium the human species finds itself again facing the resurgent specter of disease, and burdened with new zoonoses (such as HIV) that mutate rapidly, such that vaccine development has failed repeatedly and complex and expensive therapies are required to extend the life span of individuals with HIV/AIDS in the developed countries.

Critics of "health security" argue that microbes and humanity have coexisted for millennia, and besides the collapse of a few empires and the deaths of billions, the human species has managed to survive. All of this is true, yet the human species finds itself in a very different situation now: individuals can travel around the world rapidly by airplane, and overpopulation and the growth of megacities have created entirely new "disease pools" that will allow new pathogens to emerge and flourish. This brave new world is also witnessing human-induced worldwide environmental destruction that results in the release of pathogens from their ancient reservoirs in the core of rain forests, and where virulent new microbes result in the widespread destruction of aquatic life. Rapid worldwide changes may accelerate the diffusion, the lethality, and the resistance of the plethora of species within the microbial world, of which we have identified very few. While certain familiar diseases acquire resistance and conquer or reclaim territory within the human ecology, it is also likely that the natural processes of zoonotic transfer will persist and that new human pathogens will continue to emerge. The emergence of disease does not threaten the survival of the human species, yet it most certainly threatens the prosperity and stability of human societies and political structures.

In the spring of 1996 the World Health Organization declared a worldwide health emergency. The spread of ERIDs has become a crisis, and the WHO lacks the capacity to monitor, let alone contain, the various pandemics.[18]

Trends in Disease Emergence

It is important to remain as objective as possible in this type of inquiry as much hyperbole exists on the subject of health security courtesy of Hollywood, some journalists, and fiction writers. We must ask: Is the prevalence of a particular infectious pathogen rising within a given state's population and also worldwide? Is this pathogen moving into new geographic regions or reclaiming lost territory, and is it affecting new demographics within given societies?[19] What regions (if any) are particularly vulnerable to this resurgence in infectious disease, and where are the greatest increases in prevalence taking place? At what rates are these pathogens expanding their territories, both demographic and geographic?

The worldwide proliferation of HIV/AIDS since the early 1980s has resulted in a staggering amount of human suffering, death, debilitation, and fear. From the earliest genetic traces of HIV proto-DNA, culled from the tissues of a Zairean male who died in 1954,[20] the pathogen has spread relentlessly outward from its Central African epicenter to the Americas and Western Europe; it is now spreading rapidly through South Asia, East Asia, and Eastern Europe. The pace of the HIV/AIDS pandemic[21] continues to accelerate, with 33.4 million people now infected, 5.8 million new HIV infections annually, and 2.5 million HIV-induced deaths in 1998.[22]

The pace of infection increased by 24 percent from 1995 to 1998. The HIV pandemic now rivals (in absolute magnitude of mortality) the greatest plagues of history, including the Black Death of Medieval Europe and the influenza pandemic of 1918 (each of which killed more than 20 million). As of 2000, the HIV pandemic has resulted in the infection of more than 53 million and claimed the lives of 18.8 million, with 2.8 million HIV/AIDS-induced deaths and 5.4 million new infections in 1999. The number of AIDS orphans now stands at an astonishing 13.2 million, most of them in sub-Saharan Africa.[23] The contagion is relentless and continues to spread rapidly through South and Southeast Asia, Eastern Europe, and Latin America.[24]

The epicenter of the HIV pandemic is sub-Saharan Africa, where many states are now reporting adult HIV seroprevalence[25] levels in excess of 10 percent. Indeed, South Africa, Kenya, Uganda, Zambia, Namibia, Swaziland, Botswana, and Zimbabwe all have adult seroprevalence levels ranging from 10 percent to 36 percent of the population.[26] Botswana, for example, saw national adult HIV seroprevalence rise from 10 percent in 1992 to 35.8 percent in 2000, an increase of approximately 360 percent over 8 years.[27] South Africa saw cases of HIV infection rise from 1.4 million in 1995 to 4 million in 2000, with 20 percent of the population now infected.[28] This represents an increase of HIV seroprevalence in the South African population of more than 200 percent in 3 years. Some regions within these states have even higher infection levels: HIV prevalence in KwaZulu-Natal (a province of South Africa) has now reached 30 percent,[29] and Francistown in Botswana reports that 43 percent of its citizens are infected.[30] Certain towns along the border between South Africa and Zimbabwe have HIV seroprevalence of approximately 70 percent.[31]

The pandemic is expanding into Eastern Europe at an ever-increasing pace. In 1998, Russian Minister of Health Tatyana Dmitriyeva predicted that more than a million Russians would be winfected with HIV by 2000.[32] Ukraine has also seen HIV incidence soar from a modest 44 cases in 1994 to an astonishing 240,000 cases as of mid 2000, with a national adult HIV seroprevalence rate of 1 percent.[33] India is also seeing HIV spread throughout its vast population at a rapacious pace. In 1994 AIDS was practically unheard of in India; now more than 1 percent of all pregnant women tested throughout the country are HIV positive and more than 3.7 million Indians are now infected with HIV.[34] Disturbingly, by 1997 the epidemic was already firmly entrenched in regions of India such as Nagaland along the Burmese border (7.8 percent HIV seroprevalence), and nearby Manipur (over 10 percent HIV seroprevalence).[35] Indeed, except in the developed countries and in certain states such as Uganda and Thailand (which have seen some reduction in the rate of new infections), the HIV pandemic continues to expand at a rapid pace.

Tuberculosis (TB) has been making a steady comeback, and WHO declared the TB pandemic a world crisis in 1993. WHO estimates that "8.9 million people developed tuberculosis in 1995, bringing the total of sufferers to about 22 million, of whom about 3 million will have died in the same space of time."[36] Furthermore, in the absence of increased effectiveness and availability of measure to control the disease, more than 30 million TB deaths and more than 90 million new TB infections are forecast to occur by the turn of the century.[37] Tuberculosis is making inroads into the industrialized nations, particularly Canada and the United States, where it infects disadvantaged urban and incarcerated populations and then spreads throughout society. The incidence of TB in the United States is climbing. For example, in the US, reported cases had declined from 84,300 in 1953 to 22,200 in 1984, a drop of approximately 4 percent per annum. However, from 1985 to 1993, the number of cases increased by a cumulative 14 percent.[38] Similarly, Zimbabwe has reported massive increases in TB incidence, from 5000 cases in 1986 to 35,000 in 1997.[39] In 1999 the demographer Murray Feschbach noted that the incidence of tuberculosis in Russia was increasing rapidly, and based on estimates provided by the Russian Ministry of the Interior he predicted that tuberculosis would result in the deaths of 1.75 million Russians per year by 2000.[40]

Malaria continues its relentless expansion into former regions of endemicity.[41] For example, in 1989 malaria claimed 100 lives in Zimbabwe while debilitating many thousands; by 1997 malaria was responsible for the deaths of 2800 in that country, an astonishing rate of increase for a disease that was once thought to be under control.[42] Indeed, the best available estimates project that malaria currently claims 5000 lives every day in Africa, approximately 1.8 million deaths a year.[43] Estimates put the worldwide total number of deaths from malaria at upwards of 2.7 million per year and note that malaria debilitates as many as 500 million people a year.[44] The journalist Ellen Ruppel Shell claimed in 1997 that the incidence of malaria had increased by approximately 400 percent over the period 1992–1997 and noted that the disease had re-emerged in North America, moving from urban centers in California to Michigan, New York, and Toronto.[45]

Other pathogens are also re-emerging throughout the developing countries and are increasingly penetrating the porous borders of the industrialized states. For example, a new strain of cholera (designated 0139 El Tor) appeared in southeastern India in 1992. Now endemic throughout South and Southeast Asia, Africa, and South and Central America, it is spreading rapidly through Oceania. Moreover, mosquito-borne dengue fever has re-established itself in Central America and Mexico and is currently making inroads into the southern United States, particularly in Florida, Louisiana, and Texas.

Meanwhile, familiar pathogens continue to exact their toll on humanity with relentless vigor. For example, acute lower respiratory infections kill nearly 4 million children a year, and diarrheal pathogens such as adnovirus and rotavirus kill nearly 3 million infants a year. Viral hepatitis is another global scourge: at least 350 million people are chronic carriers of the hepatitis B virus, and another 100 million harbor the hepatitis C virus. According to WHO projections, at least 25 percent of these carriers will die of related liver disease.[46] Worse, many of the 10 million new cases of cancer diagnosed in 1995 were caused by viruses, bacteria, and parasites. The WHO calculates that at least 15 percent of all new cancer cases (1.5 million) result from exposure to infectious agents, and this percentage of disease-induced cancer mortality is estimated to increase as our knowledge of both infectious disease and cancer advances. New evidence is linking many other supposedly chronic or genetic diseases, such as heart disease and multiple sclerosis, to common infectious agents (chlamydia and herpes, respectively) that promote long-term disease processes within human hosts.[47] If cancer, heart disease, and multiple sclerosis are in fact induced by pathogens, the world's burden of infectious disease may be far greater than was once thought.

It is relatively easy to see that infectious disease is an agent of death throughout the developing countries. It is not often apparent that infection-induced mortality also has been on the rise in the developed countries. The United States, which is arguably the only superpower and which has enormous state capacity,[48] has seen a steady increase in mortality from infectious disease. In 1979 there were 15,360 deaths from infectious disease; in 1995 there were 77,128[49]—an increase of 502 percent.

The State of Knowledge on Health Security

The spread of lethal infections such as HIV and tuberculosis throughout significantly affected societies is comparable to the effects of a slow-acting neutron bomb that eliminates a large proportion of the population while leaving the infrastructure intact. The destruction of the population base of a country is a profound threat to that country's security, yet the literature on health security is particularly thin, likely because the concept is novel. The few works that do exist have succeeded in raising interest in the issue area and have spurred deeper analysis of the hypothesis that pathogens present a threat to national security and development.

In *The Coming Plague*,[50] Laurie Garrett claims that the worldwide proliferation of diseases poses a threat to the national security of the United States. Garrett reiterates this point in "The return of infectious disease,"[51] wherein she attempts to clarify the particular threat that ERIDs pose to the global interests and the national security of the United States. Garrett's claims have some inherent common sense, and she offers numerous examples of worldwide disease emergence. Her works are notable for having brought the issue of health security to the attention of the policy community and for having raised the possibility that the return of infectious diseases might constitute a significant threat to US interests.

Similarly, Dennis Pirages expounds on the power of infectious disease as a threat to state security and foreign policy interests. In a report titled Microsecurity: Disease Organisms and Human Well-Being, Pirages provides a blueprint for further investigations in the realm of health security and provides interesting anecdotal evidence that the resurgence of infectious disease is directly related to human-induced changes in the biosphere. This pioneering work (which had little to build upon) stands as a reasonable first attempt to clarify the issues, and it suggests many avenues for further research:

Infectious diseases are potentially the largest threat to human security lurking in the post-Cold War world. Emerging from the Cold-War era, it is understandably difficult to reprogram security thinking to take account of non-military threats. But a new focus that included microsecurity issues could lead to interesting cost-benefit thinking. Winning the war against new and reemerging infectious diseases requires both long-term and immediate changes. Educating people to think about this struggle with microbes in an evolutionary way is the ultimate solution. In the short term, policymakers need to understand the potential seriousness of the problem and reallocate resources accordingly.[52]

Though Pirages's and Garrett's theories are both intuitively persuasive, they fail to address whether the resurgence of disease will have different impacts on different societies. Do ERIDs constitute a direct or an indirect threat to states and/or societies, and do they threaten some regions of the world more than others? Recent advances have also been made by historians who have traced the effects of warfare and those of various pathogens on societies across the centuries. Though the evidence is largely (if not entirely) anecdotal, historians have done a good job of examining the effects of infectious disease on the societies in question over time.

As William McNeill proposed in *Plagues and Peoples,* microbes have been relentless adversaries of humanity and of human societies since time immemorial. Current anthropological evidence suggests that the expansion and collapse of various societies throughout history may have resulted in part from the transmission of lethal and/or debilitating pathogens. Thucydides's account of the eventual fall of Athens during the Peloponnesian Wars pays particular attention to the devastating effect that "the plague" had on Athenian governance, and by extension on the Athenian war effort:

> The bodies of the dying were heaped one on top of the other, and half-dead creatures could be seen staggering about in the streets or flocking around the fountains in their desire for water. For the catastrophe was so overwhelming that men, not knowing what would happen next to them, became indifferent to every rule of religion or law. Athens owed to the plague the beginnings of a state of unprecedented lawlessness. Seeing how quick and abrupt were the changes of fortune . . . people now began openly to venture on acts of self-indulgence which before then they used to keep in the dark. As for what is called honor, no one showed himself willing to abide by its laws, so doubtful was it whether one would survive to enjoy the name for it. No fear of god or law of man had a restraining influence. As for the gods, it seemed to be the same thing whether one worshipped them or not, when one saw the good and the bad dying indiscriminately. As for offences against human law, no one expected to live long enough to be brought to trial and punished.[53]

McNeill argued that the collapse of the Byzantine Roman Empire in the sixth century A.D. resulted from the "plague of Justinian," which was a consequence of the merging of two previously isolated disease "pools" via Asian trade routes (the Silk Road).[54] The Roman historian Gibbon recounts the devastation wrought by the plague as follows:

I only find that, during three months, five and at length ten thousand persons died each day at Constantinople; and many cities of the East were left vacant, and that in several districts of Italy the harvest and the vintage withered on the ground. The triple scourges of war, pestilence and famine afflicted the subjects of Justinian; and his reign is disgraced by a visible decrease of the human species which has never been regained in some of the fairest countries of the globe.[55]

The destruction of feudalism may have also resulted in large part from the recurrent waves of bubonic and pneumonic plague (i.e., the Black Death) that repeatedly swept Europe in the fourteenth and fifteenth centuries. Specifically, the continuing recrudescence of the plague throughout medieval Europe resulted in periodic waves of mass mortality that had a significant negative effect on the legitimacy of pre-existing structures of authority, particularly the Roman Catholic Church. As it became increasingly apparent that fealty to the Church had no effect on whether one succumbed to the plague, the legitimacy (and relevance) of the Church was called into question by Martin Luther and others. The resulting Protestant rebellion against the Catholic Church resulted in the Thirty Years' War and culminated in the Peace of Westphalia, which saw the establishment of the sovereign state as an empirical entity. In a very real sense, then, the Black Death was a progenitor of the entire system of modern sovereign states as we know it.[56] Alfred Crosby and William Denevan have constructed detailed accounts of how the merging of the American and European disease pools permitted the rapid and absolute conquest of the Americas by relatively modest European military forces. This demographic catastrophe, which derived from the importation of smallpox and other "civilized" diseases to an immunologically vulnerable population, resulted in the collapse of the Aztec and Incan empires and in centuries of subjugation of the Amerindian peoples.[57] McNeill puts the Amerindian population at the beginning of the conquest at approximately 100 million. "Starting from such levels," he writes,

population decay was catastrophic. By 1568, less than fifty years from the time Cortez inaugurated epidemiological as well as other exchanges between Amerindian and European populations, the population of Mexico had shrunk to about three million, . . . about one tenth of what had been there when Cortez landed.

Decay continued, though at a reduced rate, for another fifty years. Population reached a low point of about 1.6 million by 1620. [Such a disaster] carries with it drastic psychological and cultural consequences. Faith in established institutions and beliefs cannot easily withstand such disaster; skills and knowledge disappear. Labor shortage and economic regression was another obvious concomitant.[58]

Infectious diseases continued to play a role in the evolution of political entities. During the American Revolutionary War of 1776, smallpox helped to prevent the armies of the United States (then led by Benedict Arnold) from capturing Canada. Michael Oldstone writes:

During the Revolutionary War, the American colonial government sent an army to wrest Canada away from the English. Having captured Montreal, the colonial army, superior in number, marched on to engage in the conquest of Quebec City. But smallpox entered their ranks. The decimated American army, soon after burying their dead in mass graves, retreated in disorder from Quebec.[59]

Oldstone notes that 5500 of the 10,000 American troops originally involved in the campaign developed smallpox and died, which effectively nullified the American offensive and allowed Britain to maintain its stronghold in British North America.[60] Infectious diseases also occasionally caused significant governance problems for the fledgling United States, as became evident during Philadelphia's yellow fever epidemic of 1793:

Philadelphia had suffered a previous yellow fever plague in 1762, when a hundred had died, but now thousands were dying. Thomas Jefferson wrote from Philadelphia to James Madison in Virginia, telling about the fever, how everyone who could was fleeing and how one of every three stricken had died. Alexander Hamilton, the secretary of the Treasury, came down with the fever. He left town, but when he was refused entry to New York City, he turned to upstate New York. . . . There he and his wife were obliged to stay under armed guard until their clothing and baggage had been burned, their servants and carriage disinfected. Clerks in the departments of the federal government could not be kept at their desks. In the Treasury Department, six clerks got yellow fever and five others fled to New York; three sickened in the Post Office and seven officers in the Customs Service. Government papers were locked up in closed houses when the clerks left. By September, the American government came to a standstill.[61]

This abbreviated overview of the possible historical impact of infectious disease on the currents of history is merely intended to demonstrate to the reader the profound relationship between forces of the natural world, such as pathogens, and the evolution of human societies. It is not meant to imply that diseases have been the major force in defining the outcomes of all human history[62]; that would bring us to the shores of biological determinism, a conceptual model unlikely to take us very far. Yet it is fascinating to note that biological forces may, in fact, have had a significant effect on the broader outlines of human history, and will likely continue to do so as disease continues to proliferate around the world.

Effects of Infectious Disease on the State

Disease and Economic Productivity

The negative effects of infectious disease in the domain of economic productivity include reductions in gross domestic product (GDP) and in government expenditure per capita, decreases in worker productivity, labor shortages and increased absenteeism, higher costs imposed on household units (particularly on the poor), reductions in per capita income, reduced savings, and increases in income inequalities within a society that may in turn generate increased governance problems. Disease also generates disincentives to invest in the education of children, impedes the settlement of marginal regions and the development of natural resources, negatively affects tourism, and results in the embargoing of infected goods. The significant negative association between increasing disease levels and the economic prosperity of affected societies may lead to increases in absolute and relative economic deprivation in affected states. These effects, taken together, demonstrate how the worldwide resurgence of infectious disease is likely to produce negative outcomes for the prosperity of states.

Disease and Governance

The effects of a succession of epidemics upon a state are not measurable in mortalities alone. Whenever pestilences have attained particularly terrifying proportions, their secondary consequences have been much more far-reaching and disorganizing than anything that could have resulted from the mere numerical reduction of the population. Panic bred social and moral disorganization; farms were abandoned, and there was shortage of food; famine led to displacement of populations, to revolution, to civil war, and, in some instances, to fanatical religious movements which contributed to profound spiritual and political transformations.
—Hans Zinsser, *Rats, Lice, and History,* pp. 128–129

At the unit level, in the domain of governance, high disease incidence undermines the capacity of political leaders and of their bureaucracies to govern effectively as the infection of government personnel results in the debilitation and death of skilled administrators whose job it is to oversee the day-to-day operations of governance. Disease-induced mortality in human-capital-intensive institutions generates *institutional fragility* that tends to undermine the stability of a nascent democratic society. In Zimbabwe, an estimated 30 percent of urban adults in the 19–45 age group are HIV positive, and at least three government ministers have succumbed to AIDS in recent years.[63] Huguette Labelle of the Canadian International Development Agency estimated that as of 1999 about half the members of Zambia's armed forces and police forces were HIV positive.[64] When these individuals perish, there will be enormous negative repercussions for governance, with a likely corresponding rise in crime, civil unrest, and low-intensity violence.

Possible Systems-Level Effects

Disease exerts a negative effect on state capacity at the unit level that may produce pernicious outcomes at the systems level. Within the domain of economics, as disease produces a significant drag on the economies of affected countries, we may see chronic underdevelopment, which may in turn exert a net drag on world trade and impair prosperity. In all likelihood, owing to the nature of spiral dynamics inherent in the relationship between infectious disease and state capacity, countries with low initial state capacity will suffer greater losses over time from increasing prevalence of infectious disease within their populations. Owing to this negative spiral effect, disease's negative influence on the economic development of states may exacerbate the economic divide between developed and developing countries. Furthermore, the negative effects of infectious disease are not confined to the developing countries. At the systems level, trade goods from disease-affected regions (for example, British beef and Hong Kong chickens) may be subject to international embargo. As infectious agents continue to emerge and re-emerge, and as agricultural crops and animal stocks become increasingly infested, we should expect that presumably infected trade goods from affected states will be embargoed, tourism to affected regions may decline, and economic damage to affected states will likely intensify.

This volume demonstrates that increasing levels of disease correlate with a decline in state capacity. As state capacity declines, and as pathogen-induced deprivation and increasing demands upon the state increase, we may see an attendant increase in the incidence of chronic sub-state violence and state failure. State failure frequently produces chaos in affected regions as neighboring states seal their borders to prevent the massive influx of disease-infected refugee populations. Adjacent states may also seek to fill the power vacuum and may seize valued territory from the collapsing state, prompting other proximate states to do the same and so exacerbating regional security dilemmas. An example of this is the wide-ranging conflict in Central Africa, where the collapse of governance in Zaire (and continuing insurgency in the successor state, the Democratic Republic of the Congo) has generated a wider conflict wherein the mercenary armies of Uganda and Rwanda seek to topple the fragile government in Kinshasa. Conversely, military forces from Angola, Namibia, Zimbabwe, Sudan, and Chad have been deployed to the Democratic Republic of the Congo to crush the rebels and their masters in Kigali and Kampala.[65] Indeed, the chaos in Central Africa was so great in early 2000 that Ugandan and Rwandan forces turned on each other in their quest to dominate the ungoverned regions of the eastern DRC.

As the incidence and the lethality of diseases increase, deprivation will mount and state capacity will decline, generating more stress and greater demands on government structures. Thus, as disease prevalence increases and the geographical range of pathogens expands, the number of failing states may rise, necessitating increased humanitarian intervention by UN security forces to maintain order in affected regions. As we have seen from recent experiences in sub-Saharan Africa, the UN is unlikely to have a lasting effect in restoring order to areas where disease incidence and lethality remain high.

It is necessary to differentiate between *outbreak events* and *attrition processes*,[66] as these two phenomena may have dissimilar but significant effects at both the unit level and the systems level. Examples of classic outbreak scenarios are the bubonic plague in Surat, India (autumn 1994) and the Ebola epidemic in Zaire (spring and summer 1995). These outbreaks generated worldwide fear and panic, mass out-migrations, military quarantines to contain the exodus of infected persons, and economic damage. Attrition epidemics (HIV, tuberculosis, malaria) do not generate as much fear and out-migration as "outbreak" events, but they typically result in greater actual human morbidity and mortality and in significant long-term economic and social erosion. The distinction between these two types of phenomena is important because outbreak events and attrition processes result in somewhat different outcomes, depending on how much fear and deprivation are generated by the pathogens in question.

Disease emergence must be understood not as a singular isolated "event" but rather as a part of biological evolutionary processes taking place at the macro level. The concept of emergence as a process is important because "outbreak events" such as the plague in Surat and Ebola in Zaire are really just disease manifestations that rise above the lower threshold of our perceptions long enough to alarm us momentarily. It is best to think of these "outbreaks" as akin to upward spikes on a stock market graph. While the spikes penetrate the threshold of our perception and then retreat, the process of disease evolution and emergence continues to grow inexorably. Eventually, disease emergence, prevalence, and lethality may cross a crisis threshold, and we may be forced to take serious action to reduce the microbial threat. The only question is whether we will still have the ingenuity we will need to deal with the problem when we realize its significance and its magnitude. At the moment, the world has the wealth and the social and technical ingenuity to check the spread of disease and to limit the destruction and misery that most infectious diseases cause. Yet dealing with the proliferation of so many diverse pathogenic agents will require enormous amounts of political will, international cooperation, continued regime consolidation, and a significant redistribution of resources from the developed to the developing countries.

Case Studies

At this point, let us briefly examine several cases wherein outbreaks or resurgences of infectious diseases have contributed to economic damage and problems of governance, both at the intra-state level and at the inter-state level. One preliminary conclusion we can draw from the emergence of V-CJD (a lethal new variant of Creutzfeldt-Jacob disease), Ebola, HIV, and plague is that people are extremely risk averse when it comes to the emergence of new pathogens, and that emergence tends to generate paranoia, hysteria, and xenophobia that may affect the foreign policy of a state by impairing decision making. The recent epidemic of pneumonic plague (*Yersina pestis*) in western India during the autumn of 1994 gives an idea of how the psychological effects of infectious disease (in the form of outbreak events) may affect both an afflicted state's *state capacity* and its relations with its neighbors.

The very rumor of plague in Surat prompted a frenetic exodus from the city of more than 300,000 refugees, who might then have carried the pestilence with them to Bombay, to Calcutta, and as far as New Delhi.[67] Out of fear, Pakistan, Bangladesh, Nepal, and China rapidly closed their borders to both trade and travel from India, and some of those countries went so far as to restrict mail from India. As the plague spread, concern mounted. International travel to and trade with India became increasingly restricted. On September 22, 1994, the Bombay stock exchange plunged, and soon thereafter many countries began to restrict imports from India, placing impounded goods in quarantine or turning them back at the border.[68] As the crisis worsened, the Indian army was called in to enforce a quarantine on the affected area in western India, and doctors who had fled Surat were forced to return to work under a threat of legal prosecution by the government. In the aftermath of the epidemic (which killed 56 people), the Indian government was notified by the Centers for Disease Control in Atlanta that the *Yersina pestis* bacillus was an unknown and presumably new strain. This information was interpreted by Indian authorities as "unusual," and they promptly accused a group of rebel militants (the Ultras) of procuring the bacillus from a pathogen-manufacturing facility in Kazakhstan with the object of manufacturing an epidemic in India. This paranoia on the part of Indian officials resulted in the transfer of the inquest of the epidemic from public health authorities to the Department of Defense.[69] Beyond the acrimony that the plague fostered between India and its Islamic neighbors, the economic toll of the plague has been estimated at a minimum of $1.8 billion in lost revenue from exports and tourism.[70] While the loss of $1.8 billion may seem trivial, to a developing state like India it represents a serious blow to the economy with negative repercussions throughout numerous sectors. As we can see in the Surat event and the continuing BSE scare in Europe, infectious disease and the irrational behavior that it generates may worsen relationships between states and/or cultures.[71]

The continuing concern in Europe over BSE ("Mad Cow Disease") has resulted in the embargo of many beef-derived British products and has dictated the culling of a significant proportion of the UK's beef stocks. And the BSE scare has frightened the British population. Scientists talk about the possibility that thousands of Britons are infected with a new variant of Creutzfeldt-Jacob disease (human BSE), and in 1996 the UK's European partners summarily banned the import of British beef (in violation of EU trade law).[72] The European Union's ban on British beef products was lifted in 2000, but France continues to defy the EU by maintaining its ban on British beef products. At the beginning of 2001, relations between London and Paris remain strained over the persistent inability of these states to address the BSE issue and to limit the spread of the BSE prion pathogen in cattle.

Synopsis

In chapter 1, I summarize the concepts surrounding the emergence and the re-emergence of infectious disease, name the pathogens that are currently making inroads against our best anti-microbial defenses, discuss theories of microbial evolution that are relevant to my study, set forth my research method, and detail the various data sources and collection techniques I used. In addition, I examine the important roles of facilitating variables such as war, famine, poverty, international migration, and misuse of medical technologies as "disease amplifiers" in altering the flow of viral traffic. I then lay out the model I propose to test in order to determine whether infectious disease has a measurable effect on state capacity over time.

In chapter 2, I present the empirical findings of my quantitative analysis of the relationship between ERIDs and state capacity at the national, regional, and worldwide levels. I also examine the worldwide correlations between the various individual indicators of state capacity and ERIDs, in order to note the strength of the correlations and scale of the effects. Most important, I demonstrate the empirical existence of an asymmetrical feedback loop between population health and state capacity, with population health exhibiting a greater downstream effect on state capacity than vice versa.

In chapter 3, I analyze the effects of infectious disease on economic productivity at the state level. Here I combine empirical epidemiological data with economic indicators, and, using basic techniques of statistical analysis, I note the deleterious effect of disease on economic productivity. The profound negative effect of ERIDs on societal prosperity at the individual and macro levels will result in increasing relative and/or absolute deprivation in severely affected countries. In this chapter I employ process-tracing techniques to track the likely relations between health and development at the microeconomic, sectoral, and macroeconomic levels of a state's economy. I also demonstrate how the proliferation of ERIDs may compromise the economic development and productivity of a state, generate absolute economic deprivation at the micro level, and (in a severely affected country) increase the economic gap between the wealthy and the poor.

In chapter 4, I examine the recent emergence of infectious diseases as a security issue for the world policy community. I consider the claim that infectious disease constitutes a verifiable threat to national security and state power. I also address how the continuing emergence and proliferation of pathogens may affect regional political stability, peacekeeping, and international regimes, briefly examine certain political barriers to effective response at both the national and the international level, and examine the feasibility of locating the threat of infectious disease as a security issue within the pre-existing paradigm of environmental security.

In chapter 5, I employ process-tracing techniques to delineate the probable causal relationships among various facets of worldwide environmental change (climate change, extreme weather, patterns of land use, etc.) and the resulting likely effects on the prevalence and lethality of microorganisms and on the distribution and infectivity of their vectors (e.g., mosquitoes and rats). The balance of the evidence presented in this chapter demonstrates that humanity's increasing negative impact on the biosphere will accelerate the emergence of pathogens into the human ecology while simultaneously altering the distribution of currently known pathogenic organisms. Continuing worldwide change may also alter the infectivity and the lethality of both known and emerging microorganisms.

In the conclusion, I examine and analyze the evidence I gathered for this project, present my findings, develop policy recommendations based on these findings for dissemination to the foreign policy and international development communities, and delineate pathways for further scientific inquiry into the associations between the biological and political realms.

1

Bridging the Gap: A Consilient Methodology

A balanced perspective cannot be acquired by studying disciplines in pieces; the consilience among them must be pursued. Such unification will be difficult to achieve. But I think it is inevitable. Intellectually it rings true, and it gratifies impulses that arise from the admirable side of human nature. To the extent that the gaps between the great branches of learning can be narrowed, diversity and depth of knowledge will increase. They will do so because of, not despite, the underlying cohesion achieved. The enterprise is important for yet another reason: It gives purpose to intellect. It promises that order, not chaos, lies beyond the horizon. Inevitably, I think, we will accept the adventure, go there, and find what we need to know.

—Edward O. Wilson, "Back from chaos," *Atlantic Monthly,* March 1998

Over the centuries, science has been the cornerstone of the majority of advances in human well-being, including Hippocrates's initial inquiries into the nature of contagion and human health, Charles Darwin's hypotheses on the evolution of species, Louis Pasteur's development of antimicrobial vaccines, and Robert Fogel's thesis that reductions in morbidity and mortality impelled the industrialization of the United Kingdom.[1]

Recent research has focused on the study of complex relationships between political systems and influences on state capacity such as environmental change, resource scarcity, population, and migration.[2] In this chapter, I discuss methodological principles for the study of complex systems which include health (and specifically infectious disease, a heretofore unexamined major determinant of state capacity).

In this book I test the hypothesis that increasing levels of infectious disease exert a negative effect on state capacity, such that increases in disease prevalence result in correspondingly diminishing values of state capacity.

Thus, I seek to both understand the causal role that disease plays in determining state capacity, and determine the causal relations between the two variables. I also seek the answers to the following two questions: Can infectious disease negatively affect state capacity by generating political, economic and social instability? If so, how does infectious disease contribute to political instability and underdevelopment?

The biologist Edward O. Wilson concedes that the narrow compartmentalization of science in the nineteenth and twentieth centuries provided many benefits to society, but he bemoans the modern lack of consilience as detrimental to the greater pursuit of scientific knowledge in the years to come. Consilience is defined as the "jumping together of knowledge as a result of the linking of facts and fact-based theory across disciplines to create a common groundwork of explanation."[3] Francis Bacon, who took all knowledge to be his province, also recognized the need for the practitioners of divergent scientific disciplines to communicate their findings across the artificial boundaries between the branches of human knowledge.[4] As the Enlightenment thinkers of seventeenth- and eighteenth-century Europe understood, there is a profound need to seek scientific insight in the form of consilience at the nexus points where the disciplines meet. If we reject consilience, we risk continuing the fragmentation of knowledge; indeed, we risk creating a scientific "Tower of Babel" wherein we are incapable of communicating across disciplines.

As figure 1.1 illustrates, pathogenic microbes exist independently throughout the earth's biosphere, with the vast majority of them present in the zoonotic pool and outside of the human ecology. In a very real way these pathogens are independent variables and are exogenous to the state; they are truly global phenomena, existing at the system level. These pathogens may cross over from the zoonotic reservoir into the human ecology at any time with emergence being governed largely by the principles of chance zoonotic transmission and microbial evolution.

After pathogenic agents enter the human ecology (and become endogenized within human societies), their effects are augmented by intervening variables that I call *disease amplifiers* (DAs). These DAs generate changes in viral traffic that result in emerging and re-emerging infectious diseases (ERIDs). Thus, ERIDs are a product of the synergy between the inde-

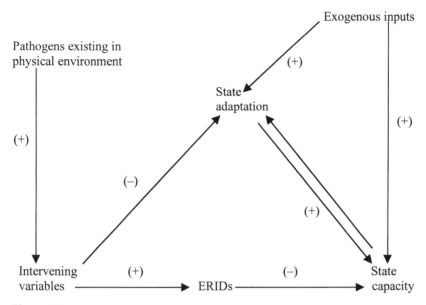

Figure 1.1
Probabilistic relations among variables.

pendent variable (pathogens) and intervening variables (such as global environmental change). These ERIDs may, in turn, have pervasive negative effects on state capacity (the dependent variable). Those effects may range from poverty to social and political instability.

States and societies may use adaptive resources to mitigate the effects of disease on state capacity. A state's ability to adapt is limited by several factors. First, the initial level of state capacity will determine the scale of the adaptive resources that may be mobilized to deal with the ERID problem. States with higher initial capacity will therefore have greater technical, financial, and social resources to adapt to crises. Furthermore, state adaptation will be affected by exogenous inputs of capital and by the social and technical ingenuity of international and non-governmental organizations. Finally, state adaptation may be compromised by certain outcomes generated by intervening variables, such as war, famine, and ecological destruction.

Exogenous inputs take the form of inputs of capital, technology, and ingenuity into the state from external sources such as international organizations and bilateral foreign aid. Exogenous inputs such as capital infusions (from the World Bank and other sources) also directly affect the resources available to a state when responding to crises, and therefore augment the efficacy of adaptation responses.

There is a positive association between state capacity and state adaptation because greater initial capacity means that there are more human, economic, and technical resources endogenized within the state that can then be mobilized to deal with various crises. The lower the initial value of state capacity (SC), the lower the amount of resources that can be mobilized to offset the crisis. This relationship operates in a reciprocal spiral such that greater initial capacity leads to greater adaptive ability, which should in turn reduce the ERID-induced loss to state capacity. Thus, in general, states that have lower SC when diseases afflict them suffer much greater SC losses than states with high initial SC. The only means by which states with lower SC can ameliorate the effects of disease is through exogenous inputs that give low-SC states both greater resources to mobilize and advanced tactical knowledge to deal with the crisis.

Although other relations between variables in the model are also important, in-depth examination of these associations is beyond the scope of this book. The relationship between pathogens in the state of nature and intervening variables is not examined for several reasons:

• Pathogens in the state of nature are generally assumed to be static in population size.

• The potential lethality and transmissibility of these pathogens is unknown until they cross over as zoonoses, are affected by intervening variables, and become ERIDs.

• The manner in which exogenous pathogens become endogenized within the human ecology has been extensively documented by epidemiologists.[5]

Research on these causal relationships is best left to microbiologists, epidemiologists, and public health scientists. I will, however, address the effects of global environmental change on projected and current shifts in disease prevalence, infectivity, and lethality (and concurrent shifts in vector distribution and behavior) in chapter 4.

In the work reported here, I did not test other certain relationships outlined in the causal diagram. Specifically, I did not analyze the relationship between the intervening variables and the dependent variable, outside of the context of infectious disease. Variables such as war and natural disasters undoubtedly have an independent and logically negative effect on state capacity, but these questions fall outside of the purview of this study. Similarly, the effects of war, environmental degradation, disasters, and migration will undoubtedly have negative effects on state adaptation, but these questions too are beyond the scope of the present book.[6] Such questions are, however, excellent avenues for further research. Finally, I did not test the relationship between exogenous inputs and state capacity. This relationship is very much in need of elaboration, although researchers working on the State Capacity Project of Peace and Conflict Studies at the University of Toronto have begun to untangle the problem.

The Dependent Variable

The political scientist Thomas Homer-Dixon has developed a coherent and comprehensive definition of state capacity, which I adopt with minor revisions.[7] He defines the state as "the government, including the center, provincial, and local levels." The term *capacity* generally refers to power and/or capability. Thus, *state capacity* refers to the capability of government. I define state capacity as one country's ability to maximize its prosperity and stability, to exert *de facto* and *de jure* control over its territory, to protect its population from predation, and to adapt to diverse crises. This definition of state capacity corresponds roughly to Homer-Dixon's multi-dimensional definition of state capacity, which consists of one set of variables that measures the state's intrinsic characteristics and a second set that measure relations between state and society. These variables are laid out in table 1.1.

State capacity includes the concept that states are entities that evolve over time.[8] This evolution occurs because of the changing factors that affect state power: land, resources, population, health, technology, human capital, prosperity, and so on. Thus, when we quantify state capacity, we should attempt to measure changes in value on a continuous scale.

For the purposes of this book, I have ranked these attributes of state capacity as follows, in order of decreasing importance:

fiscal resources

human capital

reach and responsiveness

resilience

legitimacy

autonomy

coherence

instrumental rationality.[9]

This ranking emphasizes the primacy of fungible economic power and the importance of human capital and adaptive ability in dealing with the problematic trans-boundary and internal issues of the post-Cold War era, such as global environmental degradation, crime, weapons proliferation, ethnic violence, and pathogen proliferation. Although the factors listed above are all captured by the definition of state capacity, I will operationalize state capacity by using a limited set of empirical indicators.

State capacity is the capability of government, and its level determines the state's ability to satisfy its most important needs: survival, protection of its citizens from physical harm as a result of internal and external predation, economic prosperity and stability, effective governance, territorial integrity, power projection, and ideological projection. Aside from this normative definition, which articulates the dynamic nature and needs of the state, the notion of state capacity should be quantifiable such that we can determine diachronic variance in the value of SC, determine the relative SC of states with respect to one another, and measure correlations between empirical indicators of SC and other parameters (population, resource scarcity, health, technology, environmental degradation) that may affect the value of SC.

Then how can we quantify state capacity in a meaningful way? One answer is to develop a core set of cross-national statistical indicators of SC that may then be correlated against diverse independent variables. To that end, I will correlate the following five statistical indicators for SC against two proxies for ERIDs in order to determine the empirical associations between SC and infectious disease. All indicators of SC are logically valid measures of the performance of government functions.

Table 1.1
Indicators of state capacity identified by Project on Environmental Scarcities, State Capacity and Civil Violence, University of Toronto (http://utl1.library.utoronto. ca/www/pcs/state/keyfind.htm).

Indicators of the state's (or its components') intrinsic characteristics

Human capital	The technical and managerial skill level of individuals within the state and its component parts.
Instrumental rationality	The ability of the state's components to gather and evaluate information relevant to their interests and to make reasoned decisions maximizing their utility.[a]
Coherence	The degree to which the state's components agree and act on shared ideological bases, objectives, and methods; also, the ability of these components to communicate and constructively debate ideas, information, and policies among themselves.
Resilience	The state's capacity to absorb sudden shocks, to adapt to longer-term changes in socio-economic conditions, and to sustainably resolve societal disputes without catastrophic breakdown. The opposite of brittleness.

Indicators of relations between the state (or its components) and society

Autonomy	The extent to which the state can act independently of external forces, both domestic and international, and coopt those that would alter or constrain its actions.
Fiscal resources	The financial capacity of the state or of a component of the state. This capacity is a function of both current and reasonably feasible revenue streams as well as demands on that revenue.
Reach and responsiveness	The degree to which the state is successful in extending its ideology, socio-political structures, and administrative apparatus throughout society (both geographically and into the socio-economic structures of civil society); the responsiveness of these structures and apparatus to the local needs of the society.
Legitimacy	The strength of the state's moral authority—the extent to which the populace obeys its commands out of a sense of allegiance and duty, rather than as a result of coercion or economic initiative.

a. *Utility* may be defined locally; i.e., it may reflect the narrow interests of the component and not the broader interests of the state or society.

Gross national product, per capita (current prices, 1980 US dollars)   measures the total value of goods and services produced by the state on an annual basis. The sum is divided into a per capita measure and standardized for current prices. This is a logically valid measure of SC because high values of this variable require an effective regulatory apparatus. This variable measures such aspects of state capacity as fiscal resources, autonomy, reach and responsiveness, resilience, human capital, and legitimacy.

Government expenditure (standardized currency, per capita)   measures the total fiscal outlay of the state on the provision of services (e.g. education, health care) to its population on an annual basis. This is a logically valid measure of SC because the more a state spends, the more it is able to generate a revenue stream and it is able to fund a greater number of programs. This variable measures such aspects of state capacity as reach and responsiveness, legitimacy, resilience, and human capital.

School enrollment ratio, secondary   measures the percentage of the total population of possible secondary school attendees actually receiving secondary education on an annual basis. This is a logically valid measure of SC because education is a core state function and it is expensive. This variable measures such aspects of state capacity as human capital, legitimacy, resilience, reach and responsiveness, fiscal strength, and autonomy.

Net long-term capital inflow (standardized currency, per capita)   measures the influx of economic capital into the state from exogenous sources over time. It is reasonable to assume that rational investors will seek to put their capital into politically stable and economically productive societies, and thus this variable indicates a measure of state stability and prosperity. This indicator also gives an idea as to external perceptions of state stability. This indicator is a logically valid measure of SC, because countries with low SC cannot guarantee a stable investment climate and a decent rate of return. This indicator measures such aspects of state capacity as fiscal resources, resilience, reach and responsiveness, autonomy, and legitimacy.

Military spending per soldier, per capita (standardized currency)   measures the government's annual fiscal outlay for defense. The aggregate amount is then divided by the number of soldiers in the defense forces, and then the value is adjusted so that it reflects a per capita ratio. The per capita, per soldier ratio allows a relative ranking of the amount spent on the training of soldiers and expenditures on weapons systems. High spending per soldier per capita is an indication of high-tech, capital-intensive, and training-intensive armed forces that can only be created and maintained by states that possess high state capacity. This is a logically valid measure of SC because only a state with high SC can afford to fund an efficient, high-quality defense.

These SC indicators provide us with a large data set for the period from the early 1950s to 1991. This allows us to analyze the diachronic associations between variables in order to generate conclusions about the evolutionary path of individual states. It also provides us with enough data so that we can run diachronic correlations to examine the significance of the association between variables. These five SC indicators, the data from 1950 to 1991, and the 20 countries in the sample provide us with a rich set of data points that increase both the significance and certainty of our correlations and the inferences we draw from them. Ultimately, we will be able to run multivariate regressions controlling for the independent variable (e.g., infant mortality), and an intervening variable (e.g., agricultural production) against an aggregate indicator of SC that comprises the five indicators noted above.

Political scientists who advocate interpretivist or postmodern analyses may reject the utility of attempts to quantify SC, particularly using this set of economic, demographic, and social indicators. However, the sociologist Jack Goldstone argues that empirical social indicators are important in revealing the nature of societal instability, and that economic and demographic pressures have been the core sources of rebellion and revolution over the centuries.[10]

In this book, I adopt the perspectives that Goldstone and Homer-Dixon adopted in their attempts to measure the associations between empirical indicators and SC and, beyond that, to employ qualitative means to determine the causal linkages between variables. However, some aspects of Homer-Dixon's model of SC remain difficult to quantify, particularly instrumental rationality and coherence. It may be possible to explore such non-quantifiable aspects of SC during the case studies that will eventually follow. Perhaps social scientists will need to develop new types of quantitative indicators in order to explore the mathematical associations between these aspects of SC and the various parameters that drive these dependent variables.

The Independent Variable

For the purposes of this book, I provide a specific definition of ERIDs: pathogen-induced human illnesses that have increased in incidence, lethality, transmissibility, and/or expanded their geographical range since 1973.[11] Specifically, this includes previously unknown pathogenic agents such as HIV, *E. coli* 0157 H7, Ebola virus, hantavirus, prions, hepatitis A–C), and antibiotic-resistant pathogens such as vancomycin-resistant enterococci and methycillin-resistant *Staphylococcus aureus*. Re-emerging diseases are those pathogen-induced human illnesses that were previously controlled or declining in range and/or incidence but are now expanding in range, incidence, drug resistance, and increasing transmissibility and/or lethality. Some of the re-emerging diseases are tuberculosis, malaria, cholera, dengue fever, yellow fever, schistosomiasis, rotavirus, adnovirus, and amebic dysentery. Pathogens are defined as viral, bacterial, parasitic, or proteinic organisms or agents that live in a parasitic and debilitating relationship with their human host.

It is important to think of pathogens as exogenous variables—natural agents that for the most part exist independent of humanity and for all intents and purposes have one central goal, survival. As zoonoses, microbes have historically crossed over from disease pools that exist in animal reservoirs.[12] Human activity frequently alters flows of viral traffic, and these novel pathogens may subsequently take root within the human ecology. The major human pathogens listed in table 1.2 qualify as ERIDs under this definition.

These various microbes and parasites constitute the majority of pathogens that generate significant morbidity and/or mortality in human beings. Intending to test the effect of these diseases on state capacity, I would want to employ detailed state-specific information on national prevalence rates. In an optimal scenario, standardized prevalence rates for each major disease would be available for each and every country, from 1950 to the present day. Owing to the many measurement problems detailed below, such data are not available. Since very few states collect comprehensive and composite national pathogen-specific disease prevalence indicators, we must employ proxies that measure the overall burden of disease on selected states in the sample.[13]

For many of the developing countries, even basic mortality and morbidity data are lacking. For example, many countries do not collect malaria prevalence on an annual basis; in fact, the World Health Organization has stopped collecting plasmodium prevalence statistics for all of sub-Saharan Africa because the disease is ubiquitous. Furthermore, some countries (e.g., China and Myanmar) fail to report the occurrence of certain diseases (such as HIV) owing to a lack of political transparency. (Certain governments go to great lengths to keep information about human-rights abuses and other domestic matters from being documented and to keep such information from being released to the world at large.) To complicate matters further, many diseases carry a social stigma, and physicians are often pressured into falsifying diagnoses in order to "preserve face" for the afflicted. The greatest difficulty arises from the fact that in some countries reports of disease incidence are often sporadic, and often only cover a few of the many diseases that compromise the health of that state's population. All told, these problems make it extremely difficult for the analyst to conduct a statistical analysis of the aggregate effect of infectious diseases on the stability and productivity of a society (i.e., its state capacity).[14] However, limited incidence and prevalence rates are available for selected diseases in certain industrialized countries. These data sources are listed in table 1.3, which also indicates their availability.

Given these measurement problems, the social scientist must employ indicators that serve as comprehensive proxies to measure the burden of disease-induced morbidity and mortality on societies. Such an indicator must be highly sensitive to the societal burden of disease, it must be standardized across states, it must be available for most countries over a broad span of time, and it must be comprehensive (such that it reflects mortality associated with the most prevalent pathogens in a society). In view of these requirements, the most valuable comprehensive empirical indicators

Table 1.2
Pathogenic agents and associated diseases.

Human immunodeficiency virus (AIDS)
Mycobacterium tuberculosis (tuberculosis)
Plasmodium malariae, falciparum, vivax, ovale (malaria)
Hepatitis A, B, and C viruses
Vibrio cholerae (various subtypes, notably El Tor)
Flavivirus DEN-1,2,3,4 (dengue fever)
Filoviruses (e.g., Ebola virus)
Escherichia coli 0157 H7
Flaviviridae viruses (yellow fever)
Phlebovirus bunyaviridae (Rift Valley fever)
Schistosoma mansoni, haematobium, japonicum (schistosomiasis)
Onchocerca volvulus (river blindness)
Mycobacterium leprae (leprosy)
Dracunculus medinensis (dracunculiasis)
Hantaviruses (hantavirus pulmonary syndrome)
Leishmania chagasi (leishmaniasis)
Shigella dysentaeraie, flexneri, boydii, sonnei (shigella)
Corynebacterium diptheriae (diphtheria)
Rotavirus (severe diarrhea)
Respiratory syncytial virus and parainfluenza virus type 3 (ARV)
Adnovirus (severe diarrhea)
Legionella pneumophila (Legionnaires' disease)
Cryptosporidium parvum (cryptosporidosis)
Human T-lymphotropic virus 1 and 2
Toxin-producing strains of *Staphylococcus aureus* ("flesh-eating disease")
Borrelia burgdorferi (Lyme disease)
Prion proteins (Creutzfeldt-Jacob disease)
Helicobacter pylori
Enterocytozoon bieneusi
Cyclospora cayetanensis (cyclosporosis)
Herpesvirus simplex 1 and 2 (herpes)
Treponema pallidum (syphilis)
Haemophilus influenzae type B (meningitis)
Ehrlichia chaffeensis (ehrlichiosis)
Encephalitozoon hellem
Bacillus anthracis (anthrax)
Tyrpanosoma cruzi (Chagas' disease)
Bartonella hemsellae
Encephalitozoon cuniculi

Table 1.2 (continued)

Neisseria gonorrhoae (gonorrhea)
Influenza virus A, B, C (flu)
Bordetella pertussis (pertussis)
Borrelia burgdorferi (Lyme disease)
Salmonella typhi (typhoid)
Yersinia pestis (plague)
Chlamydia trachomatis (chlamydia)
Trypanosoma brucei rhodesiense, gambiense (African sleeping sickness)
Arenavirae; sub-types Tacaribe, Junin, Machupo, Lassa, Guanarito, Sabia (viral hemorrhagic fevers)
Clostridium botulinum (botulism)
Camplyobacter jejuni
Giardia lamblia
Entamoeba histolytica (amebic dysentery)
Filarial nematodes (filariasis)

---

are *infant mortality per 1000 children* and *life expectancy (in years) at birth.* Data for these two proxies are available for the vast majority of countries over the period 1950–1991.

Infant mortality (IM) is arguably the best indicator for measuring the aggregate burden of disease on a population, as it incorporates mortality from every disease pathogen, including syncytial respiratory viruses, diarrheal rotaviruses and adnoviruses, and the pathogens that cause malaria, tuberculosis, and measles. IM measures the effect of infectious disease on the first tail of the demographic distribution of a population: children up to age 5. With the notable exception of HIV/AIDS, IM is the best indicator for measuring the burden of disease across divergent societies because the majority of global disease-induced mortality shows up in the 0–5-year age sector of the demographic curve. In layman's terms this means that the vast majority of human beings killed by infectious diseases are children below the age of 6. Indeed, Murray and Lopez demonstrate that more than 70 percent of global infant mortality is attributable to microbial and/or parasitic infection.[15] Therefore, fluctuations in IM over time typically result from the changing prevalence and lethality of infectious diseases within specified populations.

Table 1.3
Availability of disease data.

US	HIV/AIDS, anthrax, botulism, brucellosis, chlamydia, cholera, diptheria, *E. coli* 0157 H7, gonorrhea, leprosy, encephalitis, hepatitis (A,B,C), legionella, Lyme disease, malaria, measles, pertussis, plague, salmonellosis, shigellosis, streptoccal disease (invasive group A).	Weekly state and territorial disease-specific incidence data available since 1984[a]
Australia	HIV/AIDS, malaria, hepatitis (B,C), tuberculosis, cholera, diptheria, dengue fever, typhoid, syphilis	Annual national prevalence data available since 1985[b]
France	Diarrheal diseases	1990–1999
	Influenza	1984–1999
	Measles	1985–1999
	HIV	1989–1999[c]
Canada	HIV, salmonella, influenza, tuberculosis, hepatitis (B,C)	Incidence by province/month 1995–1999[d]
Global aggregate	HIV seroprevalence	1997,[e] 1998, 1999, 2000

a. Statistics for these diseases are available for the US in Morbidity and Mortality Weekly Report. Stats are given in weekly, and four week totals, according to state and overall national incidence. National prevalence levels are not similarly available for these years. See http://www.cdcc.gov/epo/mmwr/mmwr.html and http://www.cste.org.

b. See http://www.health.gov.au/pubhlth/cdi/nndss/year013.htm and http://www.avert.org/canstatr.htm.

c. Available in graph format at http://www.b3c.jussieu.fr/sentiweb. Exact values are not given.

d. See Health Canada's Communicable Disease Reports 1995–2000 at http://hwcweb.hwc.ca/hpb/lcdc/publicat/ccdr.

e. Current estimates of overall HIV prevalence at the national level for 1997 are regarded as reasonably accurate. See http://www.unaids.org/highband/document/epidemio/june1998/fact_sheets/pdfs/botswana.pdf.

Nowhere in the literature can one find a specific statement that IM is a good proxy for a comprehensive snapshot of the burden of infectious diseases on societies. This is so because medical scientists usually study a single disease pathogen and because they have never thought about the relationship between disease and state capacity. In other words, they have never had to argue that IM is a good comprehensive indicator, although most medical scientists I have spoken with agree that this is an empirically valid claim.[16]

Murray and Lopez quantify the aggregate burden of disease by including both long-term and sporadic morbidity, and disease-induced mortality. They use the measurement tool of the disability-adjusted life year (DALY) in order to look at the true effects of various diseases, injuries, and risk factors on affected populations. "DALYs," they note, "provide a common metric to aid meaningful comparison of the burden of risk factors, diseases, and injuries," and "the primary indicator used to summarize the burden of premature mortality and disability (including temporary disability) is the disability-adjusted life year (DALY)." "DALYs," they explain, "are the sum of life years lost due to premature mortality and years lived with disability adjusted for severity."[17]

Murray and Lopez demonstrate that the top two contributors to the global burden of disease are communicable diseases affecting children, namely lower respiratory infections (LRIs) and diarrheal diseases primarily caused by the adno and rotaviruses and amebic agents. Tuberculosis, measles, malaria, and pertussis also came in as the seventh, eighth, eleventh, and twenty-third greatest contributors to global death and disability, and all these illnesses are found at relatively higher levels in the youngest tail of the population curve, namely the 0–5-year age group. Murray and Lopez note that infectious disease constitutes the single greatest burden on human populations relative to all other causes of death: ". . . the three leading contributors to the burden of disease are lower respiratory infections, diarrheal diseases, and perinatal disorders. Together with measles, the eighth largest cause of burden, these childhood diseases account for 25 percent of the whole burden of premature mortality and disability."[18]

Disease-specific DALY measurements for all states over a significant period of time would be tremendously valuable to this type of project.

However, until this information is available we must use proxies that are extremely sensitive to the burden of disease. Thus, IM's sensitivity to the comprehensive societal burden of disease makes it the best available indicator for measuring the effects of ERIDs on state capacity over broad stretches of time and across a wide range of cultures and societies.[19]

However, IM will not include the entire burden of certain pathogens (such as HIV) that predominantly affect the central part of the demographic distribution curve, namely those in the 15–45-year age range. *Life expectancy* (LX) measures the total burden of disease on a specified population, covering the complete demographic curve (including both tails of the population distribution). Unfortunately, the mortality shown under LX does not replicate IM's extreme sensitivity to infectious disease, as it includes mortality resulting from accidents, suicides, and violence. However, rapid increases in the prevalence of HIV within a society will show up only in the 15–45-year portion of the demographic distribution. Thus, although the effects of the HIV pandemic on national productivity and stability are unlikely to show up in IM, they may be observed through the use of LX. "From independence in 1980 and for nearly a decade thereafter," Madavo writes, "Zimbabwe made stunning health advances. But AIDS has already erased all the life expectancy gains made since then. Further, if the worst projections come to pass, by about 2010 life expectancy will return virtually to where it stood the day I was born, in what was then Southern Rhodesia, half a century ago."[20]

Preston's detailed international statistical analyses of the major causes of mortality decline are valuable in determining the major causes of death over time. Preston expanded on previous work done with Keyfitz and Schoen[21] to examine the relative importance of various causes of death using data for 165 populations from various countries and across various time periods.[22] Preston found that in the twentieth century at least 60 percent of global mortality was in fact attributable to infectious disease. Vallin notes that Preston's estimates of the influence of disease on mortality were on the low side, as the remaining 40 percent of mortality was attributed to ill-defined causes and did not include pathogen-induced cancers. Vallin et al. also attribute considerable weight in diachronic measures of global mortality to infectious diseases, and provide evidence that reinforces Preston's conclusions.[23] Of course, variation will occur in the causes of death between different populations and over time, but diachronic and randomized statistical studies such as this should minimize those possible skewing effects. LX is therefore required as a supplementary indicator to give us an accurate picture of the effects of the HIV pandemic.

Recent medical advances have shown that some pathogens play major roles in inducing many forms of human cancer. "Up to 84 percent of cases of some cancers are attributable to viruses, parasites or bacteria. WHO estimates that more than 1.5 million (15 percent of the new cases occurring each year) could be avoided by preventing the infectious disease associated with them. About 1.2 million cancer cases (20 percent) in developing countries and 363,000 (9 percent) in developed countries are attributable to infectious agents."[24] These cancers include stomach cancers (*Helicobactor pylori*), cervical cancers (human papilloma virus), liver cancers (hepatitis B and C), AIDS-related cancers (numerous pathogens), Burkitt's lymphoma (Epstein-Barr virus), Hodgkin's disease (Epstein-Barr virus), and bladder cancer (schistosomiasis).[25] Therefore, LX compliments IM because it measures mortality resulting from both the global HIV pandemic and pathogen-induced cancers.

LX displays an inverse statistical association with IM, such that there is a significant negative correlation (−0.935) between IM and LX for the 20-country sample over the period of the analysis (1950–1991). Thus, it can be stated with assurance that IM and LX are generally "mirror proxies" that both measure the burden of disease on populations but have an inverse relation to one another. This is useful because these indicators allow us to analyze the burden of disease on the complete demographic distribution of the population within a state. IM and LX also provide us with a comprehensive snapshot of the burden of disease over a relatively broad span of time and reflect the decline over time in morbidity and mortality as measured since the early 1950s, which can then be measured against changes in state capacity over the same time period.

One caveat in regard to the use of IM and LX as proxies for ERIDs is that, although they give us an excellent idea of ERID-induced *mortality* over the decades, they only give us indirect knowledge of the *morbidity* associated with ERIDs over the same time period. For example, malaria-induced mortality will show up in IM, but we can only guess at the ratio of individuals killed as to the proportion of the population that is debilitated. This also varies according to the lethality of the disease, as malaria generally debilitates far more people than it kills, whereas HIV generally debilitates and kills those who it affects. Regrettably, a majority of states lack the ability to accurately track disease-induced morbidity within their populations. Therefore, I cannot employ the 20-country sample to ascertain the effect of specific disease-induced morbidity on state capacity. At this point in time, only a very small subset of industrialized nations (Canada, the United States, the United Kingdom, Australia) keep limited statistics on productivity lost to diseases such as HIV. Obviously, studies that measure morbidity and mortality-generated DALYs (e.g., Murray and Lopez's *Global Burden of Disease*) will be of enormous value if differentiation of pathogen weight by country per year is included in future editions. Notably, the WHO has begun to publish reasonably accurate statistics on HIV seroprevalence rates within national populations for most countries of the world for the year 1997.[26]

Theories of Causation

There is . . . a good deal of evidence that bacteria became capable of producing infections millions of years ago, and there is no reason to doubt that man from the very beginning suffered from infectious disease; and at the time when mankind had reached the period of the earliest historical records, infectious diseases of many varieties already existed. . . .
—Hans Zinsser, *Rats, Lice, and History*, p. 106

Microbial pathogens evolved from the primordial soup of life millions of years ago, along with other single-cell creatures, and thus have existed far longer than humans (much less human societies), preying on all manner of flora and fauna over the eons.[27] Thus, pathogens predate humanity, tend to exist independent of humanity in nature, and will continue to exist whether the human species endures or not. Therefore, pathogens should be seen as independent phenomena that can be affected by human actions that may then alter microbial transmissibility and lethality.

There has been some debate regarding the lines of causation in the complex relationship between ERIDs and state capacity. The principal objection voiced is that infectious disease is in fact *endogenous* and therefore caused by pre-existing human-induced conditions such as poverty, war, famine, and environmental degradation.[28] The fact of the matter is that these social conditions are actually *intervening variables* that (depending on their individual nature) may increase the transmission capacity, the infectivity, or the lethality of pathogenic agents within affected regions. However, the argument that these conditions *create* the pathogens in question is incorrect. There is significant archeo-epidemiological evidence that infectious pathogens antedated the arrival of humans (and multi-cellular life in general) and that their rapid and unpredictable evolution is guided to a large degree by complex and chaotic ecological interactions and is occasionally accelerated by human actions.[29]

The concept of pathogen emergence is critical, since new disease agents tend to exhibit the greatest virulence when first introduced to immunologically naive populations. To paraphrase Morse and Schluederberg: "Emerging" pathogens are disease agents that either have recently appeared in the population or are rapidly expanding their range.[30] Morse argues that known disease agents are "only a fraction of the total number that exist in nature."[31] Furthermore, "newly evolved" disease agents are most often the descendants of antecedent strains; this is a function of Darwinian evolution through processes of natural selection. "Given these constraints of organic evolution, then, there are fundamentally three sources (which are not necessarily mutually exclusive): (1) evolution of a virus *de novo* (usually the evolution of a new viral variant); (2) introduction of an existing virus from another species; (3) dissemination of a virus from a smaller population in which the virus might have arisen or originally been introduced."[32] Similar processes also hold for bacteria, for parasites, and perhaps for infectious proteins (prions).

However, according to Morse, pathogen evolution is not the most significant driver behind the emergence of "new" infectious diseases: ". . . over the period of recorded history . . . 'emerging viruses' have usually not been newly evolved viruses. Rather, they are existing viruses conquering new territory. The overwhelming majority are viruses already existing in nature that simply gain access to new host populations."[33] These pathogens exist in nature in disease "reservoirs" and may jump the species barrier to humanity from the "zoonotic pool" (i.e., the vast plethora of diseases that pervade all niches of life in the biosphere). Although the chance that any one particular "zoonosis" is pathogenic to humans is relatively low, the sheer magnitude of infectious agents that exist in the zoonotic pool makes the "emergence" of human pathogens more likely. Morse coined the term *viral traffic* to demonstrate how infectious agents move between species and between individuals, and he argues that most outbreaks of "new" diseases are attributable to patterns of viral traffic. Viral traffic is altered by changes in the ecological, economic, and social environment. I refer to such changes as *facilitating variables,* insofar as they may exacerbate the lethality and the transmission of ERIDs and thereby intensify the negative effects of ERIDs on state capacity.

Intervening Variables

The spread of [leishmaniasis] is accelerated by development programs such as road building, dam construction, mining and forest exploitation that bring increasing numbers of people into contact with the disease vectors. Another factor enhancing spread is the haphazard growth of major urban centers which creates conditions that increase transmission risks. A third factor is the movement between countries or regions of migrant workers who themselves act as vehicles for the disease.
—*World Health Report 1996*, p. 50

It is important to keep in mind that the effects of infectious disease on state capacity are distinctly nonlinear, as pathogens are subject to such intervening variables as ecological disruption (chapter 4), increased human mobility, poverty, technology, war, and famine. These factors often alter the flow of viral traffic, thereby producing epidemics and pandemics and affecting their courses. In this way, these intervening variables act as *disease amplifiers.* Augmentation of the virulence and the transmissibility of pathogens by these disease amplifiers generates epidemic and/or pandemic disease. These facilitating variables generally exacerbate the ERID threat, but it is important to understand the dynamics between ERIDs and these facilitating variables, as they frequently influence one another in a complex web of mutual and nonlinear interactions.[34] These interactions require the fulfillment of certain conditions that, together, are sufficient to produce ERIDs. Here I will list these facilitating variables briefly, in descending order of importance.

Migration

International and intra-state migration is playing a significant role in the diffusion of pathogens. Travelers to and from previously isolated regions may distribute previously contained microorganisms into the global population, many of whom will be immunologically naive to the emerging infectious agent. Furthermore, travelers from the developed countries bring pathogens from their sojourns abroad back into their home countries where these agents may eventually take hold within that new population. Rapid advances in transportation technologies (the ship, railway, car, airplane) have accelerated this process of global pathogen diffusion, and the profusion of international travelers for both recreational and business purposes is bound to exacerbate the problem of ERID dissemination in the coming decades.[35]

Trade

Throughout history, trade has been implicated in the worldwide diffusion of pathogens. For example, both flavidirae viruses (e.g. yellow fever) and their principal vectors (*Aedes aegypti* mosquitoes) were transmitted to the Americas from Africa courtesy of the slave trade. The mosquito vectors fed on the blood of infected slaves during the transit and then spread the contagion throughout the New World.[36] Additionally, the Pan American Health Organization believes that the recent transmission of El Tor cholera to South America was facilitated by a Chinese freighter which jettisoned its contaminated bilge water into a Peruvian harbor, after which the disease spread through seafood products and tainted regional water supplies.[37] Additionally, infected foodstuffs and livestock transported across borders have resulted in dissemination of the BSE prion to beef cattle throughout the European Community. Infected berries (cyclospora) from Guatemala were implicated in a large outbreak of diarrheal disease throughout North America during the summer of 1996.

Human Ecology

The actions of individuals within a society, and societal habits at large can also influence the course of viral traffic and lead to the emergence and reemergence of infectious disease, both regionally and globally. For example, the annual pilgrimage to Mecca is generally associated with the proliferation of cholera among the pilgrims, who then bring the bacilli back to their home countries. Other modes of behavior, particularly sexual promiscuity and the use of illicit narcotics, assist in the diffusion of many disease agents. Furthermore, the burgeoning magnitude, density, and distribution of human populations facilitates the dissemination of pathogens—particularly since, once population levels reach a new threshold, "disease pools" within those populations become large enough to sustain new infections.[38]

Misuse of Antimicrobial Drugs

Consistent misuse of antimicrobial drugs in developed and developing countries has resulted in the emergence of drug-resistant strains of parasites, bacteria, and viruses. For example, the Thai-Burmese border region is practically uninhabitable owing to the recent spread of drug-resistant strains of malaria throughout the region. Meanwhile, in the developed countries, bacterial strains such as vancomycin-resistant enterococci and methycillin-resistant *Staphylococcus aureus* are spreading throughout hospital systems, and multi-drug-resistant tuberculosis is spreading through the marginalized portion of the population. The problem stems from the fact that organisms develop drug resistance through evolutionary pressures when the pathogens in question are exposed to antimicrobial drugs. These antimicrobial agents kill susceptible bacteria, which in turn generates evolutionary pressures on those members of the species that possess a gene that provides resistance to that particular drug. These resistant microbes then expand their population to fill the ecological niches of other pathogens that were eradicated by the same antimicrobial agents.[39] Although physicians use the current drug of last resort (vancomycin) extremely sparingly, tremendous amounts of similar drugs are distributed through domestic animal feed, which results in the spread of resistant bacteria throughout the animal world. These resistant pathogens may then cross the species barrier to cause zoonoses in human populations.

Disasters

In addition to the above facilitating variables, both natural and human-induced disasters (e.g. earthquake, flood, war, famine) may also affect viral traffic in a manner that leads to disease amplification through increased transmission and/or lethality of the infectious agents and which may result in epidemics and even pandemics. The worst case of this occurred during 1918 and 1919, when the global movements of armies served as vectors for the distribution of influenza and typhus. The resulting "Spanish flu" pandemic claimed an estimated 20 million lives, and the typhus pandemic claimed nearly as many, dwarfing the mortality caused by military action.[40]

Similarly, a regional breakdown of food distribution that results in famine will also deplete the health of a population, such that infectious agents may have an easier time colonizing their hosts and may cause greater morbidity and mortality in the weakened population, as it takes the weakened host a longer time to mount an effective immune response to the invading pathogens. The greatest historical example of this synergy between famine and disease is the Great Hunger that struck Europe in 1845. This catastrophe was generated by a fungus (*Phytophthora infestans*) that destroyed the potato crops, caused massive starvation and governance problems in Ireland, and led to terrible outbreaks of typhus and cholera in affected regions, which were subsequently carried overseas to North America and Australia via infected immigrants who fled the devastation in the Old World.[41]

Data

The data I use in this analysis are taken from a random sample of 20 countries: Botswana, Brazil, Colombia, Ethiopia, Haiti, Iceland, India, Italy, Japan, Kenya, Malawi, Netherlands, Norway, Peru, Rwanda, Saudi Arabia, South Africa, Tanzania, Thailand, and Uganda. The country data used for the statistical analysis are from the World Bank Statistical Tables data set, the WHO's World Health Reports, and the UNAIDS statistical country fact sheets. Primary and secondary source epidemiological and microbiological data were obtained from the Population and International Health, and Countway Libraries at the Harvard School of Public Health. I have also used the ProMed global disease surveillance system, the US Bureau of the Census HIV Surveillance sentinel site data base, the World Health Reports, the Morbidity and Mortality Weekly Reports, journals such as *Science, Nature, The Economist,* the *Journal of the American Medical Association, New England Journal of Medicine, The Lancet, Emerging Infectious Diseases,* and numerous health-related Internet sites[42] as core data sources.

For the purposes of the quantitative analysis, I employ standardized diachronic global indicators of state capacity, such as GNP per capita and school enrollment. These measures run from circa 1960 to 1991 and are all obtained from standardized World Bank data. IM and LX data are generally available for the full sample from 1952 to 1991.

The data I use allow for the variation of both dependent and independent variables while allowing for some control over potentially confounding variables. In order to avoid selection bias in the analysis, I have randomly selected cases hoping for significant variance in the independent variable between the countries in the sample. Thus, I compare indicators from highly developed temperate states such as Iceland (with low ERID intensity) with those of tropical countries like Rwanda (with high ERID intensity). This eliminates the bias that might result from selecting only developing countries with low state capacity.

Randomizing the selection process is crucial to reducing bias. Before randomization, certain states had to be selected out of the population for inclusion in the sample because they could not satisfy the minimum data requirements. Countries such as Sierra Leone and Liberia that lacked a minimum standard of data for the selected indicators were excluded from the sample because their inclusion would have been of low utility. The sample was drawn randomly from the remainder of countries that met the minimum data requirements for the relevant indicators, even if there were occasionally significant gaps in the annual data. This randomization was generally successful, as the countries in the sample represent all climatic regions of the world, all levels of development, and most continents. This random selection of the sample should suffice to reduce the probability of bias to a reasonable minimum. Furthermore, the size of the sample ($N = 20$) is also sufficient to do a good job in terms of obtaining a "snapshot" of the correlations between the variables on a comparative cross-national basis.

Despite the advances of modern ERID surveillance technologies, there remain data problems that other scientists must consider and try to circumvent. First, a lack of transparency frequently hinders the collection of accurate field data and the dissemination of accurate statistics within the country in question. As well, political barriers may rise in order to hide the true state of affairs (i.e., the massive debilitation of the population by a stigmatized disease such as HIV/AIDS). This was commonplace with HIV/

AIDS prevalence in sub-Saharan Africa in the 1980s, and throughout South and East Asia in the 1990s. The intra-state dissemination of accurate statistics is also problematic because of the lack of technological diagnostic and communication infrastructure, and manpower, in many of the rural hospitals. Furthermore, regional authorities may have interest in exaggerating the infectious disease situation in order to receive greater amounts of aid, or conversely downplaying the gravity of the situation to avoid unfavorable reviews from their superiors and to prevent the loss of revenue from trade and tourism. This political manipulation and suppression of accurate statistics makes it difficult to get accurate disease-specific data out of many states, particularly those with authoritarian regimes (such as Zimbabwe, China, Myanmar, and the former Zaire). The greater political transparency of democratic nations allows better data collection.

At the systems level, data collection is improving as nascent global surveillance regimes such as ProMED report outbreaks and occurrences daily via electronic media. As mentioned above, the World Health Organization and the US Centers for Disease Control issue quarterly reports on the prevalence of certain notifiable infectious pathogens, and weekly updates such as the Morbidity and Mortality Weekly Report offer tallies of disease incidence within the US population. However, for the majority of the population of states the data are marred by certain inaccuracies at this level as well. First, it is very hard to obtain accurate data on the incidence of and/ or prevalence levels for certain pathogens (e.g., those that cause hepatitis) within specified national populations (e.g., Sierra Leone). Sentinel data are available for selected diseases in selected communities on various dates, but it is difficult at best to derive national seroprevalence levels from these scattered studies.[43] Second, in some cases the agencies that are expected to monitor prevalence levels have simply bowed to the enormous prevalence in certain regions and stopped collecting data on selected pathogens. This is the case in sub-Saharan Africa, where the WHO has admitted that it no longer has the capacity to monitor the prevalence of malaria. Finally, there are occasional scientific inconsistencies in the collection, interpretation, and dissemination of data from the various reporting sites to the WHO. Though the WHO attempts to harmonize the data as much as possible, it is likely that some inaccuracies will remain in the data. As local, regional, state, and WHO infrastructure improves over time, the data will improve.

Despite certain deficiencies noted above, it is possible to derive generalizable and empirically testable scientific hypotheses from the data. To ensure that my conclusions are simultaneously demonstrable and accurate, I employ statistical data analyses. Statistical analysis of empirical data provides correlations that confirm or disconfirm the various hypotheses, and it allows me to discriminate between potentially important causal linkages and ones that are marginal to the subject at hand. Quantitative techniques can indicate whether there are any potentially causal relationships.

I employ bivariate statistical analysis, using Pearson's correlation coefficient to test the strength of the hypothesized relationships between the variables. The correlations that I derive from these tests indicate the strength of the association between two variables between the values of 1 and –1, and they give the significance of the association in view of the size of the sample. Significance indicates a real and important relationship between the variables and suggests that these findings can be generalized to the entire population.

The use of t tests (tests of statistical significance) on Pearson's r (the correlation) tells whether the correlation differs significantly from 0. The above tests can either support or refute the respective hypothesis with 95 percent confidence. The margin of error based on sample size is ±10 percent. Regardless of the sample size, an α of at least 0.6 is required before it can be said that there is a strong correlation among the observed variables that constitute the computed SC variable. Having computed α as 0.64, we can attest to the firm inter-correlation between the five SC indicators that constitute the aggregate SC measure.

These statistical analytic processes can tell us much, but they cannot firmly specify the nature of the causal relations within the model. Initially, I correlate the independent and dependent variables for the entire period 1950–1991. I then lag the variables to see if the strength of the correlation changes downstream. Theoretically, disease-induced mortality and morbidity are likely to impair state capacity, but this effect is not likely to be immediate. For example, after colonizing a human host, pathogens often take differential amounts of time to generate disease within that host. Thus, the debilitating effects of certain diseases with long germinating periods (such as HIV/AIDS, hepatitis B, and hepatitis C) will logically grow stronger with the passage of time. Therefore, I lag the variables to see if the downstream effect of disease on state capacity grows or diminishes with the passage of time.

Infectious diseases' pronounced negative effect on child life expectancy will reduce the downstream availability of healthy and capable workers available to a society. By lagging the variables, I analyze the import of the differential time lag between increasing ERID values and state capacity outcomes. This will help in the prediction of downstream economic and political effects of rising disease levels, in the formulation of more effective policy measures to deal with the problem of infectious disease, and in the prediction of downstream state capacity on the basis of current population health indicators.

Since the lack of sufficient quantifiable data rules out factor analysis of the relationships among the variables, it is necessary to explore the question of causality using available non-quantifiable data. Process-tracing case studies make it possible to distinguish spurious correlations from probably causal relationships, and can help us get a handle on certain interactions that are difficult to correlate because of operationalization and measurement problems. Mapping the complex threads of causation among the independent, intervening, and dependent variables illuminates the probable causal connections among them. For example, although statistical data analysis may demonstrate a high correlation between the burden of disease on a society and that society's productivity, scientists must utilize process-tracing techniques to determine the causal linkages between the variables and the appropriate mechanisms of causation.

Falsifiability

The hypothesis that increasing infectious disease prevalence diminishes state capacity is easily falsifiable. It will be shown false if increasing levels of disease do not correspond to declining state capacity or if falling infectious disease rates do not correlate with increasing state capacity. Since most of the available data are from the most successful anti-microbial era in human history (1950–1991), one can test the hypothesis empirically by looking at how declining disease-induced morbidity and mortality has affected state capacity since World War II. If the inverse relationship holds between proxies for disease prevalence and state capacity, one can generalize that the negative association between infectious disease and state capacity will also hold over time and across geographical regions. Thus, if the hypothesis is correct, one can argue that the expanding pandemics of HIV/AIDS, tuberculosis, malaria, and hepatitis (to name just a few) will have negative implications for state stability and development in the future.

In view of the theorized empirical centrality of disease as a stressor on state capacity, any major threat to a population's health jeopardizes a state's prosperity, governance, and survival over the long term. Thus, infectious disease can be seen as a significant factor in the breakdown of governance, poverty, and state failure in seriously affected regions. Conversely, and of equal importance, declining disease rates should lead to greater state capacity and, by extension, to greater prosperity, stability, and power in healthier areas, such as the temperate zones.

My analysis of the effect of infectious disease on the populations of states and its resultant effect on states' prosperity and stability obviously has broad ramifications for most (if not all) human societies. If we can understand the relationship between rising levels of ERIDs and the associated decline in prosperity and stability of states and societies, then we gain the ability to address the break points in the chain of causation in order to formulate more effective policies for the surveillance and containment of infectious disease. We may also gain some ability to predict future events and processes that may be detrimental to a state, such as disease-related socio-economic decline, insurrection, rebellion, and (in extreme cases) state failure.

Population health is a significant *parameter* of state capacity. A parameter is defined as a phenomenon that exerts a general effect on another dependent phenomenon. In this sense, broadly defined constructs such as population, environment, poverty, and (in particular) population health may generate significant positive or negative effects on state capacity. The central concerns of any study of parameters of state capacity are to determine the importance of each parameter relative to the others and to determine how each parameter affects state capacity. Bias-free systematic studies of the other parameters will have to be completed before it will be possible to determine the relative weights of the various parameters as they affect state capacity.

2

A Smoking Gun: Preliminary Statistical Evidence

From independence in 1980 and for nearly a decade thereafter, Zimbabwe made stunning health advances. But AIDS has already erased all the life expectancy gains made since then. Further, if the worst projections come to pass, by about 2010 life expectancy will return virtually to where it stood the day I was born, in what was then Southern Rhodesia, half a century ago.

—Callisto Madavo, World Bank vice-president, in a speech titled AIDS, Development, and the Vital Role of Government (June 30, 1998)[1]

In the wake of Hiroshima and the widespread destruction of human life and property during the world wars, theorists of international relations had ample empirical evidence that war and weapons of mass destruction held the potential to cripple governments and eviscerate entire societies. With the rise of "low politics" in the post-Cold War era, political scientists are faced with a number of novel (and often competing) claims concerning the changing nature of threats to national and international security. More often than not, a lack of empirical data and analysis has plagued the evolution of new domains of international relations theory, and this is particularly true of nascent subfields such as the environmental, population, information, and health security paradigms. This chapter provides substantial empirical evidence that there is in fact a strong and significant negative association between infectious disease rates and state capacity, buttressing the claim that health security is a viable new realm for scientific exploration and analysis.

Despite the minor data problems that force us to rely on proxies for the independent variable, the statistical analysis that follows shows a clear and strong negative relationship between infectious disease and state capacity. The main question of this chapter is whether in fact we can dismiss the null hypothesis (i.e., that infectious disease has no effect on state capacity). As such the statistical analysis presented here compliments the process tracing employed in the following chapter, which should allow us to flesh out the likely causal relations between variables.

As was discussed in the previous chapter, the covariance between the proxies for disease and our computed state capacity measure (SC) will either confirm or disconfirm the null hypothesis. Using standard Pearson's two-tailed correlation to measure the covariance, we find that infant mortality (IM) does in fact correlate strongly (in a negative association) with the various measures of state capacity for the countries in the sample. Similarly, we find that life expectancy (LX) displays a strong positive correlation with the respective SC variables. Significant trends in the data indicate a strong negative association between the prevalence of infectious disease and individual indicators of state capacity within a particular society. Additionally, there are minor outliers that do not follow the general trends within each of the state capacity categories, but this is to be expected in view of the wide range of societies and cultures in our sample. I will also discuss the presence of outliers with regard to each SC variable.

Of course, the raw data employed in the analysis are derived from 20 randomly selected countries, and those data range chronologically from 1951 to 1991. National data quality ranges from excellent (e.g., Japan, the Netherlands) to rather suboptimal (e.g., Uganda, Saudi Arabia). In general, the mortality data (IM and LX) tend to be available across this time period for all countries in the sample. Therefore, measurements involving the independent variable are not subject to data gaps and do not result in significant problems for the data analysis. Conversely, certain gaps and inconsistencies do exist in the data for individual countries concerning certain SC variables at certain times. For example, there is no currently available data for government expenditure (GOVEX) in Saudi Arabia over the specified time period. Similarly, Iceland has no armed forces and therefore does not have any data for military expenditure (MX). Additionally, single-year and/or multi-year gaps exist in the data for several developing nations, particularly Uganda and Rwanda. These gaps notwithstanding, all available data for the entire time period per specified country have been employed in this analysis. To the extent that data gaps exist, they may have minor effects on the strength of the correlations; however, these same gaps will complicate the work of all social scientists who analyze these vari-

Table 2.1
Infant mortality vs. gross national product.

	Correlation	r^2
Rwanda	−0.978	0.956
Brazil	−0.956	0.913
Colombia	−0.955	0.912
Haiti	−0.950	0.902
Malawi	−0.931	0.866
Netherlands	−0.926	0.857
Botswana	−0.912	0.832
Kenya	−0.910	0.828
South Africa	−0.903	0.815
Peru	−0.899	0.808
Thailand	−0.881	0.776
Iceland	−0.871	0.758
Norway	−0.860	0.740
India	−0.853	0.727
Italy	−0.852	0.726
Saudi Arabia	−0.783	0.613
Ethiopia	−0.769	0.591
Japan	−0.760	0.578
Tanzania	−0.348	NS[a]
Uganda	0.051	NS

a. Not significant.

ables. Given the existence of imperfect data, we must be reasonably cautious in our conclusions, yet the correlations will provide the answer as to whether the null hypothesis can be discredited. The tables below display the trends in the data using a 0 year lag.

Table 2.1 shows a strong and significant trend indicating a negative association between infectious disease prevalence (represented by IM) and gross national product per capita over the period 1951–1991. Of the total sample population, 18 states show strong and significant negative correlations between IM and GNP over the selected time period. The balance of the evidence provided in the trends above gives us initial reason to question the validity of the null hypothesis. The strength of this correlation across the sample is −0.950**, significant to <0.001, with $r^2 = 0.902$.[2] Based on the strength of these correlations, we can argue that there is a significant and strong negative association between ERID prevalence and

Table 2.2
Infant mortality vs. government expenditure.

	Correlation	r^2
Tanzania	−0.978	0.955
Rwanda	−0.977	0.954
Netherlands	−0.956	0.914
Japan	−0.951	0.904
Haiti	−0.948	0.898
Thailand	−0.941	0.885
South Africa	−0.930	0.865
Italy	−0.923	0.852
Colombia	−0.891	0.794
Malawi	−0.858	0.736
Norway	−0.825	0.680
Kenya	−0.802	0.643
Botswana	−0.730	0.533
Iceland	−0.727	0.529
India	−0.719	0.517
Brazil	−0.680	0.462
Peru	−0.649	0.421
Ethiopia	−0.381	NS
Uganda	0.246	NS
Saudi Arabia	NA[a]	NA

a. Here and in subsequent tables, NA means "not available" and NS "not significant."

per capita GNP, and that this finding is generalizable to the sample population. Two of the sample countries (Tanzania and Uganda) display insignificant correlations, and in Uganda's case this is probably due to a small N. Specifically, the data available for Uganda on this variable contain several single and multi-year gaps based on national reporting to the World Bank and the International Monetary Fund. Such gaps may result from any number of exogenous factors but are probably due to the chronic unrest and internal violence that has plagued that state over the past three decades. The negative association between ERIDs and per capita GNP has direct repercussions on such measures of state capacity as fiscal resources, legitimacy, reach and responsiveness, resilience, autonomy, and human capital.

Table 2.2 illustrates a strong negative association between disease and GOVEX. Seventeen of the sample countries show a strong and significant negative correlation between IM and GOVEX. Ethiopia exhibits a trend toward this relationship; however, its correlation is insignificant.[3] Saudi Arabia has no data on government expenditure over the selected time period, and Uganda's correlation is again insignificant. The total strength of the correlation for the entire sample is −0.988**, significant to <0.001, with $r^2 = 0.976$. Thus, the global negative association between GOVEX and IM is exceptionally strong, providing additional preliminary evidence for the rejection of the null hypothesis. Based on these correlations, we can argue that increasing levels of ERIDs result in declining levels of revenue available for GOVEX: undermining the basal capability of the government to provide for the basic needs of its citizens. Therefore, infectious disease would seem to exert a negative effect on such measures of SC as reach and responsiveness, legitimacy, human capital, and resilience.

Table 2.3 shows a strong negative association between disease and military spending per capita, per soldier (MX). Fourteen of the sample countries display a significant negative association between the variables. For five of the sample countries the correlations are insignificant, and Rwanda is the only significant outlier from the general trend. Iceland has a correlation of 0 because it has no regular armed forces. The overall correlation for IM vs. MX is −0.884**, significant to <0.001, with $r^2 = 0.781$. The data suggest that infectious disease prevalence does correlate in a negative association with the ability of the state to maintain its armed forces and thereby to ensure the security of that state from external predation and internal disruption. The data suggest that infectious disease might have a major negative effect on the ability of the state to provide for national security in the classic sense of deterring external aggression, maintaining internal stability, and projecting force abroad when necessary. On the basis of these measures, we can infer that ERIDs have a negative effect on reach and responsiveness, resilience, and autonomy, and other aspects of state capacity.

Table 2.4 illustrates a strong and significant negative correlation between disease rates and secondary school education as a percentage of the eligible population. The trend is exceptionally strong. Eighteen of the sample countries show significant negative association between the

Table 2.3
Infant mortality vs. military spending.

	Correlation	r^2
Netherlands	−0.947	0.897
Italy	−0.934	0.872
Thailand	−0.903	0.815
Colombia	−0.847	0.717
Kenya	−0.840	0.706
Norway	−0.831	0.691
Botswana	−0.800	0.64
Japan	−0.800	0.64
Haiti	−0.730	0.533
Saudi Arabia	−0.690	0.476
India	−0.671	0.45
Ethiopia	−0.530	0.281
Tanzania	−0.476	0.227
South Africa	−0.452	0.204
Peru	−0.239	NS
Iceland	0	0
Brazil	0.171	NS
Uganda	0.272	NS
Malawi	0.709	NS
Rwanda	0.380	0.144

variables. Only two show insignificant correlations, and it is notable that Uganda again falls outside the general trend. The overall correlation for the sample between IM and secondary school enrollment is −0.729**, significant to <0.001, with $r^2 = 0.531$. The significance and the polarity of the correlation suggest that rising prevalence of infectious disease has a strong negative effect on the ability of the state to provide for the education of its citizens. Conversely, reducing the burden of disease would seem to allow for a greater provision of education to a state's population. The data suggest that rising prevalence of ERIDs will undermine the formation and consolidation of human capital within affected societies. Coupled with the effects of infectious disease on macroeconomic indicators, this provides us with evidence to suggest that increasing levels of infectious disease have a persistent and significant negative effect on the formation and consolidation of human capital and on aggregate national development. The nega-

Table 2.4
Infant mortality vs. secondary school enrollment (percentage).

	Correlation	r^2
Japan	−0.988	0.976
Norway	−0.988	0.976
Kenya	−0.986	0.972
Brazil	−0.983	0.966
Peru	−0.979	0.958
Saudi Arabia	−0.977	0.955
Colombia	−0.969	0.939
Netherlands	−0.963	0.927
Italy	−0.951	0.904
South Africa	−0.950	0.903
Botswana	−0.904	0.817
Haiti	−0.902	0.814
Iceland	−0.844	0.712
India	−0.820	0.672
Ethiopia	−0.806	0.65
Tanzania	−0.780	0.608
Malawi	−0.797	0.635
Rwanda	−0.779	0.609
Thailand	−0.331	NS
Uganda	−0.119	NS

tive relationship between IM and SC affects facets of SC such as human capital, legitimacy, resilience, reach and responsiveness, fiscal strength, and autonomy.

Initially, the correlations between IM and CAPIN (table 2.5) suggest that there is a weak negative association between ERIDs and the net intake of foreign capital into a state. Only four of the sample countries show strong and significant negative correlations between the two variables. Two countries show significant *positive* correlations between the variables, and the remainder of the countries show insignificant correlations or do not have data for this particular variable for the selected time period. Thus, at first glance one is tempted to conclude that there is no conclusive relationship between the variables.

Interestingly enough, when the data for CAPIN are aggregated and run together as a comprehensive sample CAPIN measure against total sample

Table 2.5
Infant mortality vs. net long-term capital inflow.

	Correlation	r^2
Rwanda	−0.877	0.769
India	−0.783	0.613
Japan	−0.680	0.462
Colombia	−0.473	0.224
Haiti	−0.464	NS
Malawi	−0.388	NS
Ethiopia	−0.380	NS
Tanzania	−0.372	NS
Kenya	−0.280	NS
Botswana	−0.247	NS
Saudi Arabia	−0.087	NS
Norway	0.153	NS
Uganda	0.188	NS
Brazil	0.368	NS
South Africa	0.510	0.26
Peru	0.608	0.370
Netherlands	NA	NA
Italy	NA	NA
Iceland	NA	NA
Thailand	NA	NA

IM, the global correlation becomes significant.[4] This is likely to be due to the fact that the mean of the data points in the sample is filling in gaps within single national data fields. The overall correlation between IM and CAPIN is −0.686**, significant to <0.001, with $r^2 = 0.471$. This suggests that increasing prevalence of infectious disease will exert a negative effect on external capital flows into a state over time. Therefore, states that bear increasing burdens of infectious disease will likely see foreign investment into their state wane as the holders of capital seek safer havens for their wealth. Thus, ERIDs have a negative effect on such measures of SC as fiscal resources, resilience, reach and responsiveness, autonomy, and legitimacy.

Life Expectancy versus State Capacity

As was discussed in the previous chapter, life expectancy (LX) is another proxy variable by which one can track fluctuations in the burden of certain infectious diseases on a society. Certain pathogens that have marked effects on LX do not exhibit a similar effect on IM, and so we can use LX to explore the correlation between ERIDs and state capacity. This is exceptionally useful in determining the prospective effect of diseases such as AIDS, hepatitis, and tuberculosis, as they have a significant detrimental effect on LX in affected societies.

As table 2.6 shows, there is a significant and strong correlation between LX and GNP over time. Of the 20 countries in the sample, 19 showed strong and significant *positive* correlations between LX and GNP. This means that, over time, rising life expectancy correlates well with increases in per capita GNP. Similarly, decreases in LX correlate with declines in GNP. This means that HIV and other pathogens that have significant negative effects on LX will probably erode GNP and undermine state capacity. Note that Uganda takes its usual role as an outlier, displaying an

Table 2.6
Life expectancy vs. gross national product.

	Correlation	r^2
India	0.976	0.952
Rwanda	0.963	0.927
Norway	0.960	0.921
Netherlands	0.958	0.917
Brazil	0.952	0.906
Haiti	0.951	0.904
Iceland	0.942	0.887
Colombia	0.940	0.884
Thailand	0.925	0.855
Malawi	0.924	0.854
Kenya	0.920	0.846
Botswana	0.912	0.832
Peru	0.895	0.801
South Africa	0.883	0.78
Japan	0.849	0.721
Saudi Arabia	0.752	0.566
Italy	0.708	0.501
Ethiopia	0.669	0.447
Tanzania	0.524	0.275
Uganda	0.035	NS

insignificant correlation between LX and GNP. The lack of reliable annual data from Uganda remains problematic and may account for the lack of significance. The overall correlation between LX and GNP is 0.950**, significant to <0.001, with $r^2 = 0.903$. The negative association between disease and per capita GNP directly affects such measures of state capacity as fiscal resources, legitimacy, reach and responsiveness, resilience, autonomy, and human capital.

Table 2.7 shows a strong and significant positive association between LX and per capita GOVEX at the national level. Sixteen of the sample countries display strong and significant correlations, Ethiopia follows the general trend, approaching significance, and Uganda takes its usual place as an insignificant outlier. The balance of the evidence suggests that HIV/AIDS and tuberculosis, which significantly affect life expectancy, will exert significant negative pressures on state capacity at the national level.

Table 2.7
Life expectancy vs. government expenditure.

	Correlation	r^2
India	0.979	0.958
Tanzania	0.979	0.958
Netherlands	0.966	0.933
Rwanda	0.953	0.908
Thailand	0.949	0.901
Haiti	0.949	0.901
Norway	0.939	0.882
Japan	0.926	0.857
South Africa	0.901	0.812
Iceland	0.891	0.794
Malawi	0.885	0.783
Colombia	0.847	0.717
Kenya	0.837	0.701
Botswana	0.710	0.504
Peru	0.632	0.399
Brazil	0.672	0.452
Italy	0.514	NS
Ethiopia	0.433	NS
Uganda	−0.396	NS
Saudi Arabia	NA	NA

Again Uganda's correlation is insignificant, and this suggests that the relatively low number of data points is affecting the correlation. Recurrent warfare in the state may be affecting the availability of N. Alternatively, inconsistencies in the reporting of data may account for Uganda's continual status as an outlier. Again, when we correlate the national data with global SC, we find a global correlation of 0.778$**$, significant to <0.001, with $r^2 = 0.605$. This implies that changes in disease-induced mortality significantly affect variations in GOVEX and that this relationship holds across time and space and is generally applicable to all states in the sample. Therefore, infectious disease would seem to exert a negative effect on such measures of SC as reach and responsiveness, legitimacy, human capital, and resilience.

Table 2.8 shows a relatively strong and significant positive correlation between LX and MX. Twelve of the sample countries show significant

Table 2.8
Life expectancy vs. military spending.

	Correlation	r^2
Italy	0.974	0.949
Netherlands	0.961	0.924
Thailand	0.943	0.889
Norway	0.924	0.854
Japan	0.899	0.808
Kenya	0.854	0.729
Colombia	0.820	0.672
Saudi Arabia	0.654	0.428
India	0.652	0.425
Haiti	0.711	0.505
Tanzania	0.513	0.263
South Africa	0.477	0.228
Ethiopia	0.459	NS
Peru	0.288	NS
Iceland	0	0
Brazil	−0.185	NS
Uganda	−0.316	NS
Rwanda	−0.371	NS
Malawi	−0.752	NS
Botswana	−0.788	0.621

positive associations between LX and MX, six show correlations that are insignificant, and there are two notable outliers (Iceland and Botswana). Iceland boasts a correlation of 0 (as would be expected, since Iceland has no armed forces). Botswana is surprising, but explainable in view of its low overall population base and its high rates of military expenditure (likely attributable to proximate military threats posed by forces in Angola, South Africa, Namibia, Zimbabwe, and Zambia). Aggregating the data into global measures, we find that LX and MX show a correlation of 0.894**, significant to <0.001, with $r^2 = 0.799$. This provides us with further evidence with which to discredit the null hypothesis, and it gives credence to the theory that ERIDs constitute a significant threat to the military aspects of state capacity, such as reach and responsiveness, resilience, and autonomy.

Table 2.9 shows a very strong and significant positive association between LX and secondary school enrollment. Eighteen of the sample

Table 2.9
Life expectancy vs. secondary school enrollment (percentage).

	Correlation	r^2
Saudi Arabia	0.994	0.891
Brazil	0.985	0.970
Kenya	0.985	0.970
Peru	0.970	0.941
Japan	0.968	0.937
Colombia	0.960	0.922
Netherlands	0.944	0.891
Norway	0.933	0.87
Iceland	0.924	0.854
India	0.924	0.854
Thailand	0.915	0.837
Haiti	0.905	0.819
Botswana	0.866	0.75
Malawi	0.863	0.745
Tanzania	0.796	0.634
Ethiopia	0.763	0.582
Italy	0.718	0.516
Rwanda	0.708	0.501
South Africa	0.912	NS
Uganda	0.082	NS

countries show significant positive association between the two variables. South Africa follows the general trend, and its correlation approaches significance. Uganda again exhibits an insignificant correlation. The global correlation between LX and secondary school enrollment is 0.876**, significant to <0.001, with $r^2 = 0.767$. Based on this, we can conclude that pathogens that exert exceptional negative effects on LX will generate significant negative pressures on this measure of state capacity at the national level. In other words, as the prevalence of lethal disease agents increases within a society there will be a corresponding drop in the ability of the state to provide basic educational services to its citizens, and this may result in the long-term erosion of human capital within seriously affected states. The negative relationship between IM and SC affects such facets of SC as human capital, legitimacy, resilience, reach and responsiveness, fiscal strength, and autonomy.

Predictably, the correlation between LX and net long-term capital inflow (CAPIN) exhibits a weak positive association at the national level (table 2.10), only five of the sample countries exhibiting strong and significant positive correlations. Indeed, four of the sample countries have no data for CAPIN, and nine states show insignificant correlations. Furthermore, both South Africa and Peru show a significant *negative* association between the variables and represent strong outliers. In the case of South Africa, this apparent effect may be attributable to the long reign of apartheid and the drop in foreign investment that accompanied it over decades. Peru's status as an outlier is enigmatic and deserves further attention in subsequent analyses. It is interesting to note that when the data are combined into global measures the correlation between LX and CAPIN is 0.682**, significant to <0.001, with $r^2 = 0.465$.

The data suggest that, over time, global improvements in public health correlate with increases in foreign capital inputs into the state. Conversely, as infectious agents take hold around the world, perceptions of disease-induced declines in productivity and stability will result in declining flows of capital into seriously affected states and regions from external sources. Thus, countries that are located in regions of the world with exceptional pathogenic virulence and prevalence (e.g., sub-Saharan Africa) will experience notable reductions in (or difficulty attracting) foreign investment over time. Inasmuch as CAPIN is a logical indicator of SC, this provides another reason for rejecting the null hypothesis. Thus, contagion has a

Table 2.10
Life expectancy vs. net long-term capital inflow.

	Correlation	r^2
Rwanda	0.895	0.801
India	0.852	0.726
Japan	0.633	0.401
Colombia	0.491	0.241
Haiti	0.471	0.222
Ethiopia	0.401	NS
Tanzania	0.360	NS
Malawi	0.307	NS
Kenya	0.258	NS
Botswana	0.247	NS
Saudi Arabia	0.138	NS
Norway	−0.197	NS
Uganda	−0.217	NS
Brazil	−0.389	NS
South Africa	−0.534	0.285
Peru	−0.633	0.401
Iceland	NA	NA
Italy	NA	NA
Netherlands	NA	NA
Thailand	NA	NA

negative effect on such facets of SC as fiscal resources, resilience, reach and responsiveness, autonomy, and legitimacy.

National Correlations

Persuant to the indicator-by-indicator evidence for these trends, it is advantageous to examine the relationship between our proxy variables for infectious disease and a computed SC measure for each state in the sample. The aggregate SC variable was computed by combining the standardized individual component variables into an additive measure (each with equal weighting) and then dividing so as to obtain a yearly mean sum. There appears to be significant variation at the national level in terms of the relations among IM, LX, and SC. Again the tendency is toward a significant negative association between IM and SC, and toward a positive asso-

Table 2.11
ERID proxies vs. state capacity.

	IM	Sig.	LX	Sig.
Botswana	−0.697	<0.001	0.717	<0.001
Brazil	−0.761	<0.001	0.760	0.001
Colombia	−0.641	<0.001	0.583	0.001
Ethiopia	−0.410	0.024	0.499	0.005
Haiti	−0.723	<0.001	0.727	<0.001
Iceland	−0.659 ·	<0.001	0.702	<0.001
India	−0.665	<0.001	0.696	<0.001
Italy	−0.738	<0.001	0.682	<0.001
Japan	−0.425	0.017	0.538	0.002
Kenya	−0.629	<0.001	0.639	<0.001
Malawi	−0.386	0.032	0.429	0.016
Netherlands	−0.886	<0.001	0.941	<0.001
Norway	−0.819	<0.001	0.915	<0.001
Peru	−0.364	0.044	0.402	0.025
Rwanda	−0.670	<0.001	0.708	<0.001
Saudi Arabia	−0.553	0.002	0.504	0.006
South Africa	−0.841	<0.001	0.844	<0.001
Tanzania	−0.763	<0.001	0.822	<0.001
Thailand	−0.797	<0.001	0.844	<0.001
Uganda	−0.462	0.023	0.327	0.119

ciation between LX and SC. The following correlations delineate these trends.

Table 2.11 shows a strong and significant negative association between IM and SC. All 20 of the sample countries show significant negative association between the variables, ranging from the strongest correlations in Netherlands, Norway, and South Africa down to Peru and Malawi at the lower end. Interestingly, and for the first time, there are no outliers (significant or insignificant); each country in the sample exhibits significant negative correlations between IM and SC. However, within the national correlations between LX and SC, Uganda rears its head again as an insignificant outlier. It is reasonable to assume that greater availability of accurate data from Uganda might drive the correlation toward the general trend of significant positive association. Perhaps inaccurate reporting of data is responsible for this apparent bucking of the overall trend of the sample.

Regional Correlations

The strong evidence of a negative association between infectious disease and state capacity at the national level makes it necessary to aggregate the data and look at the effects that ERIDs might have on SC at the regional level. Does the correlation between IM and SC hold across regions, or are some regions less vulnerable than others? One reason this question is particularly important is that those who live in the developed countries often assume that the negative association between ERIDs and state capacity is largely a feature of the developing countries, and that the global proliferation of ERIDs does not represent a threat to developed nations.

The Americas

In the data from Brazil, Colombia, Haiti, and Peru, the correlation between IM and SC (0 year lag) is -0.865^{**}, significant to <0.001, with $r^2 = 0.748$. The correlation between LX and SC for the region is 0.851^{**}, also significant to <0.001, with $r^2 = 0.724$ (table 2.12).

Europe

For the European countries in the sample (Iceland, Italy, Norway, and the Netherlands), the correlation between IM and SC (0 year lag) is -0.908^{**}, significant to <0.001, with $r^2 = 0.824$. The correlation between LX and SC is 0.948^{**}, significant to <0.001, with $r^2 = 0.898$ (table 2.13).

Asia

For the Asian countries in the sample (India, Japan, Thailand, and (by default) Saudi Arabia), the correlation between IM and SC (0 year lag) is

Table 2.12
ERID proxies vs. SC indicators, Americas.

	IM	Sig.	LX	Sig.
CAPIN	0.192	0.313	−0.211	0.347
GNP	−0.969	<0.001	0.962	<0.001
GOVEX	−0.968	<0.001	0.961	<0.001
MILEX	−0.482	0.050	0.487	0.048
SK2	−0.810	<0.001	0.809	<0.001

Table 2.13
ERID proxies vs. SC indicators, Europe.

	IM	Sig.	LX	Sig.
CAPIN	0.169	0.452	−0.167	0.459
GNP	−0.901	<0.001	0.915	<0.001
GOVEX	−0.923	<0.001	0.846	<0.001
MILEX	−0.840	<0.001	0.904	0.048
SK2	−0.974	<0.001	0.939	<0.001

Table 2.14
ERID proxies vs. SC indicators, Asia.

	IM	Sig.	LX	Sig.
CAPIN	−0.588	0.003	0.622	0.002
GNP	−0.935	<0.001	0.953	<0.001
GOVEX	−0.820	<0.001	0.801	<0.001
MILEX	−0.798	<0.001	0.804	<0.001
SK2	−0.437	0.014	0.846	<0.001

−0.709**, significant to <0.001, with $r^2 = 0.503$. The correlation between LX and SC is 0.718**, significant to <0.001, with $r^2 = 0.515$ (table 2.14).

Africa
Owing to the random selection of the sample, eight states fall into this category: Botswana, Ethiopia, Kenya, Malawi, South Africa, Tanzania, Uganda, and Rwanda. The correlation between IM and SC for this region (0 year lag) is −0.640**, significant to <0.001, with $r^2 = 0.410$. The correlation between LX and SC is 0.641, significant to <0.001, with $r^2 = 0.411$ (table 2.15).

As the four regional tables show, prevalence of infectious disease exhibits a significant negative association with state capacity across the various regions. Though there has been some speculation that disease poses only a regional threat to areas such as sub-Saharan Africa, it is evident that the problem is not necessarily localized to any particular region. Based on the data, we can conclude that the negative correlation between infectious

Table 2.15
ERID proxies vs. SC indicators, Africa.

	IM	Sig.	LX	Sig.
CAPIN	−0.739	<0.001	0.745	<0.001
GNP	−0.924	<0.001	0.927	<0.001
GOVEX	−0.692	<0.001	0.627	<0.001
MILEX	−0.608	0.003	0.623	0.003
SK2	−0.704	<0.001	0.737	<0.001

disease and state capacity holds across all regions over broad stretches of time. Thus, Europeans and North Americans should also be concerned about the potential threat that the global diffusion of disease represents to all states and societies.

It is interesting that the regions with the best data-collection capacity also boast the stronger correlations. This leads one to suspect that regions with inadequate infrastructures for collecting and disseminating data will show lower correlations than one might expect as data gaps increase in frequency (as it is more difficult to get significant correlations). This data problem may explain why the correlation appears to strengthen as you move from lower-capacity regions (e.g., Africa) to higher-capacity regions (e.g., Europe). An alternative hypothesis, that may help to explain the divergence of effect strength according to regional positioning, resides in the notion that greater standard deviation may result in insignificant correlations within certain states, and drive down the overall correlation of the South relative to the North. Specifically, IM is low and LX is high in industrialized countries and these values do not vary much. Since IM is much higher and LX generally lower in the developing countries (with larger standard errors as a result), the correlations in the developing countries are likely to be weaker: the higher correlations in the North might be attributable not to the higher quality of the data but to the data themselves.[5] This leads to the conclusion that, although the correlations remain significant and strong at the national and regional levels, the relatively greater standard deviation inherent in the Southern data is probably pulling the strength of the correlation down.

To determine whether this trend might hold, I compiled separate national data (0 year lags) for the "North" (developed countries) and the

"South" (developing countries). The "North" countries were Iceland, Italy, Japan, Norway, and the Netherlands; the "South" countries were Botswana, Brazil, Colombia, Ethiopia, Haiti, India, Kenya, Malawi, Peru, Saudi Arabia, South Africa, Tanzania, Thailand, Rwanda, and Uganda. Again following the assumption that the data are more complete for the developed North than for the developing South, I ran the correlations between IM and SC and found that the correlation for the North was -0.695**, significant to <0.001, with $r^2 = 0.483$, whereas the correlation for the South remained significant but came in at -0.483*, significant to 0.019, with $r^2 = 0.233$. A similar effect is evident in the correlations between LX and SC. The North shows a correlation of 0.743**, significant to <0.001, with $r^2 = 0.552$. The South shows a weaker correlation of 0.513**, significant to 0.012, with $r^2 = 0.263$. This finding reinforces the logical speculation that smaller standard errors within the data serve to intensify the significance of the correlations.

There may be an unfortunate tendency to misinterpret the data and claim that, because of the disparity in national and regional correlation strength, the industrialized states of the North are more vulnerable to the effects of infectious disease. Though it is true that the correlation strength is marginally stronger in the North, the correlations in the South are strong and significant. With adequate data reporting and/or similar levels of standard error, one expects, the South would show a correlation strength very similar to that of the North.

Global Correlations

In view of the strong negative association between infectious disease and state capacity, the logical next step is to examine the correlation among computed global measures for IM, LX, and SC. Comparing the sample mean from each variable for each year against the sample mean IM and LX for each year, we can compute the correlation between global IM and global SC over the period 1950–1991. The resulting correlation is -0.939**, significant to <0.001, with $r^2 = 0.882$. This demonstrates a powerful negative association between disease and SC over the selected time period, and it gives us more evidence with which to discredit the null hypothesis. In other words, increasing prevalence of infectious disease would seem to compromise state capacity.

Similarly, when global LX was run against global SC the correlation was 0.939**, significant to <0.001, with $r^2 = 0.882$. This demonstrates that increasing life expectancy correlates positively with increasing state capacity. However, it is helpful to keep in mind that IM is more sensitive to fluctuations in disease prevalence within a society than is LX. For the latter reason, I consider the IM vs. SC statistic to be more informative.

Lags

Social scientists have questioned the directionality of causation within the model. Do changes in population health affect SC, or do changes in SC affect health? If health drives SC, it will have important academic and policy implications, insofar as greater investment in population health may be a means of ensuring greater long-term prosperity and stability in a society. After the global lags between SC and IM and LX have been analyzed over the time period of the present study, the data permit further analysis to determine the nature of causality in the equation. By lagging the independent variable from 0 to 15 years, we can observe trends over time in the correlations to determine whether IM is driving SC or whether SC is driving IM and LX. Theoretically, of course, there should be a feedback loop.

When IM was run against SC over a 15-year lag period (table 2.16), the correlation was −0.939** at 0 years, increasing to −0.942** at the 8-year lag interval. After the peak of this effect (in the 6–9-year lag range), the strength of the correlation declines rapidly after the ninth year and then weakens in linear fashion until the end of the lag period at year 15 (−0.688**). Note that even at the 15-year lag interval the effect of IM on downstream SC is still powerful.

The effect illustrated by table 2.17 is even more powerful, LX being a significant driver of downstream SC. At 0 years it is −0.939**, significant to <0.001, with $r^2 = 0.882$. A secondary peak occurs in the 8–10-year lag range. Therefore, significant negative changes in the life expectancy of a national population will have significant implications for the future capacity of affected states. Thus, diseases that have particularly onerous effects on LX (such as HIV/AIDS) will have a significant detrimental effect on SC over time. Since many states in sub-Saharan Africa boast HIV seroprevalence rates ranging from 10 percent to 36 percent of the population,

Table 2.16
Global IM vs. global SC.

Years lagged	Correlation	Sig.
0	−0.939	<0.001
1	−0.937	<0.001
2	−0.934	<0.001
3	−0.933	<0.001
4	−0.935	<0.001
5	−0.937	<0.001
6	−0.940	<0.001
7	−0.941	<0.001
8	−0.942	<0.001
9	−0.940	<0.001
10	−0.764	<0.001
11	−0.755	<0.001
12	−0.758	<0.001
13	−0.739	<0.001
14	−0.734	<0.01
15	−0.688	<0.01

Table 2.17
Global LX vs. global SC.

Years lagged	Correlation	Sig.
0	0.939	<0.001
1	0.934	<0.001
2	0.929	<0.001
3	0.924	<0.001
4	0.923	<0.001
5	0.926	<0.001
6	0.930	<0.001
7	0.933	<0.001
8	0.937	<0.001
9	0.937	<0.001
10	0.937	<0.001
11	0.936	<0.001
12	0.934	<0.001
13	0.933	<0.001
14	0.933	<0.001
15	0.931	<0.001

we can expect substantial reductions in state capacity in the first half of the twenty-first century.

As expected, running SC against IM over a 15-year lag period produces a correlation of −0.939** at 0 years and a correlation of −0.924** at 4 years (tables 2.18 and 2.19). Thereafter, the correlation increases to −0.958** at 7 years, but the following year it falls apart. Correlations in subsequent years decline to insignificant levels and reverse in polarity. Only in the fifteenth year is significance again attained; however, the polarity of the correlation is opposite to the initial trend seen in the first 7 years. Conversely, SC vs. IM exhibited extreme variance in the strength, polarity, and significance of the equation over the rest of the lag period, suggesting that, although SC may significantly affect disease levels in the short term, it does not have a significant effect over the long term. This suggests that, although SC has a powerful reciprocal influence on IM during the initial 7-year range, it does not drive the incidence or the prevalence of disease within a state over the long term. This makes logical sense when one considers that high-capacity states such as the US and the UK can have higher levels of HIV infection than lower-capacity states such as Iran owing to socio-cultural factors in disease transmission (and systematic underreporting). Similarly, SC drives LX up until year 10, but again the correlation falls apart in the 11–15-year range.

This surprising evidence supports several claims regarding the hypotheses being tested here:

• The balance of the evidence allows us to firmly reject the null hypothesis, as there is a consistently strong and significant negative correlation between IM and SC, and positive association between LX and SC at the national, regional, and global levels.

• The strong and significant correlation over the lag period (the scale of the effect) indicates that the long-term effect of infectious disease on population health has a major effect on downstream state capacity.

• We can confirm that SC has an effect on infectious disease levels, but only within a short range of time (7–10 years), after which the correlations become volatile and insignificant.

Collectively, these three findings suggest that there is in fact a negative spiral dynamic or an asymmetrical feedback loop operating between

Table 2.18
Global SC vs. global IM.

Years lagged	Correlation	Sig.
0	−0.939	<0.001
1	−0.939	<0.001
2	−0.943	<0.001
3	−0.924	<0.001
4	−0.924	<0.001
5	−0.929	<0.001
6	−0.936	<0.001
7	−0.958	<0.001
8	−0.441	0.100
9	−0.506	0.065
10	−0.433	0.139
11	−0.197	0.539
12	0.066	0.847
13	0.365	0.300
14	0.578	0.106
15	0.703	0.052

Table 2.19
Global SC vs. global LX.

Years lagged	Correlation	Sig.
0	−0.941	<0.001
1	−0.941	<0.001
2	−0.942	<0.001
3	−0.942	<0.001
4	−0.955	<0.001
5	−0.959	<0.001
6	−0.957	<0.001
7	−0.960	<0.001
8	−0.721	<0.01
9	−0.754	<0.01
10	−0.704	<0.01
11	−0.530	0.076
12	−0.273	0.416
13	−0.090	0.804
14	−0.405	0.280
15	−0.601	0.115

infectious disease and state capacity—that increasing prevalence of disease reduces state capacity and, in turn, declining state capacity results in increasing levels of infectious disease. Conversely, there may be a positive spiral dynamic when low prevalence of disease permits increasing SC and greater SC correspondingly reduces the prevalence of disease in the immediate downstream range. Notwithstanding the cyclic nature of this dynamic between ERIDs and SC, the data indicates that the health of the population has a greater long-term effect on state capacity than vice versa, and thus we can reject claims that state capacity is the only thing driving the emergence and prevalence of infectious disease. We can also reasonably conclude that population health exerts a significant effect on state capacity over time, and that it will continue to do so.

Critics

Although it is true that infectious disease appears to be primarily a scourge of the developing countries, there is a disturbing tendency on the part of some Western scholars, policy makers, and media to dismiss the threat of infectious disease to their own populations. This hubris and denial is shortsighted and is bound to lead to serious downstream losses for their respective societies, as we exist in an exceedingly complex and interdependent web of life wherein changes on the other side of the world will eventually affect us. A prime example of interdependence was the global capital crash of the summer of 1998, when economic corruption and a lack of fiscal regulation in Asian economies sent the world into an economic tailspin. The natural world is of course infinitely more complex and interdependent, and as we humans continue to alter the global environment we will produce corresponding responses from that environment, such as the continuing emergence of pathogens. The recent importation of HIV/AIDS and West Nile Virus from Africa into the North American human ecology is a prime example of worldwide pathogen dissemination.

Critics will argue that only case-specific data per pathogen per year should be correlated against state capacity. However, as I pointed out at length in chapter 1, severe data limitations prevent that type of analytical undertaking at this point in time. However, with an eye to this critique, I have run US tuberculosis data for the period 1950–1991 against SC mea-

Table 2.20
Tuberculosis vs. SC indicators (United States).

	TB cases	TB deaths	TB rate	TB death rate
CAPIN	−0.684	−0.472	−0.665	−0.439
MILEX	−0.827	−0.806	−0.830	−0.803
GNP	−0.832	−0.818	−0.849	−0.819
GOVEX	−0.840	−0.867	−0.914	−0.841
SCHOOL 2	−0.792	−0.736	−0.785	−0.744
STATE CAP	−0.954	−0.924	−0.972	−0.903

sures for the United States. Despite the fact that tuberculosis is but one of many ERIDs endemic within the US population, there is a strong and significant negative association between this one disease and the state capacity of the US over this time period. The correlation between TB cases (incidence) and the state capacity of the US is −0.954**, significant to <0.001, with $r^2 = 0.910$. Table 2.20 delineates the strength of the relationship between this ERID and the state capacity of the US over the Cold War period.

The relationship between tuberculosis incidence and state capacity in the United States demonstrates the strong correlation between declining levels of infection and a corresponding increase in state capacity over 40 years, using data on one globally ubiquitous pathogen. This correlation also shows that the negative association between SC variables and tuberculosis is significant and strong for both morbidity (cases, rate of infection) and mortality (TB deaths, death rate). Of note, the correlations between the morbidity variables and SC measures are marginally higher than those between mortality and SC. This would seem to confirm the hypothesis that ERID-induced debilitation combines with mortality to exert a comprehensive negative effect on state capacity. Thus, mortality indicators in and of themselves will not give us a true picture of the toll that ERIDs exact on state capacity in a society. The strength of this relationship between tuberculosis and state capacity can be extrapolated to the rest of the world, which exhibits lower SC and in general much higher rates of TB than the United States. Thus, the US correlations can be seen as a conservative benchmark by which we can gauge the effect of a single pathogen on state capacity over a broad stretch of time.

Table 2.21
State capacity vs. tuberculosis incidence/prevalence (United States). (Cases reflect incidence; rate reflects prevalence within population.)

Years lagged (SC)	TB cases	TB rate	TB deaths	TB death rate
0	−0.954	−0.972	−0.903	−0.924
1	−0.945	−0.965	−0.876	−0.900
2	−0.935	−0.952	−0.811	−0.838
3	−0.899	−0.922	−0.718	−0.767
4	−0.775	−0.851	−0.636	−0.711
5	−0.564	−0.749	−0.558	−0.645
6	−0.281	−0.606	−0.474	−0.585
7	−0.065	−0.494	−0.611	−0.741
8	0.069	−0.402	−0.734	−0.786
9	0.116	−0.401	−0.727	−0.782
10	0.074	−0.476	−0.700	−0.787
11	0.134	−0.448	−0.724	−0.780
12	0.132	−0.339	−0.743	−0.701
13	0.036	−0.375	−0.762	−0.750
14	0.027	−0.341	−0.777	−0.711
15	0.213	−0.163	−0.909	−0.891

Table 2.21 shows the relationship between tuberculosis (both morbidity and mortality data) and state capacity in the United States over a 15-year lag period. It is interesting that in the initial 5 years tuberculosis-induced morbidity seems to generate a greater negative effect on state capacity than TB-induced mortality within the same period, although both the morbidity and mortality effects are powerful in and of themselves. The morbidity effect tends to weaken in the fifth and sixth year lag intervals, and it becomes insignificant in the seventh year. This finding concurs with the conclusions drawn in reference to table 2.20 in that disease-induced morbidity has a powerful short-term negative effect on state capacity. Conversely, TB-induced mortality over the same time period shows a weaker effect than disease-induced morbidity, with the strength of the correlations weakening significantly in the 5-year and 6-year lag intervals. However, after the 7-year interval the effect of TB-induced mortality on state capacity begins to intensify, reaching high levels of significance at the end of the 15-year lag interval. This finding might seem peculiar, but it accurately reflects the

depletion of human capital within a society as a result of lethal infectious disease agents and the significant downstream effect of death on state capacity. Thus, we can conclude that disease-induced mortality has a significant and strong long-term effect on state capacity. This is particularly noteworthy insofar as one of the major questions raised by this research pertains to which pathogens are most inimical to SC. As the data show, pathogens that induce high levels of debilitation (i.e., morbidity) in the population probably exert a significant negative short-term effect on SC. Diseases in this category include malaria (*Plasmodium vivax*), cholera, dengue fever, diphtheria, onchocerciasis, and schistosomiasis. However, pathogens that generate high levels of mortality will have a greater aggregate effect on both current and downstream state capacity. Therefore, HIV/ AIDS, hepatitis (various subtypes), tuberculosis, malaria, dengue fever, and yellow fever will generate significant negative long-term effects on state capacity.

In view of the strength and significance of these correlations, I shall now set about determining how ERIDs compromise state capacity, mapping out the causal pathways and mechanisms involved at the state level. This process-tracing approach, which permits greater understanding of the various and diverse mechanisms involved, will make it possible to formulate effective policy measures for intervention at the break points in the chain of causation.

3

Disease, Destitution, and Development

Beyond the enormous suffering of individuals and families, South Africans are beginning to understand the cost [of HIV/AIDS] in every sphere of society, observing with growing dismay its impact on the efforts of our new democracy to achieve the goals of reconstruction and development.
—Nelson Mandela, in an address to the World Economic Forum (February 3, 1997) titled AIDS: Facing up to the Global Threat[1]

Over the centuries there has been considerable debate concerning the sources of industrialization and the nature of the development of economies and societies. The most prominent and competing explanations have been modernization theory and dependency theory. It should be noted that these are not the only theories involved in the developmental debates, merely the two dominant paradigms. Modernization theory specifies that countries can industrialize if they embrace modern concepts such as free-market capitalism, urbanization, and modernity in general, while disposing of "traditional" concepts such as caste and ethnic rivalry. Dependency theory, on the other hand, argues that states in the developing countries (periphery) are held in economic thrall to the developed countries (core) in a global economic system that perpetuates the legacy of European colonialism.

I argue that the prevailing paradigms of development have generally overlooked a significant biological parameter that lies at the core of international development, specifically the burden of infectious disease on the productivity and the consolidation of human capital in a population. Following the lead of Robert Fogel, I argue that the mastery of high morbidity and mortality rates in a population has been a central driver of state prosperity and economic strength throughout recorded history. Similarly, I argue that the continuing and unchecked proliferation of emerging and re-emerging infectious disease represents a considerable threat to the economic development, stability and prosperity of states throughout the world.

Wealth is generally located in the temperate regions, with the exception of the Persian Gulf oil states. Societies in these temperate regions tend to be highly industrialized relative to those countries in the tropics. Even Canada and the Scandinavian nations are exceptionally prosperous. I argue that there is a biological foundation for development, and that this bioeconomic axiom holds both across time and globally across diverse human societies.[2]

Pathogens have historically impeded the economic and social development of many societies, particularly those that lie within the tropical regions of the world. If we think of the "burden of infectious disease" as the independent variable and "state prosperity" as the dependent variable, then we can empirically test the association between these variables to determine whether disease has an effect on prosperity, whether the effect of disease on prosperity is significant, what the nature of the association between these variables is, and whether this association holds over time and across societies. Based on the preceding empirical evidence, this chapter argues that the proliferation of infectious disease can compromise the economic and social development of countries, and that the onerous burden of disease in tropical regions may partially explain the vast economic development differential between societies in the tropics and their richer counterparts in the temperate zones.

Over the span of centuries, historians and economists have speculated that infectious disease has played a significant (if enigmatic) role in the rise and fall of societies and empires. Fogel argued that much of England's prosperity, if not the Industrial Revolution itself, resulted from the conquest of high morbidity and mortality in Britain during the late eighteenth century and the early nineteenth century.[3] This conquest of mortality and morbidity was largely the result of significant advances in public health and in the increasingly equitable distribution of food. Conversely, William McNeill notes that the arrival of the Black Death (bubonic and pneumonic plague) in Europe during the fourteenth century had significant and pervasive negative economic and social effects on the European societies of the time, generating widespread economic and political instability throughout the continent:

The buoyancy and self-confidence, so characteristic of the thirteenth century . . . gave way to a more troubled age. Acute social tensions between economic classes and intimate acquaintance with sudden death assumed far greater importance for almost everyone than had been true previously. The economic impact of the Black Death was enormous. . . . In highly developed regions like northern Italy and Flanders, harsh collisions between social classes manifested themselves as the boom times of the thirteenth century faded into the past. The plague, by disrupting wage and price patterns sharply, exacerbated these conflicts. . . . Employers died as well as laborers. . . .[4]

Sheldon Watts also notes the economically destructive power of the Black Death on the fortunes of the once powerful city-state of Venice, and its ramifications for the downstream reduction of its economic power in the international realm:

While Venice was closed down and its plague-dead leadership was being replenished from youthful entries in its Golden Book . . . Dutch and English entrepreneurs moved into its traditional marketing territories around the Adriatic and eastern Mediterranean. Once in possession they stayed. Shorn of its major markets and burdened with leaders suffering from sclerosis (young in body but old in mind), Venice soon found itself only a regional power with no economic clout. From this it was but a short step to becoming a museum city.[5]

The role of pathogens as central agents has been emphasized in the explanation of the outcomes in the Peloponnesian War, the fall of Byzantine Rome, the collapse of the feudal order in Europe, the conquest of the Americas by European forces, and even in the resolution of the US Civil War.[6] Although historians make references to the economic and social dislocation generated by the introduction of a new pathogen to the human ecology, they have not directly tested the empirical effect of infectious disease on prosperity and economic development.

At the national level we have observed strong negative correlations between ERIDs and macroeconomic measures such as GNP, GOVEX, and to a lesser extent net long-term capital inflow. Regionally and globally, the negative associations between ERIDs and each of these indicators of state capacity remain strong and significant, and improve markedly in terms of net long-term capital inflow. Taken together, these correlations indicate a strong negative association between infectious disease and economic measures of state capacity over time. This in itself is an important finding, and merits further statistical analysis as our data improve over time. However, the statistical analysis only takes us so far in our understanding of the processes by which disease undermines the *economic capacity* of a state. Process tracing at the state level allows us to map the pathways of the effect of ERIDs on microeconomic units, from households and firms to its broader effect on economic sectors (agriculture, mining, etc.) and finally to its macroeconomic effect on the state. I now examine how disease acts as the sand in the economic engine of a nation.

A Theory of Reciprocal Causation

Historically, the dominant conception of the relationship between health and prosperity in the social sciences held that improvements in population health were the product of greater prosperity. However, many medical and social scientists have recently argued that growing economic productivity often does not contribute to greater population health, since it is associated with such factors as increasing population density, exposure to toxins in the workplace, declining urban public health conditions and sanitation capacity.[7] The empirical evidence presented in the last chapter supports the reverse hypothesis, namely, that improving public health contributes to the economic productivity of a society. This growing "economic capacity" may in turn be channeled back into public health infrastructure to create a positive feedback loop. However, we must recognize that the data show that infectious disease levels have a significant downstream effect on state capacity over the 15-year lag period, whereas SC affects disease levels only in the initial 7-year lag period. Thus, improvements in public health have a greater effect on downstream SC than SC has on public health.

There are many instances throughout history where industrialization and increased economic productivity have in fact led to suboptimal health conditions for the local population. One only has to think of eighteenth- and nineteenth-century Britain to recall the barely tolerable conditions that most urban laborers lived in during the early age of industry, and the surge in environmental and infectious illnesses that accompanied massive shifts toward urbanization. Moreover, enormous inequalities persist across societies that have experienced consistent and comprehensive economic growth.[8]

Empirical research has confirmed the hypothesis that investment in basic human needs such as education and public health are investments in human capital that promote economic growth and productivity over the long term.[9] Similarly, Bruce Moon and William Dixon argue that higher rates of economic growth do not necessarily improve a state's ability to meet the basic needs of its population. Employing quantitative data for a large sample of countries over 25 years, Moon and Dixon found that "higher rates of growth did not lead to proportionately higher rates of basic needs improvement. Real product growth does seem to result in absolute gains in basic needs attainment, but the rates of change in basic needs provision do not suggest that growth is conducive to improving the provision of basic needs in developing countries. Indeed . . . higher rates of growth may have a negative impact upon subsequent basic needs improvements."[10]

Loren King tested Moon and Dixon's findings and confirmed their previous conclusions that "[economic] growth has no clear impact upon basic needs, and what effect it does appear to have is negative."[11] He concludes that "although higher growth rates do seem to exert a negative impact upon basic needs outcomes in the short term of roughly half a decade, the longer-term impact of growth upon basic needs appears to be negligible."[12] Given the mounting evidence that economic status does not determine the level of public health in the short term, and that our data support the hypothesis that rising levels of infectious disease have a significant negative effect on SC over the long term, we can conclude that neither poverty, nor economic growth are the principal determinants governing the emergence of infectious disease. In fact, the evidence leads us to posit that the prevalence of infectious disease in a society has in fact been a significant contributor to the economic decline of that society over time.

These effects are of course reciprocal in that both negative and positive feedback loops can and do occur between disease and state capacity. Countries with low or declining state capacity (e.g., Haiti, Russia) will not have, or be able to maintain, the health infrastructures to contain emerging pathogens. Thus, infection will typically spread throughout the population of countries with low or declining state capacity. The spread of contagion will deplete human capital and government coffers, which will in turn lead to diminished resources available to shore up crumbling health infrastructures. A classic example of this type of negative spiral exists in modern day Russia, which is seeing a dramatic and worrisome rise in HIV and tuberculosis seroprevalence levels fueled by its collapsing socio-economic and health infrastructure.[13]

The short-term influence of low state capacity on increasing disease prevalence is no surprise, but what is interesting is the finding that, over time infectious disease can have a reciprocal negative influence on state capacity. Anecdotal (and now empirical) evidence bears this out, demonstrated by the Black Death, which swept Europe, sparing neither peasants in the field nor the powerful elites in the city-states of Venice, Florence, and Milan.[14] Indeed, regardless of the initial capacity of the "state" in question, the Black Death seems to have struck with equanimity. Similarly, the influenza pandemic of 1918 claimed victims from the developed and developing countries alike, and initial state capacity did not seem to matter in the distribution of deaths. In fact, it can be argued that those states exhibiting higher state capacity which exhibited greater urban population densities succumbed to the Spanish Flu faster than lower-capacity states with greater proportions of the population living in rural regions.[15] Furthermore, North America and Western Europe were among the first regions to incubate the global HIV pandemic despite having the highest state capacity on the planet.

Based on the empirical evidence provided in the previous chapter we can reasonably claim that disease prevalence does in fact influence *economic capacity*, a significant facet of state capacity. Although the correlations presented in chapter 3 show this negative association at the global, regional, and state levels, it is imperative that we understand exactly how these causal processes function within states. Only if we trace these pathways will we be able to develop and evaluate policies that can mitigate the negative effect of disease on state capacity and development. Infectious disease exerts this negative effect on state economic productivity and development in myriad ways. The optimal means to analyze the general economic effect of disease is to examine its effect at the three standard levels of economic analysis: microeconomic (individuals, households, firms), sectoral, and macroeconomic.

Microeconomic Analysis

Microeconomics deals with the economic behavior of individual decision-making units in a free-market enterprise system, analyzing consumer spending and saving patterns, the maximization of profits by firms, and the pricing of resources and products. Thus, microeconomics is the study of individual components of an economy, such as firms, households, and prices of goods and services. Process tracing, which involves qualitative examination of the probable relations between variables, allows us to demonstrate how disease erodes household productivity. These maps may be able to illuminate the "break points" in the chain so that effective policy can be formulated to mitigate the negative effects of infectious disease on productivity.

Within the household unit, disease undermines prosperity and generates significant shifts in family spending and saving behavior. Households are defined as one or more individuals who represent both a consumption unit and a production unit.[16] Given their endowments of land, other wealth, and the time of their members, households engage in satisficing when they make production, consumption, and saving decisions. At the micro level, increased disease incidence and lethality exert a significant negative effect on the household by debilitating and killing productive members, which in turn generates shifts in saving and consumption and results in supply-induced and demand-induced shocks that destabilize the household as an economic (and social) unit.

It is necessary to distinguish between directly and indirectly affected households. Directly affected households are those in which a member of the family unit is ill or has died from an infectious disease. Indirectly affected households are those that directly assist affected households by taking in orphans, helping to pay funeral expenses, and providing additional labor inputs.[17] Note that disease-induced adult mortality and morbidity will tend to affect macroeconomic aggregates such as wages and saving, and so everyone in an affected society will be influenced by the resurgence of infectious disease.

Depending on their virulence and transmissibility, infectious disease reduces the number of breadwinners in the household, lowers household income, and alters patterns of consumption and saving. At the household level, pecuniary or direct costs that result from ERID-induced illness consist of personal health-care expenditures, costs of prevention, diagnosis, treatment of illness, and costs of death (funerals, mourning ceremonies, coffins). Increasing medical costs and higher funeral expenses will diminish general current expenditures, including those dedicated to saving. Households with infected members may try to increase saving rates in anticipation of paying onerous funeral costs in the near future.[18] These direct costs of death can be particularly burdensome on the poorer segments of society. For example, in southern Zambia coffins cost from $66 to $200. The family of the deceased also pays for the food, lodging, and transport of mourners. In Kinshasa, the funeral of a pediatric AIDS death costs a family an average of $320, the equivalent of 11 months' income.[19]

Other direct costs of infectious disease include the non-personal costs of educational campaigns, biomedical research, and blood screening. Arguably, the most onerous health-care costs for patients are inpatient costs incurred during hospitalization. Such costs include the treatment received (drugs, lab procedures, surgery, etc.), the number of days requiring hospitalization, and the number of episodes of hospitalization required in a year.[20] In their study of the economic affect of AIDS in Thailand, Myers et al. found that the annual cost of AIDS treatment was approximately 25,000 Baht (equal to about $1000) per case, resulting in the loss of more than 50 percent of the average annual household income.[21] Similarly onerous treatment costs are also reported in sub-Saharan Africa. In Tanzania, the average cost of an AIDS patient's illness is roughly 50,000 shillings for an adult and 34,000 for a child. Since per capita income in Tanzania was roughly 12,500 shillings in 1988, it is obvious that these AIDS-related health-care costs are becoming a tremendous burden on the household as the epidemic worsens.[22]

Disease-induced adult deaths can force vulnerable households into poverty. Even in countries such as Tanzania, where the government bears much of the burden of health costs, HIV-affected rural households in 1991 spent $60 (roughly the equivalent of a year's income per capita) on treatment and funerals. Poonawala and Cantor observed similarly deleterious effects from ERIDs on household saving and productivity. They estimated that AIDS hospitalization in Zaire costs on average 4 months' wages for the average worker, and that a funeral costs 11 months' wages.[23] For indigent families, the reduced per capita income, coupled with the needs of a chronically ill patient, usually result in substandard diets, increased labor substitution (resulting in reduced school attendance for the children of affected households), and lowered standards of living.[24]

Indirect or non-pecuniary costs result from the lost value of market and non-market output due to increased morbidity or mortality resulting from illness. Indirect costs are the forgone potential earnings of infected patients and the value of any household services they would have provided. Non-pecuniary costs also include the significance that infected individuals, their families and friends, and society place on the pain and death of affected persons, and resulting shifts in behavior to avoid transmitting or contracting disease.[25] Other disease-induced indirect costs to the household include loss of income from labor, declining agricultural inputs, reduced labor-intensive export and food crop production, reduced household assets, and rising malnutrition.[26] The combined direct and indirect costs of a lethal pathogen such as HIV can have significant long-term detrimental effects on the annual net income of the household. Ainsworth and Over have determined that in severely affected states, roughly 75 percent of annual household revenue may be lost as a result of HIV infection.[27] The UN estimates that "the indirect costs of AIDS range from $890 to $2663 in Zaire and from $2425 to $5903 in . . . Tanzania, which indicates that indirect costs represent roughly 95 percent of the total costs associated with an AIDS infection."[28]

The enormous economic burden of disease is in part a function of the synergistic interaction between various pathogens within both individual hosts and societies at large. For example, sexually transmitted diseases (herpes, gonorrhea, etc.) facilitate HIV infection, which then weakens the immune system, whereupon pathogens colonize and kill the host. Of course, the data-collection problems outlined in chapter 1 make it extremely difficult to estimate rates of co-infection throughout the developing countries. Thus, most of the economic analyses to date have focused on the effects of a single pathogen on a population. It should be noted that HIV/AIDS has received the lion's share of this recent attention, owing to its lethality and its rapidly increasing global prevalence. Despite the focus on HIV, other ERIDs (including malaria, tuberculosis, leprosy, and river blindness) also generate negative microeconomic and macroeconomic outcomes. Leprosy is one notable example of how ERID-induced morbidity affects individual productivity:

A study of lepers in urban Tamil Nadu, India, estimates that the elimination of deformity would more than triple the expected annual earnings of those with jobs. The prevention of deformity in all of India's 645,000 lepers would have added an estimated $130 million to the country's 1985 GDP. This amount is the equivalent of almost 10 percent of all the official development assistance received by India in 1985. Yet leprosy accounted for only a small proportion of the country's disease burden, less than 1 percent in 1990.[29]

Based on the evidence provided above, I argue that ERIDs in general and HIV in particular tend to generate economic "shocks" to household saving and consumption patterns. Morbidity and mortality resulting from infection erodes the economic capacity of households: it reduces the time and labor available from members of the household, it impairs the supply of education and health of the family unit, and through inheritance customs it may reduce the holdings of land, housing, and livestock available to the household.

Households adjust to these initial shocks by attempting to rationally redistribute their limited human and financial capital in order to overcome the burden of disease, and change their behavior concerning production, expenditure, saving, and investment.[30] Non-infected individuals may spend an increased amount of time caring for the debilitated, additional time working to make up for the lost productivity of the sick, and less time in school. To pay for medical care, they may also deplete their savings, liquidate assets, borrow from others, or diminish their investments. In many developing nations, affected families may have to sell assets such as land and livestock in order to maintain economic subsistence. Indeed, ill health is the cause of 24 percent of land transactions in Kenya, according to World Bank data.[31]

Despite the overwhelming (and largely justified) concern regarding the negative economic effects of HIV/AIDS, malaria and other ERIDs represent resurgent impediments to development. Though generally less lethal than HIV/AIDS,[32] malaria persistently debilitates inhabitants of tropical societies, particularly during the peak months of the rainy growing seasons. In their study on the economic effects of malaria in Africa, Shepard et al. estimated the direct and indirect costs imposed by this disease on African societies:

In 1987, a case of malaria cost $9.84 [1987 US dollars]—$1.83 in direct costs and $8.01 in indirect costs. As the average value of goods and services produced per day in Africa was $0.82, this cost is equivalent to 12 days of output. By 1995, the average cost of a malaria case is projected to rise to $16.40 [adjusted 1987 US dollars] due to increasing case severity and chloroquine resistance. At the same time, per capita output is predicted to fall to $0.77, so the burden of one case will rise to 21 days of output. In per capita terms, the burden of malaria is forecast to rise from $1.34 to $4.02. For Africa as a whole, the annual economic burden of malaria was $0.8 billion as of 1987 and will rise to $1.7 billion in 1995; it represented a 0.6 percent share of GDP previously, and a 1.0 percent share for 1995.[33]

Konradsen et al. note that malarial infection results in the loss of approximately 18 percent of annual household net income in Sri Lanka—a significant shortfall in view of the synergistic burden of disease in the developing countries.[34]

Infectious disease tends to exhibit a greater differential effect on poorer households than on rich ones. Since poorer households often bear a much greater economic burden from infectious diseases than their wealthier counterparts, infectious disease tends to reinforce income inequalities within societies and exacerbates income disparities between classes. In their study of malaria's effect on household income in Malawi, Ettling et al. observed that "very low income households carried a disproportionate share of the economic burden of malaria, with total direct and indirect cost of malaria among these households consuming 32 percent of annual household income." Conversely, malaria consumes only 4.2 percent of the annual income of an elite Malawian household.[35] The implication is that although all Malawians suffer the deleterious economic drag from the plasmodium, the economic burden of the disease falls mainly on the poor, exacerbating the income gap between the average worker and the upper classes and driving marginalized populations into deeper poverty.[36] One of the most severe effects of infectious disease on societies is that it increases both perceived and real inequalities between the rich and the poor, particularly in the case of diseases (e.g., malaria, tuberculosis, cholera) that tend to affect marginalized populations. Predictably, the economic gains from improved health are greater for poorer families, who are usually most handicapped by illness and stand to gain significantly from a decrease in the number of work days lost to illness, from improved worker productivity, from higher per capita income, from better education and nutrition,

from greater opportunity to obtain better-paying jobs, from longer working lives, and from the ability to use previously underutilized natural
resources.[37]

ERIDs and Orphans

One commonly overlooked effect of the HIV pandemic is the enormous
increase in the number of orphaned children. The direct and indirect
economic costs of caring for orphaned children will impose additional
financial burdens on afflicted societies. In 1994, Timothy Wirth, the US
Undersecretary of State for Global Affairs, estimated that "between 10
and 15 million children will be orphaned as a result of this disease (HIV/
AIDS) as we enter the twenty-first century."[38] Within those states that
display exceptionally high HIV seroprevalence rates (e.g., sub-Saharan
Africa) AIDS will result in the loss of one and frequently both parents, and
will probably claim several aunts and uncles, depriving children of stable
family structures, education, health care, and training. Both orphans and
the elderly will find themselves reduced to destitution as their sole providers of income succumb to the epidemic.

The US Agency for International Development (USAID) predicts that
the number of orphans resulting from the HIV pandemic will greatly surpass Wirth's estimates, owing to the fact that earlier demographic estimates of seroprevalence had significantly underestimated national rates of
infection throughout the developing countries. In 1997, on the basis of
recent findings of USAID studies of 23 developing countries, USAID
Administrator J. Brian Atwood predicted that more than 34.7 million children would have lost one or both parents to HIV by 2000, and 41.6 million by 2010.[39] No data are yet available for global estimates of the likely
number of HIV orphans. Aside from the immense human suffering involved, such great numbers of orphaned children will create immense financial and social strains on heavily afflicted societies. Atwood predicts
dire consequences as a result of the extreme winnowing of the adult population in many countries:

With children who have lost their parents eventually comprising up to a third of the
population under 15 in some countries, this outgrowth of the HIV/AIDS epidemic
will create a lost generation—a sea of youth who are disadvantaged, vulnerable,

undereducated and lacking both hope and opportunity. What we are seeing here are the seeds of crisis. The creation of such a large and disaffected demographic "youth explosion" could propel some of these societies to significant unrest and destabilization over the long term. The threat to the prospects for economic growth and development in the most seriously affected countries is considerable.[40]

This means that for those sub-Saharan African countries that now exhibit general population HIV seroprevalence rates of 10 percent or greater, we can expect the number of AIDS orphans in those societies to grow exponentially by 2015. In Zimbabwe, Zambia, and Botswana (which now have HIV infection levels in excess of 30 percent), one might reasonably expect that the rapid increase in orphans will generate increasing socio-economic disruption over the long term.

Based on the statistical evidence presented in chapter 2, we can reasonably conclude that the proliferation of infectious disease threatens the economic welfare of the family unit in all societies. However, the relationships illuminated through process tracing suggest that ERIDs pose a relatively greater threat to poorer, marginalized families, particularly those in the developing countries and in societies that rely on privately funded health-care systems. One of the most significant problems associated with the proliferation of pathogens is the strong possibility that it will exacerbate economic disparities between upper and lower economic strata within a society. This may contribute to increasing perceptions of real deprivation on the part of the marginalized.

In sum then, ERIDs generate the following costs to the household:

Direct Costs

• increased personal health-care expenditures, costs of diagnosis, costs of prevention, costs of treatment, and costs of death

• non-personal costs, such as costs of blood screening, biomedical research, and preventive educational campaigns

Indirect Costs

• lost value of market and non-market output due to illness

• lost potential future earnings of debilitated or dead family members and loss of household services that they provided

• the normative, emotive, and/or social value that a society places on the pain and death of infected members

• changes in the behavior of individuals in order to avoid contracting disease

Behavioral Changes

• labor substitution

• reallocation of time of household members (Greater amounts of time spent working and caring for infected members results in decreased time spent in school.)

• To pay for medical care, members reduce investments, sell household assets such as land and livestock, draw on savings, or borrow externally.

Outcomes

• lower educational attainment for directly and indirectly affected individuals (resulting in the long-term depletion of human capital for that state)

• lower consumption per capita, decreasing aggregate demand

• depletion of household income, savings and assets

• diminished level of household health

• growing inequality between prosperous and marginalized households

Households are not the only actors at the microeconomic level that are negatively affected by the proliferation of infectious disease. Individual firms, which have endowments of land, buildings, equipment, and a trained work force, are also subject to the negative effects of disease. The "environment" in which these firms operate includes market prices, levels of morbidity and mortality in the community, infrastructure, climate, rainfall, and government policies. The proliferation of infectious disease will typically affect individual firms in various negative ways: increased sick leave and absenteeism, diminished productivity, rising worker turnover, loss of highly skilled managers, augmented training costs, and larger expenditures on health and death benefits.[41] The World Bank argues that in severely affected states the work force will become younger and will lack adequate training. Tanzania and Uganda are already witnessing greater AIDS-induced absenteeism and declining productivity. The majority of macroeconomic models predict that adult AIDS-related deaths will greatly slow the rate of per capita economic growth as compared to a non-AIDS scenario.[42]

Extensive work has been done on the relationship between investment in human capital and the positive downstream effects on labor productivity.[43] Infectious diseases (notably HIV/AIDS) exert a negative effect on firms through the reduction of the local labor supply (particularly skilled workers), which over time will generate wage increases and cut the profit margins of firms. "The negative labor productivity effect will arise because sick or worried workers are less productive than happy, healthy workers. Even the productivity of those who do not have AIDS may fall as infection and illness rates among friends, families and coworkers rise."[44] This reduced labor supply and productivity combined with increasing wages will undermine the productivity and the profit margins of firms in affected regions. For this reason, multinational firms may choose not to invest in areas where disease endemicity is particularly high. As is evident from the data presented in the previous chapter, this is in fact the case: net long-term capital inflow tends to increase as disease prevalence falls. Thus, the proliferation of disease (particularly HIV) will, over time, generate disincentives to invest capital within severely affected societies. In extreme cases, exceptionally high rates of ERID infection in local populations may spur capital flight from affected regions to safer havens that have lower levels of endemic disease and hence are more productive.

Sectoral Analysis

AIDS kills those on whom society relies to grow the crops, work in the mines and factories, run the schools and hospitals and govern nations and countries, thus increasing the number of dependent persons. It creates new pockets of poverty when parents and breadwinners die and children leave school earlier to support the remaining children.
—Nelson Mandela, in AIDS: Facing up to the Global Threat

Infectious disease has a negative effect at the sectoral level of the economy, adversely affecting a plethora of economic mechanisms and generally undermining productivity throughout a society. In the formal sector, the proliferation of infectious disease threatens the expansion of industry and the private sector, which exhibits significant dependence on skilled workers, entrepreneurs and managers. In his 1997 address to the World Economic Forum at Davos, Sir Richard Sykes stated that the HIV/AIDS epidemic was already having a negative effect on the global work force, on markets, and on the overall business climate.[45] Sykes cited studies, done in Southern and Eastern Africa by the African Medical and Research Foundation (AMREF) for AIDSCAP, which concluded that the HIV/AIDS epidemic generates significant negative economic outcomes: the loss of skilled personnel, the need for greater resources to hire and maintain replacement workers, an increase in labor turnover and absenteeism, and a reduction in productivity. Reductions in labor supply resulting from increased mortality will impose shocks on industry. For example, it has been written that in Uganda "the impact of AIDS on the economy will be felt through its effect on two key inputs into economic activity—labor and capital. The most immediate impact will be through changes in both the productivity and size of the labor force. By causing premature mortality to a significant number of workers between the ages of 15 and 60, AIDS will reduce both the size and growth of the labor force. By the year 2010, there will be about 2 million fewer in the [Ugandan] labor force age group or approximately 12 percent less than without AIDS."[46] Madavo notes that, in a representative sample of 20 Zambian firms, worker mortality increased 500–800 percent between 1987 and 1992, largely as a direct result of HIV/AIDS.[47]

Further examples of the negative effect of HIV on skilled personnel include the loss to AIDS of many of the senior managers of Barclay's Bank of Zambia and the fact that in Malawi nearly 30 percent of the school-teachers are HIV positive.[48] These highly skilled workers represent significant investments in human capital on the part of their employers and home states, and it will be very expensive and time consuming to replace them. Indeed, African elites have generally been severely affected by HIV/AIDS. For example, in the former Zaire, "among the [largely male] employees at a Kinshasa textile mill, managers had a higher infection rate than foremen, who in turn had a higher rate than workers."[49] Because HIV is so prevalent in African elites, it is likely to have significant negative effects on senior management structures within firms, undercutting the reservoir of human capital within firms, sectors, and macroeconomies. Peter Piot of UNAIDS argues that HIV/AIDS costs companies operating in Kenya roughly 4 percent of annual profits, and that as a direct result of the HIV epidemic Kenya's GDP will be 15 percent less than it would have been in a non-AIDS scenario by 2005.[50]

Besides the economic shocks to firms from pathogen-induced short-ages in labor supply, Hancock and Cuddington agree that disease will undermine the economic productivity of nations as they exert general and profound negative effects on the overall size and quality of the labor force.[51] ERIDs (particularly HIV/AIDS) will affect individual sectors through both demand-side and supply-side shocks. One example of supply-side shock occurs when a company that depends on an infected labor pool manufactures products for export. Though international demand for the product is not affected by the local AIDS epidemic, the firm's labor supply and productivity are diminished, increasing costs and thus narrowing the company's profit margin.[52] Conversely, a healthy and stable work force enables employers to reduce the expense of allocating flexibility into their production schedules, permits greater investment in staff training that consolidates human capital, and provides employers with the benefits of specialization.[53] The economist Desmond Cohen argues that labor costs will rise as productivity declines because of increas-ing morbidity and absenteeism: additional training costs will also result from greater labor turnover. Firms' expenditures on health care and other social programs will also grow, such that the public and private expenditures will rise as a proportion of aggregate expenditure. Thus, Cohen posits, the ability of firms to finance capital expenditures will be diminished.[54]

Other effects of ERID-induced morbidity and mortality on firms include reduced functional capacity. Workers may not be able to do their former jobs. Labor-substitution practices may result as other workers are required to assume the former responsibilities of ill co-workers.[55] In their 1992 study of the microeconomic effects of AIDS on Thailand, Myers, Obremsky, and Viravaidya concluded that the AIDS epidemic would have a significant negative effect on the performance of the Thai economy. In addition to greater health-care costs and forgone income, HIV would probably result in a shortage of skilled labor, increased absenteeism, and significant training and re-training costs.[56] Diseases also have negative effects on the workplace at the sectoral level that go beyond mortality, absenteeism, and reduced productivity of workers. Companies and firms will experience higher recruitment and training costs as well as incurring larger medical and insurance expenditures for benefits and funerals.

Health

The resurgence of infectious disease will hurt the health-care sector in affected nations through both supply-side and demand-side shocks. As greater numbers of the population become infected and develop illness, the demand for medical care will soar, and the associated costs will drain national accounts where governments are the major providers of medical care.[57] Similarly, the increasing prevalence of infection will debilitate and kill medical professionals, who must minister to the needs of the general population. Certain pathogens, particularly HIV, have the ability to generate significant supply-side shocks within the health sector as medical personnel are infected, debilitated, and killed. Additionally, the HIV pandemic will generate much greater health-care costs, as states need to employ more health-care workers. As well, the burdens of medical insurance, disability payments, and life insurance premiums will add to the societal burden of health care.[58] Such health-sector costs are by no means limited to the developing countries, and they are undoubtedly more costly (in absolute terms) to the economies of the developed countries. The virologist Joshua Lederberg points out that nosocomial (hospital-acquired) infections result in the deaths of more than 20,000 Americans per year and cost the economy from $5 billion to $10 billion a year.[59]

In absolute terms, infectious disease is likely to have a much greater negative effect on the health-care sector in developing countries. For example, the World Bank estimates that the downstream costs of treating all current cases of AIDS in Tanzania will consume approximately 40.6 percent of that country's public health budget and nearly 25 percent of combined public and private spending. Similarly, the expense of treating current AIDS cases in Rwanda will absorb 60–65.5 percent of the public health budget.[60] This means either that far less money will be available to treat other health problems (including malaria, tuberculosis, onchocerciasis, and heart disease) or that money that would have gone into more productive sectors, such as infrastructure or education, will have to be diverted to cover national health expenditures. In many cases, the health-care system will be completely overwhelmed by the strains of disease proliferation. According to the UN, "the direct costs (drug costs, doctors fees, hospitalization care, food, etc.) of treating AIDS patients are enormous and greatly surpass available resources in Africa. For instance, it has been estimated that the direct cost of treating one AIDS patient in Zaire ranges from a low of US$132 to $1585; in . . . Tanzania, from $104 to $631. But the annual national budgets per capita for all health care were less than $5."[61]

In addition, developing countries are generally unable to afford expensive medicines required for the treatment and care of their AIDS patients. The drug AZT, for instance, was estimated to cost US$20,000 per patient per annum in 1994. In view of the low health-care funding available on a per capita basis in most of the developing countries, it is easy to see how ERIDs will drain government coffers, putting the expensive protease-inhibiting multi-drug cocktails of Western medicine out of reach for the majority of the world's inhabitants.[62] Furthermore, hopes for the development of effective and inexpensive vaccines for the prevention of HIV and medications for the treatment of AIDS have been unsuccessful, further constraining countries unable to afford the costs needed for the treatment of its AIDS patients.[63] In Thailand, Viravaidya et al. estimated HIV/AIDS health-care costs at between $658 and $1016 per year per infected person. Since the national average GDP per capita was roughly $1270 in 1991, AIDS-related costs will drain households, and the government is typically forced to ante up when the family's resources are exhausted. The estimated macro-level costs of AIDS to the Thai economy include lost future earnings of $22,000 per death and 10-year aggregate costs between $7.3 billion and $8.7 billion.[64]

The case of India is instructive. Surging HIV prevalence levels threaten to overwhelm the Indian health budget. If the HIV epidemic follows its current trend of proliferation throughout Indian society, by the year 2010 the government will have to spend about one-third more on health care than in a hypothetical non-AIDS scenario. This will necessitate an onerous $2.5 billion increase in the health-care budget.[65] Such increases in the health budget are negative for most countries, as the revenue must come from other government funds (usually those for education and other basic human services). Nelson Mandela has voiced concern that AIDS will drain the coffers of the South African government: "It is anticipated that if current trends continue then AIDS will cost South Africa 1 percent of our GDP by the year 2005; and that up to three-quarters of our health budget will be consumed by direct health costs relating to HIV/AIDS. Even creative low-cost alternatives to hospital care will leave us with a significant impact on our health-care budget."[66] Moreover, diseases such as AIDS, malaria, and tuberculosis will combine to accelerate the fiscal drain from competing sectors of government expenditure. Thus, the proliferation of infectious disease (HIV in particular) constitutes a very real fiscal problem for governments around the world, particularly those of developing countries. In a very real sense, the proliferation of disease will force governments to divert funding from other key sectors (such as education and law enforcement) to the health sector. This probably will result in higher government deficits and greater debt, and it is likely to undermine the ability of the government to provide for the basic needs of the population.

Agriculture

A major consequence of the improvement in rural health such as seems to have taken place in England in the century after 1650 was a notable increase in the efficiency of agricultural labor. Healthy people work better—and more regularly; and, as is obvious, losses to agricultural production resulting from inability to do necessary work at the right time of the year disappear in proportion as laborers cease to suffer from debilitating fevers and similar afflictions which tend to crest during the growing season. As health improved, fewer workers could therefore feed larger numbers of city folk.

—William McNeill, *Plagues and Peoples*, p. 220

The spread of disease will also have an enormous effect on the labor-intensive agricultural sector in affected regions. The UNDP notes that countries that bear the economic brunt of the HIV pandemic tend to be those that are most reliant on agriculture.[67] Diseases such as malaria, dengue fever, onchocerciasis, schistosomiasis, and HIV have the greatest ability to undercut the productivity of affected agricultural work forces. Thus, the negative consequences of HIV on the agricultural sector will be substantial throughout developing societies.[68]

The effect of disease proliferation on agricultural systems is likely to be varied and complex, depending on crop type, cash remittances, degree of labor-intensive cultivation practices, and size of holding. In sub-Saharan Africa, the absolute number of individuals infected with HIV is likely to be higher in rural than in urban areas, because the majority of the population continues to live in rural areas. Furthermore, the age groups most seriously affected by the AIDS epidemic are those that are the most productive in the labor-intensive agricultural sector.[69]

Of course, agriculture is the core sector of many developing economies, particularly in Africa, Asia, and South America. Agriculture contributes a large share of GDP, and for many countries it contributes the majority share of the value of exported products through cash crops. Increasing disease prevalence rates will similarly afflict the agricultural sector with supply-induced and demand-induced shocks. For example, as pathogens debilitate and kill workers, the semi-skilled labor supply for this sector will be reduced, necessitating either labor substitution within households and firms or the drawing of workers from other sectors. Shortages of semi-skilled labor shortages tend to get particularly acute in the rainy season, when vector-borne pathogens attain the highest prevalence within populations. However, since most developing societies possess abundant labor supplies, and since laborers can be retrained to work in the agricultural sector rather quickly, we should not be overly concerned about supply-side shocks in this sector. The only obvious concern would arise if an entire region, such as Southern Africa,[70] should suffer a rapid demographic implosion due to high prevalence of HIV in the 15–45-year age segment of its population. With HIV rates in Southern Africa ranging from 15 percent to 35 percent of the population, this remains a distinct possibility. Of course, imported labor from Northern Africa could eventually be used to offset the demographic decline, but such massive adjustment would require some time to enact.

Demand-side shocks may also compromise sectoral productivity. The citizens who succumb to disease are also consumers of agricultural products, and therefore domestic demand for these crops will grow more slowly in seriously afflicted societies. If smallholders (individuals who own and cultivate relatively small tracts of land) shift from the production of export to subsistence crops in response to disease-induced shocks, export revenues will also suffer over the long term.[71] "Those farming systems that are situated in the semi-arid tropics," Barnett and Blaikie argue, "will be most vulnerable to labor loss as a result of AIDS. . . . The farming systems of southern and eastern Africa in Tanzania, Zimbabwe, Kenya, Botswana, and Zambia seem particularly vulnerable, since seropositivity rates have already reached high levels in some rural areas of those countries. In all cases there will probably be implications for foreign-exchange earnings and urban food supplies."[72]

In one study of the Ugandan agricultural sector, production was found to be concentrated in smallholder farms and to be exceptionally labor intensive. The economist Jill Armstrong concludes that HIV/AIDS will compromise key farm production parameters such as labor availability and productivity, and that it will also limit investment in capital equipment to improve output. Thus, HIV/AIDS will reduce the amount of available disposable income that can be used to acquire agricultural inputs (e.g., occasional extra labor, new seeds or plants, fertilizer, pesticides, oxen).[73] Armstrong concludes that, as a result of increasing infection, "labor costs can be expected to increase, reflected in both market wage rates and the shadow wage rate implicit in family farm operations," and that "this, in turn, could lead to a reversal in migration from urban areas or increased migration from other regions with surplus labor."[74] Infectious disease has a number of other possible effects on smallholder agricultural production: the working day may be lengthened, land under cultivation may be reduced, cash crops may be substituted by less labor-intensive food crops, and planting and weeding may be delayed leading to poor harvests or the loss of an agricultural season.[75]

Human aversion to risk will also result in reduced agricultural productivity under certain circumstances, particularly when vector-borne pathogens are factored into the equation.[76] As a result of these vector-borne diseases, in many regions of the developing countries risk-averse farmers often forgo higher output in exchange for diminished income volatility. For example, farmers in malarious regions of Paraguay often choose to produce crops that can be grown outside the malaria season but which are of relatively lower value.[77] Thus, the desire to avoid infection may result in sub-optimal economic outcomes for smallholder agricultural producers.

Under certain conditions health investments can dramatically increase the productivity of land. For example, the reduced prevalence of malaria in Sri Lanka from 1947 to 1977 increased national income by 9 percent in 1977. The cumulative cost of containing disease was $52 million, compared with a cumulative gain of $7.6 billion in national income over the same time period. This results in an impressive gain of $140 per $1 originally invested in containment. During the exercise, regions that had been rendered unsuitable for human settlement by vector-borne disease became increasingly settled as migrants moved in, generating increased output.[78] Furthermore, the World Bank's Onchocerciasis Control Program covers 14 Sahelian countries in Africa and has been highly effective in opening new land and increasing agricultural productivity in the region. The program protects approximately 30 million people from onchocerciasis at an annual cost of less than $1 per capita, and at least 1.5 million previously infected individuals have recovered. The World Bank estimates that the program has prevented at least 500,000 cases of blindness. Furthermore, the Onchocerciasis Control Program liberated around 25 million hectares of land for resettlement and cultivation, generating a significant increase in agricultural production. The total estimated cost of the Onchocerciasis Control Program over the period 1974–2000 is about $570 million. The estimated range of increased internal national productivity ranges from 16 percent to 28 percent, and the majority of benefits will flow to those in the rural agricultural sector.[79]

Other ERIDs, such as parasitic nematodes (worms), can also have significant negative effects on the agricultural sector. In Nigeria, dracunculiasis (guinea worm disease) contributed to significant morbidity in more than 2.5 million Nigerians during 1987. Cost-benefit analyses revealed that the disease was the chief impediment to increasing rice production in Nigeria, the net effect of the disease being a reduction in rice production by $50 million in forgone revenue. Modeling suggests that the benefits of a worm-control program would exceed its costs after only 4 years.[80] The WHO is currently involved in a dracunculiasis-control program within selected regions of Africa, and the fruits of disease control are growing increasingly apparent. For example, reductions in dracunculiasis prevalence within targeted regions have resulted in a roughly 40 percent increase in food production in those regions. The land under cultivation in these areas has increased by 25 percent, and school absenteeism has declined from 60 percent to 13 percent in certain regions.[81]

One obvious lesson that can be drawn from the negative effect of ERIDs on agriculture is that the proliferation of disease threatens "food security" (i.e., the ability of the state to provide adequate nutritive resources for its population). This may lead to increasing marginalization, famine, and deprivation, which will certainly contribute to increasing poverty and human misery. As AIDS, tuberculosis, and vector-borne diseases spread, they have the potential to burden national economies that rely on labor-intensive agriculture to ensure the sustenance of their own population and to generate exports in order to increase national revenue. The proliferation of ERIDs threatens urban food supplies and foreign-exchange earnings in a number of developing nations, particularly in sub-Saharan Africa, South and Southeast Asia, and Latin America.

Education and Training

One peculiar characteristic of the AIDS pandemic is that, unlike many other pathogens (e.g., rotavirus), HIV does not spare the elite. The rates of HIV prevalence among high-income, urban, and well-educated African men are at least as high as those for low-income and rural men, and often higher. Since the elites earn, consume, and invest more, any disease affecting this group relatively more than other diseases is likely to have a greater effect per case.[82] Thus, decisions to make long-term societal investments in education are risky in Africa, as these investments in human capital are lost to HIV/AIDS with increasing frequency.[83] Cuddington argues that premature HIV-induced mortality will continue to erode national stocks of experienced workers, depleting existing reservoirs of human capital and limiting national output:

> . . . as AIDS becomes more prevalent, the perceived costs and benefits from undertaking new investments in human capital will change. Total expenditure will shift toward health care and away from schooling. To the extent that AIDS reduces expected lifetime, the incentives for individual workers or their employers to invest in education and training will also be reduced. Shifts in the relative wages of skilled and unskilled workers caused by differences in the prevalence of AIDS among various skill groups might also affect decisions to invest in human capital.[84]

In the previous chapter, I provided evidence that the level of infectious disease in a state exhibits a significant negative correlation with the percentage of the eligible population enrolled in secondary school. The cases presented below demonstrate that outbreaks and/or rising levels of disease can prevent children from attending school, or from doing well if they do attend. This provides evidence to help us interpret the aforementioned correlations, and additional evidence from which we can infer causality. As the prevalence of infectious disease continues to grow, the costs and benefits from current investments in human capital will probably shift. As a result, reduced spending on education will likely be the consequence of increasing national expenditures on health care to counter the effects of disease proliferation.[85] Since infectious diseases (particularly AIDS) tend to reduce life expectancy, the incentives for laborers or their employers to invest in training and education will diminish correspondingly. This results from the logic that there is little point in investing scarce resources in the education of someone who may be permanently debilitated by illness and therefore not likely to live to use the skills acquired through education. Furthermore, diseases may limit the efficacy of investing in human capital, as poor health tends to undermine to capacity of children to learn and acquire skills. Dasgupta has observed that youth who have been prone to illness and malnutrition tend to have learning disabilities and reduced cognitive function which is directly related to their poor health status.[86] The World Bank has found that healthier and well-fed children do much better in school, and enroll with greater frequency, than their deprived counterparts. A recent study on Jamaican children infected with whipworm showed that those debilitated by nematode infection scored 15 percent lower before treatment than healthy children in the same school. After treatment, the previously ill children achieved scores significantly closer to those of the healthy control group.[87]

Ainsworth, Over, and Cuddington expect the HIV pandemic to produce demand-side and supply-side shocks that will result in negative outcomes in the education sector. They argue that AIDS will reduce the demand for education relative to an AIDS-free scenario for a number of reasons, including reduced size of the cohort entering school and declining enrollment rates (due to the fact that affected households may find school fees too burdensome or to the fact that children may be needed as laborers or caregivers).[88] USAID data show that HIV/AIDS in Tanzania will reduce the number of children attending primary school by 22 percent and the number of children in secondary school by 14 percent from the level that could be expected without HIV/AIDS.[89] Supply-side shocks include depletion of the number of teachers available (due to increasing morbidity and mortality), increased teacher training and turnover costs, and reductions in the efficiency of the education system.[90] According to a World Bank report, "by 2010, Tanzania will have lost 14,460 teachers to AIDS. By 2020, some 27,000 teachers will have died. Training replacement teachers for the year 2020 will cost about $37.8 million (in 1991 dollars) in recurrent costs."[91] Ultimately, these disruptions of the education sector will have a significant negative effect on the downstream formation and consolidation of human capital in severely affected societies. Over time, as a result of these disruptions, the quality of the labor force will be significantly degraded, impairing long-term prospects for national growth. Demand-induced shocks to the education sector resulting from infectious disease will also have a significant negative effect on the downstream formation of human capital.

Cohen argues that rising adult mortality will also have a negative effect on training and education passed down to subsequent generations, in that rising adult mortality will diminish the passing on of acquired skills and knowledge from adults to youth, resulting in the gradual decline of labor productivity.[92]

Mining

As I have argued, infectious disease has a particularly negative economic effect on sectors associated with labor-intensive modes of production. Mining is therefore among the most vulnerable of these sectors to the increasing global proliferation of disease. Mining also tends to make a significant contribution to the economic output of many nations, particularly developing countries where resource extraction generates significant employment and revenues from export that can be used to offset foreign debt. For example, the copper industry in Zambia, which depends on young workers for its labor-intensive operations, accounts for almost 25 percent of the country's GNP and 90 percent of the country's export earnings.[93] The United Nations estimates that approximately 60 percent of the copper industry's labor force is now infected with HIV. This AIDS-induced morbidity and mortality will impair individual productivity and increase man-hours lost to illness. AIDS also will generate increased expenditures resulting from benefits for ill employees and their dependents, death benefits, and the need to train new employees. The combination of these pressures will undermine the industry's profits and will have a significant negative effect on Zambia's downstream prosperity.[94]

In Namibia the mining sector accounts for approximately 12 percent of GDP and some 3.5 percent of employment. Thus, mining is a major contributor to national output and generates more than 50 percent of national export revenues. The industry will have to cope with the direct costs associated with the epidemic, including absenteeism, health costs for employees and dependents, retraining costs, and additional recruitment costs. But the greatest costs of the epidemic will result from the loss of skilled managerial and supervisory workers. This erosion of national reserves of human capacity will be difficult, costly, and time consuming to replace.[95]

Tourism

Increasing levels of infectious disease may also disrupt tourism in severely affected regions, with attendant reductions in revenue from foreign sources. Many developing countries extract significant economic benefit from their tourism industries, particularly countries in the Caribbean basin and Oceania. The proliferation of malaria, dengue fever, cholera, and HIV may have serious and long-term negative effects on the tourism sector in many nations, particularly those in the tropics. States that depend on revenues from tourism for employment and foreign exchange are vulnerable to the myriad negative effects of disease through the reduction of labor supply, changing domestic demand priorities as disease reduces income, and demand shifts as tourists visit more benign destinations.[96]

In their study of the effect of AIDS on the Thai economy, Myers et al. concluded that "Thailand's $5 billion tourism industry may already be feeling the effects of AIDS. Tourist arrivals are down for a variety of reasons, with the fear of AIDS certain to be a significant factor in the future."[97] Aside from attrition processes such as the HIV/AIDS pandemic, outbreak events such as the sudden re-emergence of Ebola in Zaire, plague in India, and cholera in Peru generate extreme levels of fear derived from the human tendency of risk aversion, and thus tourists avoid affected regions during the outbreak period. For example, the 1991 outbreak of El Tor cholera in Peru had a significant immediate effect on tourism revenues in that country. Kimball and Davis estimate that during the outbreak tourism revenues declined between 60 percent and 70 percent in the first quarter of 1991 as compared to the first quarter of 1990.[98] Insofar as the fear of contagion can drive down tourism and deplete sectoral earnings, afflicted states may have an initial incentive not to report an outbreak, or to downplay its seriousness.

Macroeconomic Analysis

AIDS is fundamentally a development problem, not just a health problem. [Our models] predict that AIDS will reduce GDP growth by more than it reduces population growth, moving the attainment of reasonable living standards even further into the future. Regardless of the net macroeconomic impact of the epidemic, a profound distributional impact will make some households and communities much worse off, which should be of great concern to policy-makers.
—Martha Ainsworth and A. Mead Over, "The economic impact of AIDS on Africa," p. 585

The empirical evidence presented in the previous chapter clearly demonstrates that infectious disease rates show a significant negative correlation with macroeconomic national indicators such as per capita GNP, per capita government expenditure, and net long-term capital inflow. It is increasingly apparent that the current resurgence in infectious disease portends increasing poverty and economic destabilization in severely affected countries. At the microeconomic level, I have noted, ERIDs adversely affect economic well-being within families and firms, the general quality of the labor force, the formation and maintenance of human capital, and various sectors of the economy. It is logical to conclude that these microeconomic effects will, through multiplier effects, generate significant negative macroeconomic outcomes. Direct costs to the economy will be enormous, and indirect costs will include output lost as a result of increasing mortality and (to a lesser extent) disease-induced morbidity.

The four factors of production are capital, land, technology, and labor. Ainsworth argues that "if the first three of these [factors] grow at a constant rate the slower growth in labor caused by the epidemic will . . . slow the growth of output."[99] However, ERIDs act synergistically to exert negative effects on capital (both human capital and foreign investment) and land (diminishing access due to endemic infestation). This negative synergy should result in significant limits on national economic growth, and it may result in growing poverty and national economic decline (particularly within the developing countries). This supposition is borne out by the data presented in the previous chapter.

In their study of the effects of HIV on the Cameroonian economy, Kambou, Devarajan, and Over argue that the worst economic effects of HIV manifest themselves when there is significant infection of skilled urban workers and predict that HIV will result in a 2.2 percent drag on the annual national GDP growth rate in Cameroon. They posit that the growth rates of saving and investment will decline rapidly, undercutting the GDP growth rate. This contraction of real output growth will accompany the erosion of macroeconomic competitiveness in international markets. These effects have already been demonstrated in declining growth rates of exports and in increasing current account problems.[100]

Thus, the spread of disease impedes the investment of foreign capital, erodes human capital resources (thereby limiting the endogenous supply of social and technical ingenuity within a state), and renders some land and its natural resources economically useless. ERIDs may also affect technological attributes of the economy, insofar as disease-induced mortality may reduce the endogenous pool of skilled individuals (such as scientists and doctors) who would otherwise have contributed to endogenous technological innovation.

Foreign Investment

The global correlation between CAPIN and IM is $-0.686**$, significant to <0.001, with $r^2 = 0.471$. The association between LX and CAPIN is $0.682**$, significant to <0.001, with $r^2 = 0.465$. This means that declining disease rates in a state will have a positive effect on state capacity, such that foreign investors and other exogenous sources of capital may view that state as increasingly stable and profitable. Of course, correlation does not indicate causation, and this probabilistic relationship will require much deeper analysis before any claims about causation can be made.

CAPIN is one of our principal indicators for state capacity because it measures the influx of economic capital into the state from exogenous sources over time. Rational investors[101] will seek to put their capital into politically stable and economically productive societies, and thus this variable indirectly and partially measures state stability and prosperity. The evidence suggests that a high rate of prevalence of infectious diseases in a state will generate a disincentive for foreign capital owners to invest in that state. High disease rates tend to correlate with diminished state productivity, and such countries may be less able to attract exogenous capital in order to improve infrastructure and stimulate economic reforms. States with higher pathogen prevalence are, therefore, less productive and prosperous. Thus, soaring disease rates in much of the developing countries will diminish the probability of increasing foreign investment and undermine the ability of severely affected nations to generate economic growth.

Again, the global correlation between IM and per capita GNP is $-0.950**$, significant to <0.001, with $r^2 = 0.903$. The association between LX and GNP stands at $0.950**$, significant to <0.001, with $r^2 = 0.903$. GNP measures the monetary value of all goods and services produced by a nation's citizens per annum. The significant negative correlations between IM and GNP, and tuberculosis rates and GNP in the United States show a powerful inverse relationship between disease rates and economic productivity. Conversely, the positive association between LX and GNP provides further evidence to support the hypothesis. As Fogel suggested and as the data show, declining disease rates over time increase the productivity of a state. It is important to note the centrality of human capital in the economic equation of state prosperity, and understand the significant role that public health plays in the generation and preservation of that valuable human capital. Thus, we may conclude that, as public health improves, so does societal economic productivity. Conversely, we can conclude that continuing proliferation of HIV/AIDS, tuberculosis, malaria, and other diseases will undermine the economic productivity of severely affected states such as those in sub-Saharan Africa.

Another principal economic indicator of state capacity is GOVEX, which measures the fiscal outlay of the state on the provision of services (e.g., education, health care) to its population on an annual basis. As mentioned above, the correlation between global IM and GOVEX is $-0.988**$, significant to <0.001, with $r^2 = 0.976$. The correlation between LX and GOVEX is $0.778**$, significant to <0.001, with $r^2 = 0.605$. These statistical findings demonstrate that, as disease rates decrease, government expenditures increase reciprocally. The data show that, as disease rates rise in a country, government expenditures will shift to increased spending on health care and the withdrawal of funds from other sectors. This will eventually result in long-term economic decline due to falling economic productivity. As the growth rate of an economy declines, the revenues available to government will fall. This may well limit a state's economic capacity to adapt to the crisis.

Saving

Infectious disease will also affect saving at the microeconomic level. Cuddington's analysis of the effect of AIDS on the Tanzanian economy predicts that one of the outcomes of the epidemic will be a negative effect on domestic saving. According to Cuddington, infectious diseases such as onchocerciasis, HIV, and malaria will affect saving patterns in several ways. First, the immediate effect of increased medical expenditures will diminish saving as well as non-health current expenditures to a certain extent. Second, infectious diseases may negatively affect saving patterns through their pernicious effects on the life expectancy, age structure, healthiness, and growth rate of the population. The attributes of national health delivery systems will determine whether the negative saving effect burdens the private or the public sector. Cuddington argues that the decline in domestic saving will generate a corresponding reduction in the formation of capital, and that a significant decline in saving will have a correspondingly large negative effect on per capita income over the long term.[102]

In developing countries, available savings and their use will significantly affect the growth rate of GNP. There are reasons to expect that HIV and the general proliferation of ERIDs will reduce national savings, thereby resulting in reduced investment, diminished productive employment, lower per capita income, a drag on GNP growth, and in all likelihood a smaller GNP.[103] Cohen concludes that disease-induced declines in national savings resulting from domestic and exogenous sources will generate a decline in the rate of investment, precipitating a fall in the GNP growth rate. The statistics presented in the last chapter would seem to support this argument as disease levels demonstrate a significant negative association with per capita GNP over time. Ultimately, expenditures on current output will probably grow, resulting in a decline in savings. As domestic savings decline, less investment is likely.

Thus, exogenously supplied savings will decline in volume and will diminish relative to the growing needs induced by disease. Furthermore, it is probable that domestic savings will also decline as most productive sectors will be affected by disease proliferation (notably HIV). Additionally, declining foreign savings as a result of declining net long-term capital inflow will compromise national savings reservoirs over time.[104]

Trade

At the systems level, trade goods from disease-affected areas may be subject to international embargo. This has been the keystone of the growing discord between the United Kingdom and its European partners as British beef and British beef by-products have been banned by the rest of the European Community out of fear of contamination by the BSE prion that causes a lethal new variant of Creutzfeldt-Jacob disease (V-CJD) in humans. This trade embargo has seriously strained Britain's relationship with Brussels, to the extent that Prime Minister John Major once declared "diplomatic war" on the rest of the European Union in an attempt to disrupt the agenda of European unification.[105] The economic damage to Britain has yet to be measured accurately, but estimates run from US$8.4 billion to more than US$48 billion.[106]

Similarly, the re-emergence of Cholera in Peru in the period 1991–1996 had significant effects on trade and national prosperity. The epidemic generated more than 600,000 cases and 4500 deaths in Peru and spread rapidly throughout equatorial South America. Peru experienced trade-related costs resulting from the epidemic, due to canceled orders for exports of foodstuffs including fresh fruit and seafood. These export costs, including deterioration in prices of export goods, delayed sales, canceled orders, and increased inspection costs resulted in the loss of $700 million in export revenue for 1991 alone.[107]

The Indian city of Surat saw an outbreak of bubonic plague in September 1994, resulting in mass panic and rapid migration from the affected region. Because of the nature of the contagion, people became caught up in what eventually became a global epidemic of fear. Despite the fact that only 56 people perished as a result of the contagion, the economic damage to India resulting from forgone export revenues was significant. Specifically, many Indian goods, ranging from foodstuffs to fabric and diamonds, were embargoed internationally for the duration of the epidemic. Costs of the epidemic to India range from $1.3 to $1.7 billion—a significant sum in view of the persistent frailty of the Indian economy.[108]

It is important to differentiate between outbreak events and attrition processes when we evaluate the potential for ERIDs to disrupt trade. Attrition processes are highly unlikely to generate the significant levels of fear that may lead to an international boycott of a country's exports. Conversely, outbreak events tend to generate high levels of fear, which, in combination with the generalized human aversion to risk, result in extreme (and often inappropriate) measures, such as trade restrictions on Indian diamonds. Once the hysteria associated with an outbreak event dissipates, normal trade patterns will probably resume. Attrition processes, on the other hand, are likely to have greater negative long-term effects on trade, as every factory worker felled by contagion fails to produce a tradable good every minute, day, or year, depending on the nature of the good in question.

National Costs

Despite its high state capacity, the United States is increasingly vulnerable to the effects of disease proliferation. The US National Science and Technology Council estimates that the annual financial cost of common infectious diseases in the United States exceeds $120 billion. This figure includes morbidity and mortality associated with intestinal infections ($23 billion in direct medical costs and lost productivity), with food-borne diseases ($5 billion–$6 billion in medical and productivity costs), with sexually transmitted diseases ($5 billion in treatment costs, excluding AIDS), with influenza ($5 billion in direct medical costs, $12 billion in lost productivity), with antibiotic-resistant bacterial infections ($4 billion in treatment costs), and with hepatitis B virus infection (more than $720 million in direct and indirect costs).[109] Furthermore, many Americans suffer from hospital-acquired infectious complications. Approximately 2 million such cases occur every year in the United States, resulting in approximately 70,000 related deaths. The spread of these nosocomial infections imposes economic costs on the order of $10 billion a year.[110] In the case of Thailand, Sawert et al. found that "indirect costs resulting from morbidity and mortality due to the TB epidemic . . . are US$317 for a treated patient and US$1900 for a patient who remains undiagnosed. Death of an HIV-infected TB patient causes an economic loss of US$3490 to society, while the death of a non-HIV-infected patient results in a loss of US$19,400."[111]

Malaria

According to recent USAID estimates, more than 85 percent of malaria cases occur in sub-Saharan Africa, where the disease is responsible for approximately 2.5 million deaths per year. The negative economic effect of malaria on the region is substantial and increasing: for example, the direct economic cost of malaria in Africa for 1987 was $800 million; it rose to $1.7 billion by 1995, and it was projected to reach $3.5 billion by 2000. Moreover, USAID estimates that health-care costs for malaria on an out-patient basis account for approximately 40 percent of current national public health expenditures in sub-Saharan Africa.[112] USAID predicted in 1997 that the region could expect a 7–20 percent annual increase in the burden of malaria-induced mortality and morbidity in the coming years.[113] Shepard et al. pointed out in 1991 that the direct and indirect costs of disease are often greater than the amount of economic aid provided to afflicted regions by international donor agencies: ". . . in 1987 the cost of malaria in sub-Saharan Africa was about $791 million per year. This figure is projected to rise to $1.684 billion by 1995. By comparison, the entire health assistance to Africa of a major bilateral donor, the US Agency for International Development, was only $52 million for all conditions."[114]

Ettling and Shepard's study of malaria's economic cost to Rwanda demonstrated that malaria's drag on the national GDP rose from 1 percent in 1989 to an estimated 2.4 percent in 1995—a 140 percent increase over 5 years.[115] Following the projected trajectory of increases in malaria incidence, the cost of malaria to the Rwandan GDP could conservatively be expected to reach a minimum of 3.36 percent by 2000. Recent studies by the World Health Organization in Burkina Faso, Chad, Congo, and Rwanda show that the cost of an average case of malaria in sub-Saharan Africa is equivalent to about 12 days' productive output. The total cost for the area in 1995 was projected at $1.684 billion, equal to 1 percent of GDP (having risen from $791 million—0.6 percent of the GDP—in 1987).[116] This represents an increase in costs to the regional GDP of 66.7 percent from 1987 to 1995. To extrapolate conservatively from the trend line, malaria alone will exert a drag of 1.67 percent on the regional GDP by 2003, and an onerous 4.64 percent by 2012.

Of course, one must consider that the effect of malaria differs from state to state. South Africa has a relatively minor malaria problem compared to the tropical states in the Great Lakes region of Central Africa. Shepard estimates that malaria incidence in Rwanda increased an average of 21 percent every year through the 1980s (an eightfold increase since 1979), while malaria incidence in Togo increased by a relatively modest 10.4 percent per annum over the same time period. Furthermore, malaria's resistance to quinine increased from 0 to 30 percent for the whole of Africa, and rose to an astonishing 66 percent in Rwanda, over the same time period. Regional resistance to another powerful anti-malarial agent (fansidar) is estimated at 34 percent.[117] Malaria is not confined to the African continent, and its spread bodes ill for other tropical regions, particularly South Asia. One detailed study concludes that malaria causes the Indian economy to lose between 500 million and a billion US dollars per year.[118] As malaria spreads through South and Southeast Asia, Oceania, and Latin America, we should expect to see mounting damage to the economies of those affected regions.

HIV/AIDS

We have every reason to assume that the epidemic in South-East Asia will soon be just as widespread as it is in Africa. And that East Africa's experience—a slow down of its economy—will be replicated in Eastern Europe and the developing countries of Asia and Latin America.
—Peter Piot, in address to World Economic Forum, February 3, 1997[119]

The significant economic costs resulting from the HIV pandemic are becoming clearer as it drains government coffers and markets in both developing and developed countries. Hellinger notes the burdensome costs imposed by HIV infection on the American health-care budget. He estimates that the lifetime cost of treating a person with HIV from the time of infection until death is approximately $119,000.[120]

Hanveldt et al. compared the societal effect of HIV/AIDS with other selected causes of male mortality to determine the indirect costs of lost future production in Canada. Over the period 1987–1991, these authors assert, the HIV/AIDS epidemic resulted in a loss to the Canadian economy of the equivalent of US$2.11 billion:

Assuming a 2 percent annual growth in earnings and a 3 percent annual real discount rate. . . . Deaths due to HIV/AIDS accounted for 2.11 billion in 1990 US$. Future production loss due to HIV/AIDS more than doubled during the period from 1987 to 1991, from 0.27 to 0.60 billion 1990 US$. Our findings demonstrated HIV/AIDS mortality is already having a dramatic impact on future wealth production in Canada. If the past trend continues, the production lost in 1994 should exceed 0.86 billion 1990 US$ and will account for more than 10 percent of the total annual loss for men aged 25–64 years.[121]

In 1993, D. C. Lambert estimated the costs of AIDS-related deaths in France. He concludes that the annual cost of AIDS-induced mortality in France was between US$10 billion and US$12 billion in 1989 and between US$18 billion and US$20 billion in 1992. Based on the trend line of the epidemic, he argued that the costs of HIV to the French economy would be between $32.4 billion and $36 billion for 1995.[122] Furthermore, Newton et al., who have examined the past and potential effect of HIV/AIDS in nineteen English-speaking nations of the Caribbean, estimate that the total annual costs of the epidemic will approach $500 million (in constant 1989 US dollars), or 2 percent of GDP, in the low scenario, and will exceed 1.2 billion, or 5 percent of GDP, in the high scenario.[123]

Using a sample of 56 countries over the period 1980–1992, Bloom et al. estimated the effect of HIV on the Human Development Index and concluded that HIV resulted in the loss of 1.3 years' human development progress per country. Some countries in particular have borne an enormous toll: Zambia has lost 10 years' development, Tanzania 8 years, and Malawi and Zimbabwe approximately 5 years.[124] (Because seroprevalence has increased greatly since 1992, the negative developmental effects will probably be significantly greater than the data presented by Bloom et al. suggest.)

Recent studies by USAID conclude that AIDS will infect 25 percent of Kenya's population by 2005, and that it will reduce Kenya's GDP by 10 percent.[125] Cuddington argues that HIV/AIDS may reduce Tanzania's GDP in the year 2010 by 15–25 percent in relation to a counterfactual no-AIDS scenario.[126] Dayton concurs, noting that the presence of AIDS in Tanzania will probably reduce the average real growth rate in the period 1985–2010 by between 15 percent and 28 percent, from 2.9 percent to 4.0 percent per annum. Over 25 years, this decreases potential output by between 15 billion and 25 billion 1980 Tanzanian shillings. The net effect of HIV on growth of potential GDP per capita is estimated at a reduction of 12 percent (vs. a counterfactual non-HIV scenario).[127]

Desmond Cohen argues that Botswana will witness a dramatic decline in its Human Development Index ranking as a result of HIV. Human development indicators in 2010 will decline below 1996 levels.[128] Cohen also posits that HIV/AIDS will probably result in a net loss of 10 percent to Namibia's Human Development Index indicators over the period 1996–2006, and that the lion's share of these losses will be incurred by the most deprived and marginalized Namibians.

Peter Piot has warned that several of the most promising emerging markets, particularly China, India, and Thailand, are likely to replicate the experience of sub-Saharan Africa in a few years, which would be a disaster for the global economy.[129] Myers et al. predict that the negative macroeconomic effects of HIV/AIDS in Thailand will continue to slow growth: "The total annual health care costs plus the value of lost income is projected to grow from $100 million in 1991 to $2.2 billion by 2000 in the high scenario and from $97 million to $1.8 billion in the low scenario. Over 10 years, $8.7 billion will be lost as a result of AIDS illness and death in the high case, $7.3 billion in the low case. These annual cost, both direct and indirect, equal about 16–18 times the per capita GDP."[130]

A recent study commissioned by the UNDP's Regional Bureau for Asia and the Pacific has examined the detrimental effect of the HIV/AIDS pandemic on development as measured by the Human Development Index. The study anticipates that the HIV pandemic will cost Thailand approximately 9 years' human development, and will cost Myanmar (Burma) 5 years' developmental progress between 1992 and 2005. India, which will soon be the HIV/AIDS capital of Asia, will forgo a year's development progress by 2005, and the loss will accelerate thereafter.[131]

Piot has called the worldwide economic effect of AIDS roughly equivalent to 4 percent of the GDP of the United States or the entire economy of India.[132] In the 1994 version of the UNDP's Human Development Report, the cumulative direct and indirect costs of HIV/AIDS throughout the 1980s were estimated at $240 billion. According to that report, "the social and psychological costs of the epidemic for individuals, families, communities and nations are also huge—but inestimable." The report goes on to predict that "the global cost—direct and indirect—of HIV and AIDS by 2000 could be as high as $500 billion a year—equivalent to more than 2 percent of global GDP."[133] Occasionally, critics argue that rising levels of infectious disease will in fact concentrate wealth in the hands of survivors and thereby raise per capita GDP and the overall standard of living in affected societies.

However, models developed by Ainsworth and Over predict that the Malthusian hypothesis under which survivors will experience rising GDP is erroneous, and that the AIDS/HIV epidemic (among others) will in fact reduce GDP growth per capita across many scenarios.[134]

Based on the evidence culled from the studies of state capacity, we can reasonably conclude that the global proliferation of ERIDs will impose a general drag on the productivity and prosperity of seriously affected states. Under extreme conditions of endemic pathogen infection within the national population pool (e.g., most countries in sub-Saharan Africa), disease has the potential to destabilize economies and push entire regions into economic decline. Cohen warns that HIV's "impact on the economic, social and political systems may be fundamental and structural. The consequences of system collapse are not something that economists can predict or even comprehend. Such collapse, however, may pose a threat to the continued functioning of some countries with high rates of seroprevalence."[135] Unfortunately, social scientists have no idea where the threshold of collapse may lie, after which the system may rapidly slide into a negative spiral dynamic.[136] Available models are based on the anecdotal evidence compiled by historians and on their observations of the effects that various forms of pestilence had on local populations at distant points in time. In view of the rapid and significant changes in population density, urbanization, migration, environmental decay, and travel times that occurred in the twentieth century, we have no clear idea of the levels at which pathogen seroprevalence in local populations may push societies across a poorly demarcated threshold into a negative economic (and social) spiral.

From the evidence presented above, it is reasonable to speculate that one of the main barriers to the development of pathogen-laden tropical areas is the economic burden that disease inflicts on those societies. If we extrapolate from Fogel's arguments it becomes apparent that one reason for the significant gap between the developed states of temperate regions and the generally underdeveloped tropical states is the intensity of infectious disease in tropical regions.[137] Such arguments are taken as obvious within the medical community but have yet to be recognized by the community of scholars of international development in the social sciences.

The strong association between health and prosperity is certainly evident in sub-Saharan Africa, which is the area of highest ERID prevalence, and not surprisingly the poorest region of the world as well, despite the presence of significant natural resources. Besides having the highest prevalence of endemic regional pathogens, sub-Saharan Africa is also host to the most virulent sub-epidemic of the AIDS pandemic. Now that the HIV pandemic is thoroughly entrenched in Africa, we should be concerned about the economic instability that the epidemic will bring in its wake as it spreads through South and Southeast Asia and Eastern Europe. The UNDP has predicted that economic losses resulting from AIDS could soon exceed total foreign aid to seriously affected states.[138] From the experience of sub-Saharan Africa and the data we now have, it seems reasonable to predict that as infectious disease continues to proliferate we will see increasing poverty and economic polarization between social classes within societies.

High rates of disease impose costs on the family unit, reduce per capita income, reduce saving, reduce government revenues and fiscal resources, divert government expenditure from more productive sectors into health care, produce disincentives to invest in child education, impede settlement of marginal regions and the development of natural resources, negatively affect tourism, and occasionally result in the embargoing of presumably infected trade goods, producing a general negative effect on the state economy. If many states are similarly affected within a region, such as sub-Saharan Africa, the net effect will be the underdevelopment of the region as a whole, which may in turn impose a net drag on global trade.[139]

Reviewing the evidence, we can draw the following conclusions regarding the economic effect of infectious disease on national productivity:

• Infectious diseases impede the formation and consolidation of human capital.[140]

• Disease-induced morbidity and mortality will generate supply-side and demand-side shocks to households, firms, and even to entire sectors. These shocks will reverberate across sectors and will tend to destabilize national economies, resulting in declining standards of living, per capita income, and buying power.

• Disease may result in diminished levels of foreign capital inflow and may generate incentives to place trade embargoes on countries with high ERID prevalence.

• Disease may increase and/or reinforce perceived and real income inequalities within afflicted societies. Such increasing inequalities may generate
absolute deprivation and perceptions of relative deprivation in marginalized segments of society, possibly leading to increasing social dysfunction
through crime, rioting, and low-intensity violence.[141]

Ultimately, the global proliferation of infectious disease poses a significant
long-term threat to the economic capacity of states, as disease-induced
economic shocks force a contraction of the frontier of national production
possibilities and threaten the development prospects of many societies.
Indeed, infectious disease is already undermining hard-won economic and
social gains throughout the developing countries, particularly in tropical
regions. The available evidence suggests that the negative effects of infectious disease on economic productivity are likely to be greatest in the
developing countries (owing to initially low state capacity, geographical
endemicity, and lower endogenous adaptation capacity). Infectious disease constitutes a significant long-term threat to the economic stability of
states and possibly entire regions, particularly those within the tropical
zones of the planet and those with low or declining state capacity (e.g., the
former Soviet Union).

4

Infectious Disease and Security

Swords and lances, arrows, machine guns, and even high explosives have had far less power over the fates of the nations than the typhus louse, the plague flea, and the yellow-fever mosquito. Civilizations have retreated from the plasmodium of malaria, and armies have crumbled into rabbles under the onslaught of cholera spirilla, or of dysentery and typhoid bacilli. War and conquest and that herd existence which is an accompaniment of what we call civilization have merely set the stage for these more powerful agents of human tragedy.
—Hans Zinsser, *Rats, Lice, and History,* pp. 9–10

The history of human societies is replete with evidence that shifts in the equilibrium between humans and their microbial predators can lead to significant societal destabilization and to subsequent transformation. The destruction of pre-Columbian societies in the New World, the collapse of Byzantine Rome, and demise of the feudal order in Europe are all attributable in part to the destruction wrought by various "plagues" on immunologically vulnerable populations.[1] Thucydides's account of the oscillations of Athenian power during the Peloponnesian Wars pays particular attention to the devastating and destabilizing effect of "the plague" on Athenian society and, by extension, on the Athenian war effort.[2] In view of the empirical fact that pathogenic agents are engaged in continual co-evolution, emergence, and recrudescence, this historical dynamic between pathogens and humanity is unlikely to change in the near future. In fact, it is increasingly likely that humanity's increasing degradation of the biosphere and changes in the human ecology will foster the emergence and proliferation of pathogens that will thrive in the world's changing environment.[3]

In this chapter I examine the claim that infectious disease constitutes a verifiable threat to national security and state power. I also develop an

understanding of how the continuing emergence and proliferation of
pathogens may affect international matters such as regional political stability, peacekeeping, and international regimes. I briefly examine certain
political barriers to effective response at the national and the international
level. Finally, I examine the feasibility of locating the threat of infectious
disease as a security issue within the present paradigm of environmental
security rather than creating a separate sub-discipline of health security.[4]

The Social Contract and National Security

Rousseau and Hobbes argued that a social contract has historically
existed between the state and the governed.[5] In essence, the citizen declares
his or her fealty to the state, and in return the state guarantees to protect
the citizen from predators internal (i.e., criminals) and external (foreign
armies).

As I have argued above, the destruction of the populace by an ecological predator (in this case, pathogenic agents) constitutes a distinct threat
to the well-being of the populace as guaranteed by the state. Since infectious disease results in far greater population mortality than typically
results from war, the resurgence of older miasmas and the emergence of
novel and lethal pathogens constitutes a very real threat to the security of
the population of the modern state.

Interdisciplinary research of the type I am reporting here requires a fundamental reconceptualization of standard definitions of national security.
Constrictive definitions that focus exclusively on the relative military
capabilities of states are increasingly sterile in the face of the many global
challenges of the post-Cold War world. Threats to human welfare such
as global environmental degradation, resource scarcity, and population
growth present policy makers with difficult choices having to do with collective action. In view of the current inclusion of diverse issues (such as
migration and the environment) in the security debate, does it not make
sense to also include infectious diseases, whose immediate effects on the
state can be more direct, more immediate, and far more destructive than
the effects of population movement?

As the import of trans-boundary threats to state stability and to the survival of the human species increases, concepts of security must transcend

traditional militaristic definitions. In 1983 the political scientist Richard Ullman argued that "defining national security merely in military terms conveys a profoundly false image of reality [and] causes states to concentrate on military threats and to ignore other and perhaps more harmful dangers."[6] Ullman redefined a threat to national security as "an action or sequence of events that (1) threatens drastically and over a relatively brief span of time to degrade the quality of life for the inhabitants of a state, or (2) threatens significantly to narrow the range of policy choices available to the government of a state or to private, non-governmental entities (persons, groups, corporations) within the state."[7]

For the purposes of my research, I adopt Ullman's definition, which includes potential non-military threats to national security. This is reasonable and logical, insofar as the emergence of a pathogen may result in a particular event (a temporally circumscribed outbreak) or in a sequence of events (slow and steady proliferation) that will significantly degrade the quality of life for inhabitants of a state. There is now ample evidence that infectious diseases (particularly HIV, malaria, and TB) have significant deleterious effects on the quality of life of a populace—effects that are reflected in declining life expectancy and in increasing poverty. Furthermore, I have argued that as disease intensity grows it will correspondingly reduce state capacity, increase economic deprivation, and deplete the reservoir of human capital within seriously affected states. This long-term depletion of human capital will undermine national prosperity and effective governance, thereby diminishing the range of policy options available to the state. In these two respects, infectious disease constitutes a real threat to the national security of all states, but particularly those that are most vulnerable to the ravages of disease—that is, states with low endogenous capacity. Under extreme circumstances (such as the exceptionally high HIV prevalence in sub-Saharan Africa), infectious disease exhibits the capacity to generate catastrophic numbers of human deaths over a relatively brief span of time. The absolute expected mortality in this region resulting from HIV/AIDS greatly exceeds deaths resulting from any one conflict in this region in recorded history. Aside from the absolute destruction of populations that may result from high levels of infection, extreme pathogen-induced burdens on human health may result in the widespread economic and political destabilization of societies, states, and entire regions.[8]

The literature of the field has developed two principal hypotheses that link environmental and demographic change to intra-state violence: the *relative deprivation* hypothesis and the *state weakness* hypothesis. The deprivation hypothesis argues that certain processes, such as environmental scarcity and demographic growth, may have a significant negative long-term effect on individual living standards and quality of life within a society, inducing either relative or absolute deprivation.[9] The argument is that increasing deprivation eventually translates into increasing frustration that in turn generates increasing aggression by disaffected individuals and collectivities. Thus, greater deprivation may increase the probability of social violence and political chaos.[10] As Eckstein and Kahl have noted, however, the deprivation hypothesis is incapable of explaining political violence in and of itself.[11] Specifically, it generates an excessive number of false positives in its prediction of sub-state violence. If the hypothesis were true, most poor nations of the earth would be caught up in an eternal maelstrom of political chaos and violence, and this is simply not the case. In all likelihood, this lack of rebellion derives from the fact that the poor often lack the organizational capacity, economic resources, and opportunity to rebel. Thus, not every state that suffers from poverty is exceptionally prone to chronic internal violence. Indeed, conflict seems to occur more frequently when mounting deprivation is combined with declining state capacity, which generates increasing probability that the desire to redress perceived or absolute inequalities between classes, ethnicities, and elites may provoke collective violence.[12]

The state weakness hypothesis suggests that intra-state organized violence tends to occur when stressor variables (e.g., poverty, environmental scarcity) create both opportunities and incentives for citizens to engage in collective violent action against the status quo. These stressors create increasing competition between groups within the general polity for increasingly scarce resources, thus creating additional incentive for violent action against competitor groups or against the state. Additionally, stressor variables may increase demands on the state to provide services, simultaneously reducing state capacity, increasing institutional fragility, and undermining the cohesion and legitimacy of the state.[13] Thus, the prospects for the success of rebellious action improve, providing greater incentive for collective violence.

As I demonstrated in chapters 2 and 3, the proliferation of infectious disease may significantly reduce both individual and societal prosperity, producing more absolute deprivation and more relative deprivation in seriously affected populations. Furthermore, I argue that pathogen-induced declines in population health generate increasing poverty at both the individual level and the macro level, and that they widen economic disparities between social classes in a society. Rapid negative change in the health status of a population and pathogen-induced demographic collapse may therefore figure in the destabilization of states. Thus, this study compliments both the deprivation hypothesis and the state weakness hypothesis.

One caveat: Although disease may be a significant contributor to the preconditions for sub-state violence and state failure, it is unlikely to generate these effects in and of itself. It is important to recognize that disease may combine with other stressors (such as environmental degradation and scarcity) to magnify both relative and absolute deprivation and to hasten the erosion of state capacity in seriously affected societies. Thus, infectious disease may in fact contribute to societal destabilization and to chronic low-intensity intra-state violence, and in extreme cases it may accelerate the processes that lead to state failure.

Of related interest is the recent work of Kalevi Holsti on the changing nature of conflict since 1945. Holsti has found that the incidence of inter-state war has declined precipitously since the nineteenth century, and that the current principal foci of violence are at the intra-state level.[14] If Holsti's calculations are correct, political scientists concerned with the study of conflict must shift their focus to the growing incidence of intra-state violence and must develop theoretical models that explain the recent collapse of states such as Sierra Leone and the former Zaire. Holsti emphasizes this need for a conceptual shift in security studies:

Overall[,] . . . strategic studies continue to be seriously divorced from the practices of war. . . . Most fundamentally, the assumption that the problem of war is primarily a problem of the relations *between* states has to be seriously questioned. The argument . . . is that security *between* states in the Third World, among some of the former republics of the Soviet Union, and elsewhere has become increasingly dependent upon security *within* those states. The trend is clear: the threat of war between countries is receding, while the incidence of violence within states is on an upward curve.[15]

In addition to the shift in the loci of conflict from the inter-state to the intra-state level, the political scientist Mohammed Ayoob notes that the majority of these recent conflicts now occur in the developing countries.[16] This is, of course, consistent with the finding that states with low endogenous capacity should be more vulnerable to stressors on their economies and institutions of governance. Thus, the proliferation of infectious disease directly threatens institutions of governance in the developing countries and raises the probability of intra-state violence in seriously affected regions.[17]

This is no excuse for complacency in the developed countries. In the United States, deaths from infectious disease have doubled to 170,000 per annum since their historic low in 1980.[18] Thus, in that period, infectious disease has re-emerged as a direct threat to the well-being of the US population. Despite their enormous technological and economic power, it is extremely unlikely that the developed countries will be able to remain an island of health in a global sea of disease. In fact, the proliferation of HIV throughout European and North American societies from the early 1980s through the mid 1990s shows that even high-capacity states may be initially vulnerable to pathogen emergence. Europe's growing inability to contain the spread of the BSE prion and the recent emergence of West Nile Virus near New York City testify to the continuing vulnerability of even the most affluent societies to infectious disease. In this respect, global interdependence applies to the microbial threat just as it applies to the pervasive degradation of the biosphere. Unilateral, isolationist policies will only compromise the prosperity and well-being of all peoples over time.

Furthermore, the destabilization of the developing countries affects the interests of the developed nations in myriad ways, and there is evidence that US policy makers are cognizant of the threat that the resurgence of infectious disease poses to the broader security and foreign policy interests of United States. In the Clinton administration's national security strategy of "engagement and enlargement," the proliferation of infectious disease was identified as a novel threat to American foreign policy interests, particularly to the central policy pillars of global economic growth and the expansion and consolidation of stable and functional democracies throughout the developing countries and in the former Soviet Union:

New diseases, such as AIDS, and other epidemics which can be spread through environmental degradation, threaten to overwhelm the health facilities of developing countries, disrupt societies and stop economic growth. Developing countries must address these realties with national sustainable development programs that offer viable alternatives. US leadership is of the essence to facilitate that progress. If such alternatives are not developed, the consequences for the planet's future will be grave indeed.[19]

President Clinton appointed the National Science Council on Emerging and Re-Emerging Infectious Diseases to determine the direct and indirect threat of infectious disease to the security and prosperity of the United States and to further evaluate the potential effects of pathogen proliferation on American national security and global foreign policy interests. According to the council's subsequent report:

The improvement of international health is a valuable component of the US effort to promote worldwide political stability through sustainable economic development. Thus, the effort to build a global disease surveillance and response system is in accord with the national security and foreign policy goals of the United States.[20]

Former Undersecretary of State for Global Affairs Timothy Wirth was also keenly aware of the threat that HIV/AIDS poses to state stability and prosperity:

It is . . . evident that as the pandemic spreads, HIV/AIDS has potentially devastating impacts on whole sectors of societies. In the most vulnerable nations, these trends could have devastating consequences for sustainable development and contribute to conflict and instability. [W]e must understand the pandemic for its ability to affect the social, economic, and political fabric of many nations and, thus, its implications for US foreign policy, American leadership, and global cooperation. Viewed in the context of national security interests, many countries are today waging (and losing) a war with this infectious disease.[21]

On January 10, 2000, US Vice-President Al Gore, UN Secretary General Kofi Annan, and US Ambassador to the UN Richard Holbrooke convened a special session of the UN Security Council to deal with the HIV/AIDS pandemic, which was subsequently recognized by much of the international community as a novel and growing threat to both national and international security. In his impassioned address to the Security Council, Gore argued as follows:

For the nations of sub-Saharan Africa, AIDS is not just a humanitarian crisis. It is a security crisis—because it threatens not just individual citizens, but the very institutions that define and defend the character of a society. This disease weakens work forces and saps economic strength. AIDS strikes at teachers and denies education to their students. It strikes at the military, and subverts the forces of order and peacekeeping. AIDS is one of the most devastating threats ever to confront the world community. The United Nations was created to stop wars. Now we must wage and win a great and peaceful war of our time—the war against AIDS.[22]

The balance of the evidence suggests that disease will generate a pervasive negative effect on political polarization and promote competition between elites within a climate of declining fiscal resources and increasing deprivation. The probability of intra-elite conflict will increase as a result of the absolute decline in resources available to the state, which is reflected in declining national fiscal measures such as per capita GDP, in declining foreign investment, and in an eroding savings base (see chapter 3). Under the rubric of environmental scarcity, Thomas Homer-Dixon suggests that, in the context of declining resource availability, political elites will attempt to capture increasingly scarce renewable resources such as water, crop land, and timber. There is every reason to assume that this dynamic of intra-elite competition will hold in the context of increasing economic scarcity, wherein elites must increasingly compete over their portions of an ever-diminishing economic pie. Though I have previously argued that class-based conflict between elites and the poor is one possible result of increasing disease prevalence,[23] the potential for intra-elite violence is also increasingly probable and may carry grave political consequences, such as coups, the collapse of governance, and planned genocides.

Disease-induced declines in productivity, prosperity, and the general well-being of the populace are bound to have a negative effect on the perceived legitimacy of ruling elites. Lower classes may engage in increasing anti-governmental activity if the state is perceived as weakening, and aspiring factions of the middle and upper classes may see eroding governmental legitimacy and declining state capacity as a window of opportunity to displace the ruling elite. In many cases, the resulting turbulence may impede the consolidation of democratic institutions and processes of governance within seriously affected societies. Disease-induced intra-societal competition may also have a pronounced negative effect on the formation of civil society within affected regions, such that inter-class competition and intra-elite competition erode the fundamental basis for the construction and consolidation of civil society. Thus, the continuing proliferation of disease agents threatens to impede and/or destabilize nascent democratic transitions throughout the developing world. In certain cases, elites may be forced to respond to increasing challenges from within their societies by cracking down on dissent and imposing draconian measures to stabilize the state, which may precipitate a slide back into authoritarian structures of rule. Moreover, certain regimes under pressure may engage in either the scapegoating of minorities (e.g., Zimbabwe), or the pursuit of foreign military adventures (e.g., Rwanda, Uganda) in an effort to distract their populations and deflect criticism away from ruling elites. Ultimately, the increasing burden of disease promises significant problems for national and regional governance in severely affected areas. This has wide-ranging implications for the development and consolidation of nascent democracies throughout the developing countries and in the former Soviet Union.

After the unprecedented meeting of the Security Council to address a public health issue, the National Intelligence Council of the United States issued a comprehensive report detailing the US government's position. That report states that infectious disease constitutes a significant and evolving threat to both the broader foreign policy concerns and the national security of the United States.[24] Concurring with the findings presented herein, it asserts that "the infectious disease burden will add to political instability and slow democratic development in sub-Saharan Africa, parts of Asia, and the former Soviet Union, while also increasing political tensions in and among some developed countries."[25] It continues:

The severe social and economic impact of infectious diseases, particularly HIV/AIDS, and the infiltration of these diseases into the ruling political and military elites and middle classes of developing countries are likely to intensify the struggle for political power to control scarce state resources. This will hamper the development of a civil society and other underpinnings of democracy and will increase pressure on democratic transitions in regions such as the [former Soviet Union] and sub-Saharan Africa where the infectious disease burden will add to economic misery and political polarization.[26]

US policy makers are increasingly accepting of the wisdom inherent in the doctrine of "preventive defense" articulated by former US Secretary of Defense William J. Perry, wherein the United States is currently adopting a wide-ranging and proactive stance in its bid to ensure global stability.[27] Colonel Patrick Kelley of the US Army recognizes that "since the end of the Cold War, the United States is increasingly accepting its role in global security as one of securing peace and prosperity through efforts directed toward states that are failing or at risk of failing. Even if these states do not pose a direct military threat, their failure clearly has a ripple effect well beyond their borders."[28] It is evident that the Clinton administration regarded the global proliferation of infectious disease as a significant threat to the national security of the United States and to global security within the context of the doctrine of preventive defense. Secretary of Health and Human Services Donna Shalala commented:

The catastrophic effects of AIDS are endangering not only the security of these countries, but also their fragile health systems. We also know that a crumbling health infrastructure leads to crumbling stability of societies. We also know the relationship between AIDS and political stability which is indirect but real, and as [Holbrooke] had pointed out, AIDS has affected political stability. . . . Imagine how important it is to fight this pandemic and how much we believe that the US has a direct self-interest in fighting this disease.[29]

This view is not yet widely shared by everyone within the apparatus of the US government. Although a growing community of legislators in the Republican-dominated houses of Congress are increasingly receptive to the arguments put forth by intelligence officials and by academics, there are many who remain opposed on partisan grounds. For example, when asked if he viewed AIDS as a national security threat, Senator Trent Lott responded: ". . . the answer is no, I don't. I guess this is just the president trying to make an appeal to, you know, certain groups. But no, I don't view that as a national security threat. Not to our national security interests, no."[30] Lott's speculation that the rise of infectious disease to the realm of national security resulted from the Clinton administration's interests in placating certain domestic constituencies did not serve to clarify or advance the debate. Furthermore, such beliefs carry the potential to mire a grave global issue in the partisan intransigence so commonly exhibited within US institutions of governance. In truth, it is rather unlikely that the Clinton administration elevated issues of public health to the lofty realm of national security merely to court the favor of a very small portion of the American population.

Let us return for a moment to Rousseau's notion of the social contract. The HIV/AIDS epidemic in sub-Saharan Africa threatens the population base of most states throughout the entire region. Any understanding of national security should be predicated on the protection of the population of the state, for without a populace there can be no industry, no surplus revenue for taxation, and ultimately no reason for government. Therefore, the destruction of the population by any source constitutes a direct threat to the contract between state and citizen, and if the state cannot guarantee the citizen an adequate degree of protection from death and/or debilitation then that state has not honored its part of the bargain. Of course, there is a significant degree of human agency involved in the proliferation of infectious disease (particularly HIV): human beings act as vectors of transmission, and elements of human behavior (such as war, trade) serve to accelerate disease proliferation. Moral and legal obligations notwithstanding, state power and stability will weaken as its population base erodes as a result of the proliferation of infective agents. This view was echoed by security officials at the highest levels within the Clinton administration. For example, National Security Advisor Samuel Berger said: "The countries . . . that have enjoyed solid growth in Africa now are beginning to see that growth erode because its work force is not able anymore to function in the economy and the cost of the disease (HIV) to the government is becoming overwhelming. Those countries begin to unravel. They are unstable. They're more likely to engage in conflict with their neighbors. And before long, we have something, a situation which is really tumultuous."[31]

Direct Effects

Aside from the effects of disease on poverty and governance, disease has historically exhibited direct negative effects on military forces through the debilitation and/or death of military personnel. The presence of infectious disease in foreign military theaters has resulted in the exposure of troops to previously unknown pathogens. Such exposure to novel or recrudescent pathogens affects military readiness, force structure, and recruitment. Patrick Kelley warns that in certain cases military forces from the developed countries are at increased risk of contracting exotic pathogens from foreign military theaters owing to "differential immunity":

The fact that our troops tend to grow up under good hygienic conditions further means that upon reaching adulthood they tend to be 'immunologic virgins' compared with members of many potential opposing forces who spent their childhood in hygienic squalor. As a result, some infections, to which our opponents may have almost universally become immune during childhood, can pose a significant health threat to a deployed US force. The military effect of differential immunity was well illustrated in the colonization of the New World. . . .[32]

Operationally significant examples of exotic pathogens infecting US military forces during training and during operational deployment include outbreaks of primaquine-tolerant vivax malaria after troop deployments in Somalia, dengue fever during and after operations in Somalia and Haiti, and malarial recrudescence along the demilitarized zone on the Korean peninsula.[33] The resurgence of vivax malaria in the DMZ in Korea has implications for US servicemen deployed in that area, and its reappearance has caused US soldiers to be placed on anti-malarial prophylaxis for the first time in 20 years. Kelley comments: "The [1992–1995] US mission to Somalia . . . was marked by hundreds of cases of dengue fever and primaquine-tolerant vivax malaria. Under the right tactical circumstances, such illnesses could significantly affect military capabilities, especially when key individuals are incapacitated. Fortunately, effective personal protective measures are available, though they are usually underutilized."[34] Perhaps one of the greatest historical examples of military vulnerability to infection is the influenza pandemic of 1918–19, which killed more than 20 million people, including at least 43,000 US military personnel[35:]

During mid-October 1918, the US Army and Navy experienced over 6000 influenza-related deaths per week, largely in recruit camps. In spite of the ongoing World War, this outbreak necessitated suspension of about 143,000 inductions into the service. The effect on the Germans was also significant: the thousands of cases in German divisions during the summer of 1918 greatly weakened the German's capability to mount a successful offensive against the Allies.[36]

Of course, troop movements themselves often serve as "vectors" (modes of transmission) for new pathogens to move rapidly to areas where the population has little natural immunity to them. During World War I, malaria was transmitted as far north as Arkangelsk, Russia, because the troops involved in the war served as vectors for pathogen dissemination. Subsequently, the twin influenza and typhus pandemics of 1918 claimed almost 40 million lives as they circled the globe along with the moving armies.[37] World War II saw enormous morbidity of Allied troops in the Pacific theater due to malaria. During the Korean War, US troops were exposed to the Seoul Hantaan virus—a virus that subsequently traveled via troop supply ships to the United States, where it is now endemic.[38] The fact that troops often act as vectors of transmission may have downstream effects on how military forces are permitted to operate in foreign theaters. For example, forces known to exhibit high prevalence of certain pathogens (such as HIV) may not be acceptable in international peace-keeping operations. Kelley points out that in the wake of the Gulf War US personnel who had served in the region were not permitted to donate blood because many were found to be infected by a novel variant of leishmaniasis.[39]

Policy makers are increasingly aware that troops involved in peacekeeping operations often are vectors for the proliferation of infectious diseases (particularly HIV) throughout indigenous populations. US Ambassador to the UN Richard Holbrooke argues that future peacekeeping efforts must try to limit the spread of disease through troop vectors:

> We have now stated that we will never again vote for a peacekeeping resolution in the Security Council which does not contain a section on AIDS . . . and here we get into one of the ugliest truths that every one knows about AIDS—it is spread by UN peacekeepers—I say that with the greatest of reluctance, but it is true. So we are demanding that the UN include in all its preparation for peacekeeping, actions to combat AIDS. But we are not likely to be very successful because almost none of the troop contributing countries will agree to have their troops tested.[40]

Thus, warfare (and peacekeeping) can act as a direct disease "amplifier," creating those physical conditions (poverty, famine, destruction of vital infrastructure, and large population movements) that are particularly conducive to the spread and mutation of disease. According to the microbiologist Paul Ewald, the density and high mortality rates of tightly packed soldiers in the trenches of the Western front may have actually spurred the evolution of the 1918 influenza into its highly transmissible and lethal form:

> If the conditions and activities at the western front were responsible for the enhanced virulence of the 1918 pandemic, the timing and spatial pattern of virulent disease should accord with virulence enhancement at the western front. That is, the increased virulence should have occurred among troops at the western front while mobility-independent transmission was occurring. When the activities allowing this transmission ended at the end of the war, the virulence should have gradually declined as the mobility-dependent transmission favored the milder strains. . . . The first appearance of influenza with the corresponding characteristics [exceptional virulence and transmissibility] can be traced to troops in France near the western front. This origin is noteworthy because influenza pandemics typically spread from east Asia. During the several months just before and just after the end of the war, mortality per infection was about 10-fold higher. During the three years

after the war, the virulence gradually declined to normal levels. Our knowledge about the timing and spatial pattern of the pandemic therefore accords with virulence enhancement at the western front.[41]

The evidence suggests that the spread of infectious disease throughout military populations jeopardizes military readiness, international cooperation, and the ability of a state to preserve its territorial integrity. At the intra-state level, disease depletes force strength through the loss of skilled military personnel, reduces the supply of able draftees or recruits, and imposes costs that constrain military budgets, all of which impair the state's capacity to defend itself against a potential aggressor and limits the state's ability to project power abroad for both peacekeeping and coercive measures. The premature death and debilitation of a significant proportion of a state's population erodes worker productivity, undermines state prosperity, and induces a great deal of psychological stress in the populace. The destructive effect of disease-induced mortality in human-capital-intensive institutions generates institutional fragility and undermines the legitimacy of authority structures and ruling elites, thus impairing the state's ability to govern effectively, and may compromise transitions to democratic forms of governance. Disease-induced poverty, misery, military weakness, and governance problems may contribute to policies of repression and a slide toward increasing authoritarianism as the weakening state seeks to maintain order. In extreme cases disease may act as a significant stressor that tips the balance and may precipitate state failure, although disease is likely to generate this effect in combination with other stressors such as pre-existing inter-ethnic hostilities. This was problematic for the Clinton administration's strategy of "engagement and enlargement," which placed a premium on the establishment and strengthening of democratic regimes around the world. In summary, at the state level, the emergence and resurgence of infectious disease may have significant implications for state survival, stability, and prosperity.

At the regional level, the continuing proliferation of pathogens will induce widespread poverty that will create a significant drag on regional productivity and prosperity. The HIV/AIDS epidemic in sub-Saharan Africa has generated significant declines in productivity in many countries, and this has resulted in economic stagnation throughout the entire region. As increasing poverty threatens the political stability of entire regions such as sub-Saharan Africa, we are seeing more regional political disruption and violence. State collapse and inter-state war are now commonplace in sub-Saharan Africa, which is now reeling under the deepening shadows of HIV/AIDS, malaria, and tuberculosis. It is no coincidence that this strife-ridden region is home to the highest HIV seroprevalence on the planet, and it is likely that the continuing warfare will accelerate the spread of pathogens, which will in turn generate increasing instability. The negative spiral of declining population health, impaired governance, and increasing poverty will necessitate increased humanitarian intervention by UN security forces to maintain or re-establish order in affected regions. As we have seen from recent experiences in Central and West Africa, the UN is unlikely to have a lasting effect in restoring order to areas where pathogen prevalence and lethality remain high, and its credibility as an actor capable of inducing stabilization continues to decline. Indeed, many nations that supply peacekeeping forces are increasingly reluctant to commit troops to such perilous areas.

Power

In view of the numerous negative effects that high pathogen prevalence may have on a society (including declining productivity, increasing poverty, class competition, and declining capacity of the state to govern effectively), what is the likely effect of disease proliferation on state power, in both an absolute and a relative sense? In absolute terms, the increasing colonization of human hosts within a society by pathogenic microorganisms is likely to gradually erode the level of absolute power of the state. This erosion of state power results primarily from the decline of productivity and the erosion of human capital within the state. Since economic resources are fungible and easily translated into other resources (such as weaponry and infrastructure), the erosion of the economic base of the nation threatens its long-term ability to mount an effective military force either for the projection of power beyond national borders or for purposes of defense against potential aggressors. If we measure power in terms of empirical indicators (such as GNP, trained military personnel, and the number of tanks, warplanes, and nuclear weapons), high rates of disease prevalence will induce a decline in a state's level of absolute power over the long term.

This erosion of power at the state level makes it easier to contemplate how rising levels of infection might compromise a state's relative power with respect to its rivals. For example, let us imagine two geographically adjacent states, A and B, that for all practical purposes are identical. The population of state A displays exceptionally high HIV/AIDS seroprevalence (30 percent); the population of state B is also infected but exhibits a much lower seroprevalence level (10 percent). Over time the population base of A will experience much more death and debilitation, undercutting economic productivity, savings, and endogenous human capital. Bloom and Canning estimate that a 5-year decline in the life expectancy of a state's population will results in a drag of between 0.3 percent and 0.5 percent on the annual growth of the national economy.[42] As a result, the long-term economic growth trajectory of B will exceed that of A, perhaps substantially. Thus, over the years B will have a greater base of endogenous resources in the form of economic and human capital, both of which contribute to state power. In a very real sense, after years of the pathogen-induced destruction of the populations of both states, B will have suffered relatively less damage and will be more powerful than A. This is not necessarily to imply that B might attack its weakened neighbor simply because of the relatively rapid erosion of A's power base, but B will now enjoy an advantage in the relative distribution of capabilities between the two states.

How might this power differential play out in a regional sense? Empirically, the global burden of disease is greatest within the continent of Africa, and sub-Saharan Africa in particular. Of course, this is also the current epicenter of the global HIV/AIDS pandemic, which is exacting the greatest toll of all diseases in terms of the destruction and debilitation of populations. One possibility is that the burden of disease will increasingly cripple African economies and erode both state capacity and power in the region. Thus, the relative gap in power between Africa and other (less affected) regions of the world will increase. However, as the HIV/AIDS pandemic continues to spread through the areas of the former Soviet Union, South Asia, East Asia, and Latin America it may have long-term consequences for the global distribution of capabilities. The net effect could be that high-capacity regions in the developed countries (e.g., Western Europe and North America) will enjoy even more power with respect to other regions. Increasing inequities in the global distribution of power may not bode well for the long-term stability of the international system. To that end, it should be obvious that it is in the long-term interest of all states, including those in the developed countries, to develop effective strategies for international cooperation in order to mitigate the trans-boundary threat of disease proliferation.

Surveillance and Control Regimes

The leadership of the United States (the current hegemonic power) on trans-boundary security issues such as the emergence and proliferation of infectious disease is crucial. However, the United States will not be able to effectively address and contain this growing threat without the active co-operation of the international community. In a positive sign, certain other countries (notably Canada and the United Kingdom) have recently pledged increased funding toward the development of both national and global disease surveillance systems. Unfortunately, many national policy makers (e.g., those in Russia and China) have yet to recognize the unique threat of infectious disease to national security and prosperity, let alone participate in the construction and consolidation of nascent global disease surveillance and control regimes. Indeed, in many of the regions that exhibit the greatest prevalence of lethal pathogens within their societies (sub-Saharan Africa) there is a persistent and worrisome official culture of denial when it comes to acknowledging, let alone addressing, the problem of disease.

Cooperative international legal agreements on the containment of infectious disease outbreaks have existed since the Black Death swept through the city-states of Italy in the fourteenth century. Mark Zacher and David Fidler argue that the practice of regarding infectious disease as an international threat and the subsequent emergence of norms and codified international law to deal with these issues constituted some of the first international regimes to govern trans-border problems.[43] Despite this legacy of international law dealing with stemming the tides of infection, international surveillance regimes are still at a very early stage, with initiatives coming from civil society and from state-centric militarized sources. The ProMED surveillance network is a global civilian-based epidemiological surveillance network based on individual physicians' reporting disease outbreaks via the Internet to a central facility, whereupon significant epidemiological events are transmitted via e-mail.[44] A militarized epidemiological surveillance system is the Global Epidemiological Information System (GEIS), which uses a number of military bases around the world to gather and analyze data on pathogen prevalence and emerging disease outbreaks for the US Department of Defense.[45]

Aside from the construction of a global surveillance system, which is still very much in its infancy, the global response to the proliferation of infectious disease has been uncoordinated and fitful at best. State actors are of course central to this analysis, as they are principally affected by the spread of disease agents through their populations. To this end, certain multilateral organizations (such as the Group of Seven) have increasingly committed themselves to the development of mechanisms for disease surveillance and control. Other bilateral initiatives, including the US-European Union New Transatlantic Agenda, the Gore-Mbeki Commission, and the Gore-Chernomyrdin Commission, have seen the issue of infectious disease rise to the upper reaches of the international agenda.[46]

International organizations (such as the World Health Organization and the World Bank) and non-governmental organizations are also crucial players in the global response to the continuing proliferation of emerging and re-emerging infectious diseases. The WHO has a mandate to regulate international health matters, which includes prioritization of various global health issues, international coordination of health surveillance systems, and emergency response to outbreaks. Though the WHO has enjoyed notable successes over its history, including the practical eradication of smallpox and the near eradication of polio, it been criticized in recent years for its persistent underestimation of the prevalence of pathogens, its bloated bureaucracy, and its lack of focus.[47] Despite the WHO's shortcomings, the 1999 appointment of Gro Harlem Brundtland to the position of secretary general is a positive sign. Brundtland has seen fit to expand the WHO's efforts to control the expanding malaria pandemic, and she has instituted a broad series of reforms that includes the augmentation of the Emerging and other Communicable Diseases Surveillance and Control Division (EMC). Increased funding of the EMC permits greater cooperation with other UN actors (such as the UNAIDS Program and the UN Children's Fund) and with state institutions such as the Pasteur Institute (in

France) and the Centers for Disease Control and Department of Defense (in the United States).[48]

The increasing recognition that declining public health results in increasing poverty has spurred the World Bank to increase its intervention within the health sector, with an eye to the control of infectious disease. Despite increasing budget allocations dedicated to disease prevention and control, the actual amount dedicated to such activities amounts to $800 million, which is still far below the minimum level required to make any serious impact on global disease proliferation.[49] Meanwhile, other UN agencies are devoting increasing resources to the various pandemics currently underway. Under the leadership of Peter Piot, the UN AIDS Program (known as UNAIDS) has a mandate to increase national, regional, and global capacity to respond to the HIV/AIDS pandemic. Other UN agencies involved in the fight against disease proliferation include the UN Development Program, the UN Children's Fund, the UN Educational, Scientific and Cultural Organization, the Food and Agriculture Organization, the UN High Commissioner for Refugees, the International Labor Organization, the UN Family Planning Agency, and the World Food Program. Inter-organizational cooperation on these issues is improving, and infectious disease prevention and treatment are seen as an increasing priority within budget allocations.

Barriers to Effective Response

It is, of course, important to understand the various phenomena that may impede an effective international response to the various pandemics and to HIV/AIDS in particular. I have previously mentioned the pervasive denial, lack of transparency, and lack of accurate collection and dissemination of data in many countries. However, there are other specific problems that emanate directly from the concept of state sovereignty.

Sovereignty

According to Kenneth Waltz, "to say that a state is sovereign means that it decides for itself how it will cope with its internal and external problems, including whether or not to seek assistance from others and in doing so to limit its freedom by making commitments to them."[50] This is a useful point of departure for our analysis of sovereignty's role as a barrier to effective response to the various pandemics. The inviolability of the state is guaranteed by the Charter of the United Nations, which holds that any state is a sovereign entity and thus other states have no legal basis for intervening in the internal affairs of another unless invited to do so by the host state or explicitly authorized by the UN. This notion of sovereignty has in fact had important negative ramifications for the continuing proliferation of the global infectious disease threat, particularly since concerned state and non-state actors may not intervene in seriously affected countries without that country's explicit permission to do so. In the case of states such as South Africa and Zimbabwe, where there remains an enduring culture of denial regarding HIV/AIDS, this means that the international community has little choice but to stand by and watch the ruling elites of these countries preside over the destruction of their populaces. Moreover, the governments of Russia and China have opposed the inclusion of public health matters within the global security agenda on the ground that such an inclusion would result in increased external intervention within their internal affairs. Holbrooke once commented:

We were pleasantly surprised when one by one the fourteen nations of the Security Council agreed to talk about a health issue [the HIV/AIDS pandemic] and so on January 10 [2000] a health issue was discussed for the first time. Just for the record. . . . [Many] African nations wanted to do this from the beginning . . . The French were expected to oppose but did not. The real problem came from China and Russia, and to understand why, particularly Russia you need to understand that . . . they are concerned that any such discussion gets in their internal policies. Furthermore, lets be frank about it there is a lot of denial going on about whether they themselves have a problem. . . .[51]

Since the proliferation of the HIV/AIDS pandemic in sub-Saharan Africa threatens regional governance (already to such an extent that international peacekeeping forces have intervened), and since increasing infection levels will accelerate the rate of transmission of the HIV pathogen to other regions of the world, the international community has a direct and growing interest in convincing or coercing misguided and/or irresponsible governments to tackle the epidemic. This may be carried out by a carrot-and-stick approach, with financial and technological incentives used to obtain compliance from recalcitrant regimes. In extremis, fiscal institutions such as the IMF and the World Bank may make additional loans to non-compliant regimes conditional on effective action to slow the spread of contagion within national borders.

Environmental Security

Although there are a growing number of advocates for the development of a distinct "health security" paradigm, it is equally valid to see the threat of infectious disease as a valuable component of the pre-existing "environmental security" paradigm. Historically, researchers have been unable to show direct lines of causation that demonstrate how environmental degradation has reduced national security or impaired state survival. Certain individuals, particularly the political scientist Jessica Tuchman Mathews and the ecologist Norman Myers, have developed intellectually flimsy arguments in order to include environmental concerns in the security agenda. Their reluctance to define the concepts "environment" and "security" does not help move the intellectual discussion forward, nor does it help in constructing an appropriate and proactive policy agenda. We need specifically defined notions of "environmental security" if we are to advance the debate beyond the realms of rhetoric and hyperbole. The political scientist Marc Levy argues, correctly, that only environmental phenomena that directly affect the national security interests of the United States should be included under the rubric of environmental security[52:]

Direct physical threats provide the most compelling rationale for considering environmental degradation to be a security risk, but they receive the least attention as security threats. Environmental degradation constitutes a direct physical threat to US security interests when environmental damage results directly in the significant loss of life or welfare of US citizens, or otherwise impairs our most important national values. A thinning of the ozone layer that threatens to kill and blind hundreds of thousands of Americans is easy to identify as a security risk.[53]

Levy concludes that the negative effect of global environmental change on human health is the only direct threat to the national security of the United States. This echoes Ullman's definition of non-militaristic threats to security, and it is relatively easy to see that the global proliferation of infectious disease constitutes a significant direct threat to the survival and welfare of citizens in both developed and developing countries.

Insofar as the current proliferation of disease pathogens (and of many cancers and chronic illnesses) is directly induced by global environmental change, the link between environmental change and security becomes clearer.[54] The emergence of HIV/AIDS has claimed countless American lives, and hantavirus, *E. coli,* and drug-resistant tuberculosis continue to debilitate and kill Americans. In this sense, environmentally induced public health threats do constitute a direct threat to US security, and this is the most direct link possible between environment and security. As global environmental degradation continues to accelerate and as disease-induced population mortality increases, the saliency of the paradigm of environmental security increases accordingly.

One significant problem with the current security literature, however, is the tendency to focus solely on the security and the national interest of the United States. Much of the literature reflects this bias and tends to overlook the many threats faced by other markedly different states and societies around the world. Obviously the United States has less to fear from the direct threat of infectious disease (or other environmentally induced health threats) to its population than do developing countries with much lower endogenous capacity. Thus, the least developed nations with the least capacity to respond to public health threats are the states that face the greatest direct "environmental security" threats if we include infectious disease under that rubric. This profile fits most tropical states—particularly those in sub-Saharan Africa and South Asia, where the burden of disease has historically been greatest. This means that the paradigm of environmental security will be of exceptional importance to those in the developing countries who are more directly threatened by global environmental degradation as it affects the health of their populations. The evidence suggests that environmental change and disease proliferation may contribute to widespread instability in developing countries. Therefore, infectious disease may be usefully included within the "environment and security" debate as both a direct and an indirect threat to national security and stability.

Conclusion

. . . of all the problems that we face in the world today, I really think that [the HIV/AIDS pandemic] is the most important, and I believe that . . . if it is not dealt with

it will clearly wreck the economies of Africa and the Sub-continent. [AIDS] will spread, you can't draw a wall around Africa and commit continental triage. It won't happen.
—Richard Holbrooke[55]

Instability in the developing countries affects the national interest of the developed countries, whether we like it or not. Global economic interdependence has increased to the point that the collapse of the economy of Thailand or Indonesia can precipitate a global economic crisis, as happened in 1997. Thus, disease-induced economic decline in both developing and developed countries will have a negative effect on the global economy. Similarly, regional instability and violence threatens the national interests of developed countries when they deploy peacekeeping forces in war-torn regions to re-establish peace and effective governance. The evidence suggests that the Clinton administration's designation of infectious disease as a threat to the national security of the United States was justified. However, only further diligent and unbiased analyses of the interactions between infectious disease and national security in the form of detailed case studies will bear out these initial conclusions. Furthermore, I have argued that environmental degradation and public health problems interact synergistically to threaten national security and national interest through both direct and indirect processes, and I concur with Levy and Pirages that the environment-health nexus provides a valuable point of departure for further inquiries into the notion of environmental security.

Population health does in fact significantly affect state capacity. This means that the natural world can have significant although admittedly difficult-to-observe effects on human social structures. This provides additional ammunition for the theories of scientists, such as Sir Francis Bacon, William Whewell, Edward O. Wilson, and William McNeill, who have consistently argued that great truths may be found when we investigate the possibility of discovering consilient knowledge that lies between the great branches of scientific endeavor. Conversely, the continued fragmentation and compartmentalization of knowledge in the sciences as a general trend may lead us to bypass certain avenues of consilient scientific investigation, which may in turn induce a greater ignorance of the perils that may await humanity as we continue to alter our planet's ecology.

5

Environmental Change and Disease Proliferation

The concept of perfect and positive health is a utopian creation of the human mind. It cannot become reality because man will never be so perfectly adapted to his environment that his life will not involve struggles, failures, and sufferings. . . . The less pleasant reality is that in an ever-changing world each period and each type of civilization will continue to have its burden of diseases created by the unavoidable failures of adaptation to the new environment.

—René Dubos, *Man Adapting* (Yale University Press, 1965)

Humanity is confronted with a world out of balance. Human activity has resulted in significant deterioration of the biosphere, ranging from deforestation to acid rain, to the depletion of global fish stocks and the most rapid extinction of species seen since the demise of the dinosaurs. I argued in the previous chapter that infectious disease, broadly defined as a threat to the national security of the United States, dovetails with the literature of "environmental security." As was detailed in the introduction, environmental change facilitates the zoonotic transmission of pathogens from the state of nature into the human ecology. Thus, it is useful to examine the extent to which global environmental change may affect the relationship among vectors, pathogens, and human hosts. The purpose of this chapter is to examine the pathways by which environmental change may act as a disease amplifier over the long term.[1] Specifically, I argue that continuing and accelerating global environmental change will have significant negative effects on the health and prosperity of human societies, which in turn will increase stress on state capacity and increase human deprivation. I also argue that it is time to consider microbial evolution as an additional component of the spectrum of environmental problems that we now face. I will attempt to sketch the probable relations and interactions among climate events, regional ecology, and human behavior—including patterns of migration, changes in land use, and transmission of infectious diseases.

The goal of this chapter is to map the synergistic dynamic between global environmental change and its effects on pathogens themselves and the vectors that distribute such microorganisms. Though such global change is induced by human actions, I will not be dealing with the issue of whether increasing global temperatures are in fact human induced or whether they are reflections of natural variance. Regardless, the evidence shows that the climate is in fact warming, and this warming will have specific and measurable effects on disease replication and transmission.

Human-induced degradation of the biosphere will have long-term negative effects on human health, including the continuing emergence and reemergence of lethal pathogens (such as HIV and Ebola virus), the proliferation of "chronic" diseases (such as asthma), and the rapid spread of various cancers.[2] Though cancers have historically been associated with environmental toxicity or radioactivity, mounting evidence suggests a relationship between the proliferation of human pathogens and the increasing prevalence of cancers, with the disease agent often inducing cancerous cell mutation and growth. It is important to keep in mind that the links among ecological disruptions are not historically novel. Over the broad span of history, disease has often accompanied man's disruptions of his environment. Anthony McMichael concurs that oscillations in the health of human societies over history (notably the emergence of diseases) have reflected the dynamics of local ecological disruption:

> The collapse of the agriculture-based civilization of Mesopotamia 5000 years ago, the drought-assisted epidemics of plague in densely settled parts of Egypt, Italy and Africa in the second and third centuries A.D., the Black Death of fourteenth century Europe and the decimation of remote aboriginal populations by infectious diseases from European settlers and invaders—all these testify to the potentially disastrous impact upon human health of the disturbance of ecosystems.[3]

The rather obvious point is that we humans have known for some time that ecological disruption will have significant negative long-term consequences for the health of human populations. What is novel is the absolute magnitude of environmental degradation occurring on a global scale and its increasing rapidity.

Climate Change

In the aggregate . . . the direct and indirect impacts of climate change on human health do constitute a hazard to human population health, especially in developing countries in the tropics and subtropics; these impacts have considerable potential to cause significant loss of life, affect communities, and increase health-care costs and lost work days.
—Intergovernmental Panel on Climate Change, 1998[4]

The World Health Organization regards global climate change as a significant threat to human health in the new century.[5] Reiter defines climate as the "long-term summation of the atmospheric elements—radiation, temperature, precipitation, humidity, and wind—and their variations."[6] Variation in these atmospheric conditions will have significant effect on the multiplication, dispersal, and survival of microorganisms.[7]

The Intergovernmental Panel on Climate Change (IPCC) argues that temperatures in the tropics may increase by as much as 3°C by 2050 as a result of greenhouse gas emissions unless human activity changes substantially.[8] The UN estimates that mean surface temperature of the planet will rise by between 1.5°C and 3.5°C by 2100. Regardless of which model is more accurate, this projected change is significant and will probably have widespread effects on numerous ecological systems. One expected result of the warming is significant changes in precipitation levels, with both dramatic increases and decreases according to geographical position (the greatest variation projected to occur in the tropics). According to our current understanding of the phenomenon, climate change may increase the frequency and intensity of weather events (e.g., storms, floods). Climate change may also cause sea level to rise as a result of oceanic thermal expansion and the melting of large ice formations. Indeed, the mean sea level is projected to rise by 15–95 centimeters by 2100. Such an increase in sea level will increase societal exposure to coastal flooding and storm surges. Furthermore, the warming may result in the shift of climatic zones, and their attendant ecosystems and agricultural zones, toward the polar regions by as much as 550 kilometers by 2100.[9]

Haines et al. estimate that global warming will shift standard isotherms toward the polar regions, and as a result vector-borne diseases will shift their ranges accordingly, with yellow fever at the 10°C isotherm, vivax malaria at 16°C, and falciparum malaria at 20°C.[10] Furthermore, when humidity is high, dust particles may serve as sites for the transmission of bacteria, with redispersion affected by precipitation and wind patterns. Thus, higher relative humidity will ultimately increase microbes' survival rates and their infectivity.[11] For example, the prevalence of poliomyelitis tends to increase during the summer months. Tromp and Armstrong have noted that the incidence of poliomyelitis in the United States increases dramatically when the relative humidity rises above 28 percent. Similarly, in tropical regions the incidence of poliomyelitis is highly correlated with the advent of the rainy season.[12] Furthermore, high humidity may protect microorganisms from the destructive effects of ultraviolet radiation.[13]

According to Ford, transmission of trypanosomiasis is significantly altered by variations in temperature, humidity, and rainfall, by patterns of land use, by distribution patterns of humans and livestock, and by migration.[14] Cholera is another pathogen that proliferates under conditions of increasing warmth. The bacillus, dormant in cold water, multiplies at an increasingly rapid rate as the water warms, the optimal reproductive isotherms ranging from 15°C to 27°C.[15]

Shope articulates the ecological parameters that generally affect pathogen transmission and replication:

> ... the infections that will spread with climate change have some commonalities. They are focal, and their distribution is limited by the ecology of their reservoir, be it arthropod, snail, or water. They usually have a two- or three-host life cycle, meaning that in addition to infecting people, they infect a vector and frequently also a wild vertebrate animal host. Either the vector or the host, or both, are the reservoir. The range of the reservoir is delineated by temperature and sometimes water. In order to survive global climate change ... the agents will need to have reservoirs that will survive; they will probably survive by moving in a polar direction ... in order to find a temperature range that is ecologically permissive.[16]

Thus, climate change will affect the distribution of pathogens throughout human populations, such that vector-borne pathogens (e.g., those that cause malaria and dengue fever) may increase their latitudinal range and may also reach altitudes where the disease had not previously been a concern. Whereas significant victories against malaria (and other vector-borne diseases) were recorded in the 1950s and the 1960s, the disease has made a significant recovery since 1973, returning to areas where it was previously thought to have been eradicated. The *Plasmodium* parasite cannot reproduce at temperatures below 16°C, and so malarial transmission is confined to the range of the 16° winter isotherm. Thus, as global minimum temperatures continue to increase, the isotherm border will extend into higher latitudes and altitudes, affecting immunologically naive populations and generating increased morbidity and mortality in vulnerable regions.[17] Preliminary evidence shows a correlation between rainfall anomalies and outbreaks of disease, particularly vector-borne diseases. Indeed, in the Kenyan highlands the El Niño Southern Oscillation has had a pronounced effect on the recrudescence of epidemics of malaria.[18]

Temperature increases may also affect the prevalence of schistosomiasis within human populations, as environmental parameters (notably temperature) affect the water phase of the parasite's interaction with its snail host. For example, when temperatures fall below 9°C the snail host typically remains free of parasitic colonization. Temperatures in the range 35–39°C result in death of the snail host. In fact, the temperature range that favors water-and-snail transmission of the parasite is 26–28°C. Furthermore, excessive precipitation can flood the snails from their typical ecological niches, but in most cases rainfall enhances snail survival rates. Snail populations typically reach their zenith during the rainy season.[19]

Owing to climate change, some vector-borne disease may also return to immunologically naive populations that have been unaffected by such parasites for a very long period of time, through the dynamics of recrudescence. Lacking naturally acquired immunity, such populations would be exceptionally vulnerable to the re-introduction of pathogens into the local human ecology, and thus both transmission and lethality of the pathogen will be enhanced. Variation in local climatic conditions has affected malaria incidence in Rwanda. Patz and Epstein note that record high temperatures and precipitation levels in 1987 resulted in the proliferation of malaria throughout higher-altitude zones where *Plasmodium* had not previously been endemic. It would seem that malaria incidence in such high-altitude transitional regions was markedly affected by increases in minimum temperature. Thus, even relatively minute increases in minimum temperature may facilitate the proliferation of malaria throughout immunologically naive urban highland populations. Among the cities that may be affected by temperature-related change are Nairobi and Harare. Current models of climate change predict that the risk of malaria epidemics may increase dramatically in both tropical and temperate regions. Patz and Epstein estimate that more than a million additional fatalities per year could be attributed to the effects of climate change on disease incidence by 2050.[20]

According to IPCC models, global warming trends will significantly increase the geographic zone of potential malaria transmission, increasing the vulnerable proportion of the global population from 45 percent to 60 percent in the latter half of the twenty-first century. The models also predict intensified transmission, with a 10–15 percent increase in infection rates in areas where the *Plasmodium* parasite is already endemic. This greater rate of transmission derives from increases in temperature that also increase the biting rate of arthropod vectors (e.g., mosquitoes)[21] and simultaneously decrease the extrinsic incubation period of the pathogen in question, with the net effect of increasing the absolute number of vectors that are infectious at a given time.[22] Thus, temperature change can substantially influence vector infectivity by altering the period of infectivity, the maturation time, and the processes of pathogen replication.[23] In other words, global warming will expand the range of diseases such as malaria and dengue fever and simultaneously increase the number of infected individuals within that range, vastly increasing the burden of that particular disease on human populations.[24]

Koopman's recent research on dengue fever prevalence in Mexico, derived from population samples taken from 70 sentinel sites in varying locations, demonstrates that an average temperature increase of 3–4°C augments the rate of transmission of the dengue virus by approximately 200 percent.[25] In addition, increased temperature and rainfall in Australia would allow various vector-borne diseases to extend to higher latitudes (or higher altitudes). Thus, the Australian National Health and Medical Research Council is increasingly concerned that malaria, which was eradicated from Australia decades ago, could be re-established through climatic change[26]:

... given the effect that warmer temperatures have in accelerating the extrinsic incubation period of many vector-borne diseases, this may in turn increase the probability of the parasite's evolving increasing resistance to chemoprophylaxis and other control measures. As Darwinian evolution predicts, this occurs because a smaller incubation period allows for greater production of absolute numbers of the pathogen within a set span of time. As the absolute number of pathogenic agents increases, so does the probability that random genetic variance will confer properties of genetic resistance upon a few organisms. When non-resistant parasites are destroyed by prophylaxis the resistant organisms will proliferate to fill the now-vacated ecological niche.[27]

Of course, the warming of the atmosphere will affect precipitation levels and thus will affect the distribution of surface water and patterns of flooding. This may negatively affect the hygienic quality of water supplies in many areas, and with increasing deviation from the norm it may increase the spread of such water-borne diseases as dysentery, cholera, and diarrhea.[28] Studies of the cholera organism, *Vibrio cholerae*, have revealed how its survival, particularly in oceanic waters, "is greatly enhanced by its sheltering beneath the mucous outer coat of various algae and other phytoplankton, which are themselves very responsive to climatic conditions and nutrients in wastewater."[29] Of course, many diarrheal illnesses are caused by a plethora of bacteria (e.g., *Salmonella* and *Shigella*), viruses (e.g., rotavirus), and protozoa (e.g., *Giardia lamblia*). The majority of these microorganisms can survive in aquatic environments for months, and increased precipitation will tend to augment their dissemination throughout population pools. As the global environment continues to change, increases in diarrheal illness are most likely to occur in communities with insufficient clean water and poor sanitation. Thus, the most impoverished countries are at the greatest risk of environmentally induced rapid increases in the prevalence of such pathogens.[30] Furthermore, climate change may have the unanticipated effect of re-activating residual pockets of the plague bacillus in temperate regions.[31] Gillett argues that the geographic distributions of the majority of unicellular parasites are highly correlated with variation in temperature.[32] These microorganisms include trypanosomiasis (sleeping sickness), filariasis (also known as elephantiasis), onchocerciasis (river blindness), schistosomiasis, leishmaniasis, hookworm, guinea worm, and various tapeworms. Furthermore, the prevalence of vector-borne viral infections, such as dengue fever and yellow fever, is also affected by both surface water distribution and temperature. The WHO's recent modeling of the response of schistosomiasis to prevailing global warming patterns and trends suggests that the burden of this particular pathogen on the human species will increase by an additional 5 million cases per year by 2050.[33]

Of course, climate change will not always generate increases in the local burden of disease, as the climate may become inhospitable to some pathogens in their historical regions of endemicity. The result of this will be the relocation of the pathogen to areas that are more favorable to the survival of its vector hosts and that permit adequate replication and transmission. "If the temperature in the tropics of Africa and South America rises sufficiently," Shope argues, "it is likely that some of the present foci of schistosomiasis will be too hot to support the parasite. Areas of Africa on the east and west coasts already have high temperatures, and it has been suggested that this is the reason why *Biomphalaria* has not colonized these zones. On the other hand, other areas in Europe, Asia, and the Americas, now too cold to support the host snails, can be expected in the future to be favorable ecologically for schistosomiasis."[34]

Liehne argues that climate change will produce higher winter temperatures and increased summer rainfall in temperate Australia, extending the season favorable to the reproduction and survival of the mosquito *Culex annulirostris*. Such change will result in far higher populations of the vector and may result in the increased incidence of epidemic polyarthritis. Increasing precipitation may allow the increasingly frequent crossing of specific "threshold associations" between vectors and hosts. This may increase the frequency of outbreaks and/or epidemics of Australian encephalitis. By one account, "if this threshold is exceeded only in those years with major spring floods associated with intense [El Niño Southern Oscillations], then the incidence of Australian encephalitis epidemics will depend on the changes to the [ENSO] resulting from the greenhouse effect."[35]

Extreme Weather

Theoretically, global warming will generate increasing frequency and intensity of extreme weather events.[36] Extreme weather patterns have been implicated in the emergence of new infections, ranging from the 1994 hantavirus outbreaks in the southwestern United States to the emergence of West Nile virus near New York City during the autumn of 1999. The medical ecologist Paul Epstein argues that the latter was directly related to extreme weather events, such as the prolonged drought in the area through the summer of 1999 and the subsequent intense rainfall in the early autumn resulting from Hurricane Dennis. It would seem that the West Nile virus had established a reservoir of infection within the local crow population, which was then transmitted to humans and other animals by mosquitoes. These linkages remain speculative, but we do have an historical association between extreme weather and the recrudescence of various encephalitic pathogens in the United States. Furthermore, the West Nile virus somehow traveled from North Africa to North America, although the vector for this recent trans-oceanic exchange is not currently known.[37] In another example, the pulmonary hantavirus epidemic in the southwestern US was related to a surge in the population of rodents, which serve as vectors for the virus. Extremely high precipitation in 1993 after 6 years of drought resulted in a dramatic increase in food for the local deer mouse population, which then increased dramatically, bringing the mouse-borne virus into increasing contact with humans.[38]

Other diseases, such as Murray Valley encephalitis, are also likely to flourish in the context of climate change:

A higher prevalence of this virus is strongly linked with the creation of large non-immune host populations (particularly bird populations, and perhaps mouse plagues) such as occurs after a drought breaks. Increased waterbird breeding will mean more potential carriers, extended area of endemicity, and increased potential for outbreaks in tropical Australia, the Northern territory, the Murray-Darling Basin, and South Australia. . . . The new distribution and incidence will depend not only on vector-vertebrate host distribution but also on the degree of man-vector contact. It is probable that the disease will migrate south.[39]

Furthermore, a Johns Hopkins School of Public Health analysis of the relationship between extreme precipitation and water-borne disease outbreaks in the United States since 1940 has found that a positive temporal and spatial correlation exists between high precipitation and disease occurrence, with the highest correlation in autumn.[40]

Long-term studies of the relationship between precipitation and disease incidence in the United States suggest that there is a statistically significant positive association between periods of extreme precipitation and outbreaks of waterborne disease generated by pathogens such as hepatitis, *E. coli*, and cryptosporidium.[41]

Finally, droughts or floods may destroy crops and threaten regional food supplies. Climate change may also exert a negative effect on agricultural production through long-term changes, such as reduced soil moisture, and in the short term through extreme weather events such as droughts, floods (and erosion), and tropical storms.[42] Patz argues that climate-induced sea-level rise might also compromise food production through the combination of flooding and rising salinity of farmland in coastal areas.[43] Moreover, as global environmental change accelerates we can reasonably expect proliferation of insectile and microbial pests that compromise food security; this will, in turn, accelerate the decline of basal human health in affected areas.

The El Niño Southern Oscillation

The 1997/98 El Niño-related extreme weather events spawned "clusters" of disease outbreaks in many regions of the globe. In the Horn of Africa extensive flooding led to large outbreaks of malaria, Rift Valley fever and cholera. In Latin America, extreme weather was associated with outbreaks of malaria, dengue fever and cholera. In Indonesia and surrounding island nations, delayed monsoons—and the compounding effects of local farming practices—led to prolonged fires, widespread respiratory illness, and significant losses of wildlife.
—Paul Epstein[44]

The term "El Niño Southern Oscillation" (ENSO) refers to periods of acute and persistent warm weather that have significant effects on global climate patterns. Marked changes of air pressure in the Pacific induce periodic oscillations between remarkably warm waters in the eastern Pacific ("El Niño") and subsequent periods of cooler waters ("La Niña"). The ENSO cycle starts with a notable decline in the strength of prevailing trade winds in the Pacific and a subsequent shift in precipitation patterns. There is significant variance in the periodicity of ENSO events (2–7 years), and the cycle typically lasts 12–18 months. The Southern Oscillation is generally linked with extreme weather all over the world, and it has been implicated as a major cause of severe and prolonged periods of drought in Southeast Asia, Southern Africa, and Northern Australia. Conversely, the Southern Oscillation is typically associated with excessive rainfall and flooding in Peru and Ecuador.[45]

The El Niño Southern Oscillation is a climate phenomenon that has contributed to erratic global weather patterns and to extreme events ranging from droughts to floods, and its activity has been associated with various outbreaks of disease.[46] El Niño is increasingly associated with the transmission of vector-borne disease in particular. In transitionally malarious areas, rainfall, humidity, and temperature are the basic parameters that govern disease transmission. In such transitional zones, malaria transmission tends to oscillate; as a result, the local population typically lacks significant protective immunity to the parasite. Thus, serious epidemics may occur when local weather conditions facilitate transmission. Of course, precipitation and temperature variation may alternatively promote or inhibit the growth of vector populations, thereby affecting the distribution of pathogens throughout the region. For example, "Malaria is now controlled in Punjab, but it is still a serious problem in more arid areas in Western Rajasthan and Gujarat in India and Pakistan. There, too, the epidemics are linked to excessive rainfall. However, in some regions, malaria epidemics are linked to below-average rainfall."[47] Again, the point is that local climatic deviations from the norm are likely to result in the emergence of new pathogens as endemic, and they may result in the recrudescence of pathogens that had been dismissed as controlled or eradicated.

Patz argues that exceptional precipitation associated with ENSO events has triggered outbreaks of Murray Valley encephalitis and Ross River virus in Australia.[48] Similarly, ENSO has been associated with outbreaks of eastern equine encephalitis in the United States[49] and of West Nile encephalitis in Southern Africa,[50] and with cyclical malaria epidemics in Argentina[51] and Pakistan.[52] El Niño has also contributed to significant patterns of drought in areas proximate to the Indian Ocean, generating acute food scarcities that compromise human health.[53] According to the Weekly Epidemiological Record: "Quantitative leaps in malaria incidence coincident with ENSO events have been recorded around the world; such epidemics have been documented in Bolivia, Colombia, Ecuador, Peru and Venezuela in South America, in Rwanda in Africa, and in Pakistan and Sri Lanka in Asia. Historically, in the Punjab region of northeastern Pakistan, the risk of malaria epidemics increases five-fold during the year after a major El Niño, and in Sri Lanka, the risk of a malaria epidemic increases four-fold during an El Niño year."[54]

The strong correlation between the ENSO event of 1987 and the subsequent massive rise in malarial infection throughout Rwanda suggests that the increasing frequency and intensity of ENSO events will generate an increase in the incidence of diseases such as dengue fever, malaria, dysentery, and cholera. The incidence of malaria tends to increase by up to 20 percent in Colombia in the year after an El Niño event.[55] Moreover, satellite data have contributed to our growing knowledge regarding the association between El Niño events in the early 1990s and cholera outbreaks in Peru and along the Bay of Bengal during that period.[56]

Recent studies of the relationship of diarrheal disease to ENSO show that the incidence of such diseases in Peru increased by approximately 200 percent during the 1997–98 El Niño season. A recent study of 57,331 children in Peru by a research team from Johns Hopkins University found that increases in diarrhea cases between 1993 and 1997 were associated with even minute increases in local temperature, the effect being somewhat greater in winter, even though the aggregate climate was cooler. During 1997–98, El Niño increased winter temperatures in Lima by approximately 4°C.[57] According to William Checkley, who led the Johns Hopkins team, the incidence of disease increased by approximately 8 percent for every 1°C increase in the ambient temperature. Checkley concludes that global warming may potentially augment the global burden of diarrheal disease by millions of cases with each 1°C increase in ambient temperature.[58]

On a similar note, there is a growing body of evidence that El Niño events are associated with increases in the incidence of cholera. This may be due to the heating of surface water and/or to the contamination of groundwater that usually follows increased precipitation and flooding. Epstein argues that the current increases in oceanic algal blooms and associated cholera epidemics may be the result of "climatic perturbations" of ecosystems that have already been subject to exogenous stressors such as habitat destruction, pollution, and/or the invasion of non-indigenous species.[59]

According to the WHO, initial evidence suggests a link between ENSO and the incidence of dengue fever in nations where ENSO has a marked effect on weather patterns (e.g., many Pacific Rim states). The unusually high incidences of dengue fever and dengue hemorrhagic fever in Southeast Asia in 1998 probably were due in part to ENSO-related extreme weather, and the emergence and spread of Murray Valley encephalitis in the temperate regions of southeast Australia in 1998 were associated with high precipitation, which typically accompanies La Niña. Historically, El Niño has resulted in excessive precipitation in the Pacific coastal region of South America, and it is notable that Ecuador, Peru, and Bolivia suffered serious malaria epidemics after heavy rainfall associated with the 1983 El Niño.[60] In Venezuela and Colombia, malaria cases tend to increase by more than one-third following dry conditions associated with El Niño.[61]

The WHO reports that the 1997–98 El Niño generated exceptional amounts of rainfall in northeastern Kenya and southern Somalia, which in turn induced severe outbreaks of Rift Valley Fever, malaria, and cholera in those areas.[62] The unusually strong El Niño of 1997–98 has also been associated with outbreaks of Japanese encephalitis in Vietnam, Malaysia, Nepal, Papua New Guinea, and in Australia's Cape York region. El Niño is also implicated in large outbreaks of dengue hemorrhagic fever in Thailand, Indonesia, Vietnam, Malaysia, Singapore, Fiji, the Cook Islands, New Zealand, and mainland Australia.[63]

El Niño has also been implicated in outbreaks of disease in the United States. As mentioned above, ENSO generated a significant increase in precipitation levels in the Four Corners area in 1992–93. This increased rainfall contributed to a sharp increase in the production of pinyon nuts, which in turn generated an explosion in the local mouse populations (20 times normal levels).[64] These mice serve as a vector for the transmission of hantavirus to humans, and as a consequence of the increased frequency of mouse contact with the human population the area experienced a significant outbreak of hantavirus pulmonary syndrome (Sin Nombre virus) in 1993. After the return of normal precipitation levels, the mouse population declined rapidly and infection rates from hantavirus in the region plummeted.[65]

The lesson to be taken from the growing body of eco-medical evidence is that the absolute amount of precipitation is not the key to the proliferation of disease agents and their respective vectors of transmission. Rather, it is the variance—the deviation from the norm—that affects vector growth and often accelerates pathogen reproduction rates, which in turn may precipitate epidemics. Thus, ENSO may precipitate increased patterns of rainfall in a territory, which may then contribute to the emergence of pathogens and vectors that thrive in such an increasingly humid environment. Simultaneously, ENSO may render another region increasingly arid, which may then contribute to the emergence and proliferation of pathogens and vectors that thrive under such conditions. Thus, the deviation from the norm in terms of climate and extreme weather events is likely to contribute to changing patterns of disease prevalence on a global scale. As disease patterns shift, there is increased probability that immunologically naive populations will be infected by pathogens that have not been previously recognized as endemic, the usual result being more morbidity and mortality in affected populations.

Land Use

The construction of dams in three African river deltas—the Nile, the Senegal and the Volta—has led in recent years to schistosomiasis infection in up to 75 percent of local villagers, and even among people as far as 500 kilometers upstream of the dams.

—World Health Report 1996[66]

Other patterns of human-induced ecological change can also have a significant negative effect on human health. For example, the expansion of irrigation systems throughout warm arid areas has generated a significant increase in the prevalence of schistosomiasis, which is prevalent throughout vast areas of Northern Africa and throughout South and East Asia. Irrigation zones usually provide a greater range of microclimates that affect both vector populations and the general dynamics of disease transmission. Warmer temperatures also increase the reproduction rate and transmissibility of the schistosome parasite within the snail host. Therefore, increases in temperature will result in the spread of the disease over a longer proportion of the year, increasing the absolute burden of that particular disease on affected societies.[67]

According to the WHO, schistosomiasis (also known as bilharzia) has doubled in global prevalence since the middle of the twentieth century, primarily as a result of the rapid and significant construction of irrigation systems in tropical climates. During the course of this disease, blood flukes (schistosomes) colonize the blood vessels of the urinary bladder and the intestines, inducing extensive inflammation and tissue damage. The eggs of the parasites are subsequently excreted and typically end up in the shallow, warm water of canals, ditches, and irrigation channels, where they then infect their other host species: water snails. Increases in temperatures and in precipitation are logically expected to influence this cycle and exacerbate the exposure of human populations to this illness. "In Egypt, for example, the water snails tend to lose their schistosome infections during the winter months (January–March). However, if temperatures increase, snails may spread schistosomiasis throughout the years, thus increasing the already heavy parasite burden in rural Egypt."[68]

The construction of the Aswan High Dam in 1971 resulted in a significant rise in the burden of disease for populations living above and below the dam. The increase in local water supply and irrigation systems has resulted in the increasing prevalence of both schistosomiasis[69] and Bancroftian filariasis in the area.[70] A dramatic increase in schistosomiasis resulted from the construction of dams and irrigation canals in the Senegal River basin, where local workers experienced a rise in infection from 0 to more than 95 percent prevalence in only 3 years.[71] It has been suggested that the construction of the Three Gorges Dam on the Yangtze River in China may be promoting the emergence and reemergence of parasitic worms and contributing to the proliferation of their snail vectors. The vast majority of the Chinese population living in proximity to the Yangtze have historically been at high risk of such helminth infection.[72] Owing to the mobilization of the population against schistosomiasis during Chairman Mao's patriotic health campaigns, the number of infected persons in the region was reduced from 10 million in 1955 to 1.52 million in 1989.[73] The Three Gorges Dam will affect the provinces of Sichuan and Hubei through the creation of a reservoir area of 50,700 square kilometers, submerging 220 counties and displacing approximately 1.4 million people. The construction of the dam and reservoir will increase the prevalence of the *Oncomelania* snail vector and the overall incidence of schistosomiasis throughout the area. When the dam is complete, the permanent new high water level in the reservoir area will increase groundwater levels and local snail populations. There may be unprecedented distribution of the snail vector and the schistosome parasite via lateral canals from Sichuan to Hubei and downstream, probably resulting in a significant future expansion of the disease throughout the region.[74]

Shifts in land use and water use resulting from environmental degradation or economic development can also increase the amount of contact between disease agents and their human hosts. For example, changing patterns of land use in Haiti have resulted in increasing parasitic hookworm infection. Such intestinal worm infections have soared in the community of Leogane, where these types of parasitic infections historically exhibited exceptionally low prevalence rates. It has been asserted that the increase is probably a consequence of local deforestation, which has led to the accumulation of silt in a certain river. This has resulted in flooding, which has altered local drainage patterns and saturated the soil in certain communities. These changes in the local ecology would seem to have generally facilitated hookworm transmission in the area. Hookworm prevalence increased from 0 to 12–15 percent over the period 1991–1997.[75]

The construction of dams may have also contributed to the establishment of novel emergent pathogens in immunologically naive populations. One clear example is the Rift Valley fever virus, which spread into the populations of Egypt and Mauritania after 1977, debilitating hundreds of thousands of people and killing hundreds. "Apparently, the still waters created by the Aswan dam on the Nile and the Diama dam on the Senegal river favored the development of these epidemics by fostering vast increases in the mosquito population."[76] Schistosomiasis prevalence increased dramatically with the introduction of irrigation technologies in the wake of the construction of the Volta Lake dam in Ghana.[77] According to one report, seroprevalence of schistosomiasis in the population of the Nile region between Aswan and Cairo surged from 5 percent before the dam's construction to 35 percent afterward.[78]

Patz and Epstein note that the recent global proliferation of oceanic algal blooms is a direct consequence of wetland destruction, poor erosion control, excessive use of fertilizers, and coastal sewage dumping, in combination with the gradual increase of mean sea surface temperatures over 100 years. They argue that the proliferation of toxic algal blooms results in increasing incidences of human shellfish poisoning and fish kills. Extraordinarily high concentrations of algae in the coastal waters off Peru in the early 1990s coincided with the emergence of the virulent El Tor strain of cholera throughout Peru and neighboring countries in 1993–94.[79] Of course, it is notable that the draining of wetlands throughout the United States resulted in a dramatic reduction in the incidence of yellow fever and malaria throughout the country. Thus, some changes in land use can actually benefit local populations by reducing potential exposure to disease pathogens and their vectors. However, there are many other negative and wide-ranging ecological consequences related to the destruction of wetlands, and it is advisable to consider the greater ramifications before destroying such ecosystems.

On another note, Daily and Ehrlich posit that the use of chemical agents for the purposes of agriculture has contributed to the unpredictable emergence of virulent new pathogens, including viral strains that result in hemorrhagic fever:

Intensification of agriculture in the Pampas of Argentina led to the introduction of herbicides after World War II to fight weeds that competed with maize production. The resultant change in the grass flora favored a mouse, *Calomys musculins,* which was the natural reservoir of the Junin virus, the cause of Argentine hemorrhagic fever. In contrast, a shift from cattle raising to subsistence agriculture encouraged another small mouse, *Calomys callosus,* in eastern Bolivia, which was the reservoir of the Machupo virus. The latter invaded the human population causing Bolivian hemorrhagic fever.[80]

Ewald argues that human land-use patterns have also been a major factor in the spread of the typically avian oropouche virus (a cousin of Rift Valley fever virus) from its African base to Amazonia, where it is now established in the local ecology:

. . . over the past few decades, [oropouche] has caused about 200,000 cases of disease, apparently by way of mosquito-like midges. The midges, like the mosquitoes transmitting Rift Valley Fever, probably multiplied to great numbers because of human activities. In this case, expansion of cacao plantations increased the numbers of the minute midge breeding ponds that formed in discarded cacao shells.[81]

Moreover, deforestation and the movement of large numbers of people into forested or recently deforested areas has often resulted in increased transmission of vector-borne disease into immunologically naive human populations. For example, the deforestation of the Brazilian interior and the concurrent migration into that area has resulted in a 500 percent increase in malaria prevalence throughout the region, and a notable shift in species dominance from *Plasmodium vivax* to the far more lethal *P. falciparum.*[82] Extensive forest clearance throughout Latin America has increased the incidence of leishmaniasis as a result of increasing populations of both the sandfly vector and animal reservoirs.[83]

Degradation and exploitation of forests bring humans into increasing contact with zoonoses that may have not yet entered the human ecology. When contact occurs, these pathogens may cross over from animals into humans through the process of "zoonotic transfer." The most lethal pathogens known to humanity are in fact historically recent biological crossovers of this type. Significant examples include HIV and Ebola virus (derived from primate populations) and falciparum malaria (derived from avian species).[84] The epidemiologist Mary Wilson argues that the introduction of new technology, innovative farming methods, and pesticides may have a significant and persistent effect on regional disease patterns. The destruction of forests, the construction of dams, and the development of transportation infrastructure in heretofore inaccessible regions have all been linked to population movements and subsequent shifts in the distribution and frequency of a plethora of human pathogens.[85]

Moreover, increasing urbanization is problematic, since certain pathogens can thrive only when absolute urban population levels exceed a specific threshold. For example, the development of agricultural practices approximately 10,000 years ago induced the formation of towns and cities that exhibited population densities sufficient to sustain epidemics of smallpox, cholera, influenza, measles, and polio.[86] In 1950 only London, Shanghai, and New York had populations exceeding 10 million. Current estimates show that more than 23 cities have surpassed that number, and current projections hold that more than half of humanity will live in urban centers by 2010.[87]

The effective endogenization of a parasite within a human populations requires a basal reproductive rate greater than 1.[88] That is, each infected individual must infect more than one other. The exact threshold will vary according to the specific attributes of both the parasite and host populations. For example, measles was unable to endogenize itself in human populations until thresholds of 200,000 to 500,000 persons were surpassed in urban centers.[89] Continually increasing population thresholds (and densities) in urban centers will permit the emergence and establishment of novel pathogens within the human ecology. It is equally important to note that the continuing growth of the absolute human population on this planet increases the absolute number of contacts between humans and pathogen reservoirs in the form of infected fauna. This, in turn, raises the statistical probability that zoonotic pathogens may jump the species barrier and establish themselves within human populations.[90] Ewald also agues that increasing population density will probably increase the lethality of infectious diseases, as increased frequency of transmission increases pathogenic lethality.[91] Wilson is also concerned that global trends in urbanization may increase the probability of transference of pathogens between urban and rural population pools and, moreover, may permit the spread of entirely new pathogenic agents:

[Megacities] will have the population density to support persistence of some infections and contribute to the emergence of others. Many of these areas are located in tropical or subtropical regions, where the environment can support a diverse array of pathogens and vectors. Also developing are huge periurban slums, populated with persons from many geographic origins. Poor sanitation allows breeding of arthropod vectors, rodents, and other disease-carrying animals. Crowded conditions favor the spread of diseases that pass from person to person, including sexually transmitted infections. Travel between periurban slum areas and rural areas is common, paving the route for the transfer of microbes and disease. Transfer of resistance genes and genetic recombination may also occur in and spread from crowded environments of transients.[92]

Thus, an increasing aggregate global human population, urban population, and population density will typically combine to act as disease amplifiers by promoting pathogen emergence, enhancing transmission, and increasing lethality.

The expansion of urban habitats into previously undisturbed areas can also affect the exposure of human populations to vector-borne diseases and increase the incidence of human illness. It has been argued that ecological changes associated with growing urbanization have been associated with significant increases in Rocky Mountain spotted fever in the late 1970s, with the increasing prevalence of Lyme disease from the 1980s on, and with the increase in ehrlichiosis in the 1990s, throughout the United States.[93] The effects of urban growth on human exposure to pathogens is exhibited in the dynamic of murine typhus proliferation in the southern and southwestern United States as well. Moreover, the destruction and fragmentation of natural habitats displaces animal populations and often forces them into greater contact with urban populations, which increases the probability of zoonotic transference and the emergence of novel pathogens into the human ecology.[94] Mackenzie attributes the increasing incidence of Ross River virus in parts of Australia to the increasing encroachment of urban populations into or near wetlands and other areas conducive to the propagation of the mosquito vector.[95] Finally, the proliferation of human waste in close proximity to burgeoning urban human populations may have significant long-term repercussions for human health, as waste-disposal sites incubate vector populations ranging from mosquitoes to rodents. Gubler argues that discarded consumer products (which often collect standing rainwater) tend to facilitate large-scale arthropod propagation and serve as residences for rodents.[96]

Ozone and Health

Destruction of the ozone layer results from reactions between atmospheric ozone and compounds in chlorofluorocarbons, other halocarbons, and methyl bromide.[97] The continuing depletion of the ozone layer has increased the amount of malign ultraviolet B radiation striking the Earth's surface.[98] Though the most apparent human illnesses linked to UV-B exposure are melanoma (skin cancer) and cataracts,[99] UV-B also results in the suppression of the immune systems of living creatures, including humans.[100] This UV-B-induced immunosuppression will generally increase the susceptibility of the human species to colonization by pathogens, leading to the increasingly rapid emergence and proliferation of infectious disease throughout human societies. Immunosuppression will also tend to increase human vulnerability to cancers and chronic illnesses (many of which are pathogen-induced), increasing the aggregate burden of disease on humanity. "UV-B irradiation depresses the skin's contact hypersensitivity, reduces the number and the functions of immunologically active cells (langerhans cells) in the skin, stimulates the production of immune suppressing 'T-suppressor' cells, and alters the profile of immunologically active lymphocytes (white cells) circulating in the blood."[101] Though such immunosuppression may increase infection rates for many skin diseases, the UNEP has warned that immunosuppression resulting from increased irradiation may in fact accelerate the progression of AIDS in infected individuals.[102] Furthermore, increased exposure to solar radiation (among other ecological changes) may in fact accelerate the processes of microbial evolution:

New mechanisms of genetic plasticity of one microbe species or another are uncovered almost daily. Spontaneous mutation is just the beginning. We are also dealing with very large (microbial) populations, living in a sea of mutagenic influences (e.g., sunlight). Haploid microbes can immediately express their genetic variations. They have a wide range of repair mechanisms, themselves subject to genetic control. Some strains are [rendered] highly mutable by not repairing their DNA; others are relatively more stable. They are extraordinarily flexible in responding to environmental stresses (e.g., pathogen's responses to antibodies, saprophytes' responses to new environments). Mechanisms proliferate whereby bacteria and viruses exchange genetic material quite promiscuously. Plasmids now spread throughout the microbial world. They can cross the boundaries of yeast and bacteria. Lateral transfer [of genetic information] is very important in the evolution of microorganisms. Their pathogenicity, their toxicity, their antibiotic resistance do not rely exclusively on evolution within a single clonal proliferation.[103]

Resistance

Of course, humanity is generating many changes throughout the biosphere. Aside from changing the chemical contents of the atmosphere and altering land use, we are proudly affecting the environment of the microbial world through the introduction of chemical compounds into the microenvironment. Increasing microbial resistance is typically the result of the increasing use of manufactured anti-microbial agents that have been introduced into the human, animal, and insect ecologies. The continuing misuse of antibiotics and pesticides has also resulted in the increasing prevalence of drug-resistant microorganisms. The persistent misuse of anti-malarial drugs throughout Southeast Asia has led to exceptionally high local resistance in the parasite to quinine and its derivatives. There is also increasing evidence that human activities have led to the emergence of an entirely novel type of pathogen: infectious proteins called prions, which are capable of inducing BSE in cattle and the lethal variant known as Creutzfeldt-Jacob disease in humans. New strains of resistant pathogens are emerging. Vancomycin-resistant enterococci and methycillin-resistant *Staphylococcus aureus* are proliferating throughout health-care facilities in the developed countries.[104]

The problem of resistance results from the synergy of social, economic, and behavioral factors, including improper use and unnecessary prescription of antibiotics by health professionals, untrained practitioners, and the general public. Other general practices leading to increased resistance are inadequate surveillance mechanisms, poor pharmaceutical quality, and the lack of hygienic conditions. The crux of the resistance problem stems from principles of Darwinian evolution as applied to the microbial world. The use of anti-microbial agents provides selective pressures that accelerate the process of microbial evolution, leading to the emergence of resistant strains.[105] Lederberg explains the complex biomechanical synergies involved in the transfer of genetic qualities of resistance from one microbial agent to another as follows:

Recombination mechanisms are quite promiscuous. Conjugation, which can occur between bacteria of widely varying kinds, is most often recognized by plasmid transfer and every now and then by mobilization of chromosomes. Conjugation can even occur across kingdoms, between a bacterium and a yeast, or between a bacterium and a plant. Some bacteria can deliver DNA intercellularly to their host animals. Plasmid interchange [movement of tiny bits of DNA from one species to another] is not just a laboratory curiosity; it is the mechanism for rapid spread of antibiotic resistance from widely different species, one to another. It adds even greater cogency to our concerns about the less than optimally advantageous use of antibiotics (e.g. in animal husbandry). The mechanisms exist to make it easy not only for single antibiotic resistance but whole blocks of resistance to be moved from one bacterium to another.[106]

Many medical professionals across the globe are unaware of the downstream evolutionary implications of the overprescription of antimicrobial agents. "This combines with false or misleading information distributed by drug companies, inner-city poverty, and the casual availability of antibiotics through pharmacies and black markets."[107] The problem has been exacerbated by the massive quantities of antibiotics now fed to livestock populations in order to increase their growth rate and adult size. Microorganisms within livestock develop resistance to these persistent doses of antimicrobials. These resistant organisms may then cross over into human populations through zoonotic contact, through the ingestion of contaminated foodstuffs, or through the drainage of animal wastes into local water resources.[108]

Another area of growing concern is the long-term potential for pathogens to cross over and become endogenized within the human ecology as a result of xenografting and xenotransplantation. Xenotransplantation, the transfer of animal organs or tissues into human recipient hosts, has the potential to save many thousands of lives per year. Much as HIV/AIDS, Ebola, and falciparum malaria are historically recent (and lethal) zoonoses that have crossed over from animal reservoirs into the human species, xenotransplantation could lead to the diffusion of new pathogens throughout the human species, thus creating the potential for new epidemics.[109]

Biodiversity

The annals of the history of public health are replete with stories of the discovery of plant-derived agents that have been extremely useful in diminishing the burden of disease on human societies. A notable example is the anti-malarial agent quinine, derived from the bark of the Peruvian quinchona tree.[110] More recently, the WHO has reported that extracts of the Chinese herb qinghao produce the artemisinin compound, which has proved effective against drug-resistant strains of malaria.[111]

Degradation of the biosphere increases the rate of extinction of rare flora and fauna. This reduction in global biodiversity will have significant negative consequences over the long term as it compromises the integrity of the global genetic reservoir, inhibiting our ability over the long term to create effective new anti-microbial agents and medicines.[112] For example, curare liana bark has given us the alkaloid d-turbocuarine, an effective treatment for chronic illnesses such as multiple sclerosis and Parkinson's disease; and the rosi periwinkle of Madagascar is the source of two effective anti-cancer agents used to combat lymphocytic leukemia and Hodgkins disease.[113] The preservation of biodiversity will also help to guarantee the long-term preservation of the world's food stocks.

Genetic diversity in flora populations renders them less vulnerable to colonization by pathogens, which inevitably results in the destruction of crops. (The classic example of this dynamic is the Irish potato famine.) Pathogen-induced destruction of food crops also may lower the basal health of populations and significantly compromise human immune systems, making possible the proliferation of microbial colonies and cancers in human hosts.[114]

Migration and Trade

Neither migration nor trade falls under the specific rubric of global environmental change in a strict sense, yet these two phenomena are strongly associated with the global diffusion of pathogens and should be included in the larger discussion of disease emergence and proliferation. One of the greatest problems associated with the spread of infectious disease has to do with the increasingly large and rapid flows of people and goods throughout the biosphere, facilitated by increasingly rapid transportation technologies such as the airplane. Many pathogens and vectors have jumped from their initial zones of endemicity and re-established themselves in new geographical areas and new population pools. With the increase in inter-continental travel, we can expect increased microbial traffic between peoples that in the past may have had limited contact.[115] It has been demonstrated that international travel is highly correlated with the global proliferation of HIV/AIDS.[116]

West Nile Virus had never been present in North America before the summer of 1999. That mosquito-borne encephalitic viral infection had historically been confined to North Africa and the Mediterranean region. Its sudden appearance in the New York area in 1999 surprised and alarmed the public health and policy communities.

There are many competing hypotheses as to how West Nile Virus became established in the local fauna (particularly the crow population). These range from the importation of infected livestock to transmission via infected travelers or immigrants. It will be some time before we can be sure of the path of transmission to the New World, but we can state with confidence that global movement of peoples and goods has contributed to the emergence of this lethal new pathogen in North America. Similarly, it can be argued that the dissemination of HIV outside its African base of historical endemicity was directly facilitated by international travel technologies that carried the virus from Africa to North America and Europe.[117] Transportation technologies (particularly trucking) were instrumental in distributing HIV throughout sub-Saharan Africa and play a role in the current expansion of the HIV pandemic throughout South and East Asia.

Australia has also recently experienced problems with the importation of dengue fever, which is not historically endemic to that area. According to Mackenzie, importation of the virus into the Australian population is largely a function of the continual movement of people between Papua New Guinea and north Queensland for purposes of work, education, and recreation.[118] Argentina reported the re-emergence of dengue fever in

1997, the last previous epidemic having occurred in 1916 in Entre Rios province. Dengue fever was reported as officially eradicated in 1963 by Argentinean authorities, but the virus and its mosquito vector (*Aedes aegypti*) have re-established their endemicity as far south as Buenos Aires and Rosario, where there is now local transmission of the virus in urban areas. It has been suggested that the resurgence of dengue fever throughout Argentina is probably associated with the continuous human traffic with Bolivia, Paraguay and Brazil, where dengue fever has re-established endemic status.[119]

Pathogen transmission is also associated with mass migrations such as religious pilgrimages. For example, the proliferation of cholera has often been associated with the Haj. As recently as the early 1970s, a pilgrim to Mecca brought smallpox back to his native Yugoslavia, resulting in 174 cases and 35 deaths.[120] In another case, Islamic pilgrims from South Asia transported a pathogenic strain of group A *Neisseria meningitidis* to other pilgrims at Mecca in 1987. The newly infected migrants carried the disease back to Africa, where it generated epidemics in 1988 and 1989.[121]

The accelerating combination of travel and trade has been said to allow for the "mixing of diverse genetic pools at rates and in combinations previously unknown."[122] The transportation of microbes from one population pool or zoonotic reservoir to another is no new phenomenon. Historians have noted the devastating effect of imported European diseases on immunologically naive indigenous populations in the Americas and Australia after the "discovery" of these territories by European forces.[123] As an example of how population mobility has increased over the centuries, Grubler and Nakicenovic estimated that the average distance traveled by a member of the French population per day had increased by a factor of approximately 1000 between 1800 and 2000.[124] This means that the absolute probability of pathogen mobility between population pools, and indeed from one ecosystem to another, is increasing synergistically alongside humanity's increasing mobility.

The movement of refugee populations also has significant implications for the spread of disease. Complex humanitarian emergencies usually lead to sparse and mobile living quarters (camps and shelters) that display attributes conducive to the spread of disease, such as lack of clean water and food, lack of adequate sanitation, crowding, and limited medical care.

One glaring example of the synergy between disease and refugee populations is that of the movement of more than a half-million Rwandan refugees into camps in Zaire in 1994. At least 50,000 refugees died in the first month of resettlement as a result of the rapid spread of cholera and shigella dysentery through those camps.[125]

Trade has played its part in the dissemination of pathogens and their vectors for many centuries. According to the historian William McNeill, the establishment of vast trade networks between India and the Middle East at the core, and Europe and China at the periphery, led to the importation of pathogens into immunologically naive European and Chinese populations. Indeed, between 200 and 600 A.D. Roman populations experienced exceptional mortality from infectious disease, which implies that Roman society had been exposed to one or more novel pathogens. This pattern of exceptional mortality was repeated in China during the same period, but no record exists of similar pathogen-induced destruction in Indian and Middle Eastern centers. The obvious implication is that novel pathogens from the core regions were transported via trade activity to the peripheral regions, where they induced severe mortality. This dynamic is remarkably similar to the destruction of indigenous American populations through the importation of virulent European pathogens in the early 1500s.[126]

Yellow fever, historically endemic to Western Africa, has spread throughout the Americas over the centuries. The prevalent theory is that the disease was carried to the Americas aboard colonial slave ships that transported the dominant vector: the *Aedes aegypti* mosquito.[127] The first recorded outbreaks of the disease in the Americas occurred in 1648 in Havana and on the Yucatan peninsula.[128] A modern example of vector migration via trade is that of the Asian tiger mosquito (*Aedes albopictus*), a vector for the dengue fever and yellow fever viruses. Tiger mosquito larvae traveled across the Pacific in small pools of water present in used tires that were shipped back to the United States for retreading. Since its introduction, the tiger mosquito has spread rapidly throughout the Americas, and the dengue virus that it transmits has followed suit in synergistic fashion.[129]

There is also preliminary evidence to link the construction of transportation infrastructure with the proliferation of malaria throughout regions where its prevalence was historically extremely low or non-existent. Malaria did not exist in the western highlands of Kenya until approximately 1910.[130] In 1901, the completion of a railway running from Lake Victoria through the highlands and across to the Kenyan coast, and increased road infrastructure throughout the region, led to the gradual proliferation of mosquitoes from low-altitude endemic regions into the immunologically naive populations of the highlands.[131] It has been suggested that the spread of malaria was also facilitated by clearing of the forests to permit the growth of tea plantations and other agriculture, along with an influx of infected laborers.[132]

Nonlinearity

Even though many . . . global environmental changes may entail effects upon health not previously encountered, we cannot defer social action until we "know" those end-effects. By the time the health consequences of ecosystem disruption are clearly evident in human populations it may be too late to reverse or repair the damage. The dynamics of ecosystems do not obey the linear orderliness of physical systems; instead they are influenced by feedback systems and critical loads. Limits, once exceeded may [rapidly] lead to decline or collapse.
—Anthony McMichael[133]

Western thought systems unjustifiably emphasize humanity's belief that it has a right and an obligation to "master" the natural world. Of course, during the seventeenth century Spinoza and Locke took issue with the anthropocentric point of view.[134] The medical ecologist Anthony McMichael notes that there is a widely held "assumption that we are dealing with simple systems that conform to a mechanistic Newtonian world in which relationships are obligingly linear."[135] But, he continues, "ecosystems are not like that. At some point an external load will overwhelm the system's resistance and rapid change or collapse then ensues. . . . Thresholds in non-linear systems are difficult to anticipate. Once such a threshold is passed the momentum of induced change continues, and feedback mechanisms that amplify or constrain the change may be activated. If regenerative powers or absorptive capacities are long exceeded, the system may collapse, causing what the catastrophe theorists call (with nice understatement) a 'discontinuity.'" Thus, we have no clear idea as to whether the stresses that humanity is now exerting on the biosphere will at some point exceed natural thresholds and generate a shift to a significantly different equilibrium state. In a microbial sense this means that the ever-accelerating destruction of ecosystems, the increasing aggregate populations and their densities, increased human mobility, and misuse of antimicrobial and anti-vectoral agents may precipitate the emergence of entirely new and lethal pathogens. The emergence and proliferation of HIV is a clear function of this type of synergistic dynamic, and the continuing spread of BSE (caused by prions) is linked to unsustainable animal husbandry practices. Of the problems associated with microbial evolution, and the human pressures that accelerate such Darwinian processes, Lederberg writes:

We are engaged in a type of race, enmeshing our ecologic circumstances with evolutionary changes in our predatory competitors. To our advantage we have wonderful new technology; we have rising life expectancy curves [except in areas of high HIV prevalence]. To our disadvantage, we have crowding, we have social, political, economic, and hygienic stratification. Affluent and mobile people are ready, willing, and able to carry afflictions all over the world within 24 hours notice. This condensation, stratification, and mobility is unique, defining us as a very different species from what we were 100 years ago.[136]

Paul Ewald's innovative theories concerning the evolution of infectious disease may shed more light on the complex environment-pathogen-host interactions that are likely to result under scenarios of global biosphere degradation. The evidence presented above establishes a link between temperature increases and a shortened extrinsic incubation rate coupled with increased biting activity of many arthropod vectors. Increases in humidity, precipitation, and human waste are also likely to generate larger vector populations. Ewald argues that the most virulent strains of malaria tend to occur where the biting activity of the vector is greatest. For example, biting activity at the southern edge of the Sahara desert is rather low owing to local environmental constraints on the vector population (e.g., low humidity, low host population density). As a result, the local virulence of malaria is extraordinarily low. In regions where biting density is extremely high, the virulence of *Plasmodium* reflects this dynamic with similarly elevated virulence. Since global environmental change is expected to generate significant long-term shifts in abiotic phenomena (temperature, humidity, water resources, etc.), we can reasonably expect attendant shifts in pathogenic virulence. Of course, these shifts will vary on a regional basis, with some areas experiencing declining biting densities and infectivity and thus declining virulence. Other areas will see increased vector populations, greater biting rates, and shortened pathogen incubation periods, which will synergistically combine to generate higher pathogen virulence.[137] Large urban centers will also increase the frequency of transmission and thereby permit greater expression of the pathogen's lethality. Thus, the lethality of pathogens such as malaria is likely to increase as greater population pools and density thresholds are crossed.

The use of anti-microbial and anti-viral agents is accelerating the evolution of pathogens and contributing to greater resistance across strains. The crux of the problem is that these chemical agents are useful in the clinical treatment of patients who would otherwise be killed or permanently damaged by pathogenic infestation; however, from an epidemiological perspective we are simple accelerating the great historical evolutionary race between pathogens and the human species. Ewald argues that, instead of resorting to technological quick fixes (as is our penchant), we should use the processes of biological evolution to our advantage and attempt to "domesticate" pathogens. Domestication involves reducing the frequency of contact between a pathogen and the human host, which will in turn result in increasingly diminishing virulence over time. In this way, we may able to selectively breed out traits for virulence over the long term without having to resort to "microbial warfare" strategies that only serve to exacerbate downstream problems, such as resistance. Unfortunately, in many areas of the world increased frequency of vector-host contact is increasing the virulence of many pathogens, increasing mortality from sexually transmitted diseases (HIV/AIDS, herpes, syphilis, etc.). Ewald notes that in areas where sexual transmission of the pathogen is high its virulence increases accordingly. In Senegal, where social and cultural constructs limit sexual activity (and therefore the frequency of sexual transmission), the virulence of STDs, particularly HIV/AIDS, is much lower than in high-transmission areas such as Southern Africa. Ewald's findings imply that by limiting the frequency of transmission we can actually reduce the virulence of the pathogen. Therefore, simple strategies such as the construction of mosquito-proof housing and the increased use of condoms will ultimately reduce the lethality of pathogens spread by arthropod vectors or through frequent sexual contact.[138] Of course, construction of adequate housing is problematic in states with low endogenous resources, and getting people to change their beliefs and sexual habits is difficult.

A caveat: Empirically measuring the projected health effects of global environmental change is exceptionally difficult because environmental change will affect different pathogens in a number of ways, altering zones of endemicity, transmissibility, and lethality. Some pathogens will flourish, new pathogens will emerge, and some pathogens may decline. Moreover, these fundamental shifts in the microbial world will be governed by a number of factors, including migration, provision of clean urban environments, "improved nutrition, increased availability of potable water, improvements in sanitation, the extent of disease vector-control measures, changes in resistance of vector organisms to insecticides, and more widespread availability of health care."[139] The balance of the evidence available at this point in time leads to the conclusion that human-induced global environmental changes will significantly alter the global distribution of pathogens and their vectors and, in many cases, provide increasingly permissive environments for the proliferation of pathogenic agents throughout the human ecology, thereby increasing the aggregate burden of disease on humans and other species over time. Of course, human ingenuity can be employed to prevent and to mitigate the consequences of environmentally induced disease proliferation. We shall simply need to engage in greater analysis of the linkages between human-induced environmental change and disease emergence, with the obvious goal of limiting activities that increase opportunities for pathogens to emerge. With scientific analysis, and (one hopes) with ecology-minded foresight and policies, humanity should be able to slow the emergence of pathogens.

Conclusion

The gravity of the HIV pandemic and its potential for widespread destruction of life, prosperity, and stability have finally been recognized by the majority of nations, as is evident from the resolutions presented to the General Assembly of the United Nations in January 2000. It is my hope that the evidence I have amassed may, in some way, be employed by the global policy community to better understand the possible effects of the proliferation of disease, and perhaps to design policy mechanisms that may mitigate some of the widespread damage already being wrought by these modern "plagues."

I have presented the following major arguments:

· The increasingly rapid proliferation of pathogens constitutes a significant and direct threat to human life and welfare. The direct effect of disease will generate increasing mortality and morbidity and, in certain cases, will result in the continuing destruction of a significant proportion of a state's population. I find Richard Holbrooke's assertion that the HIV pandemic may constitute the greatest challenge facing humanity in the twenty-first century perfectly reasonable in view of the evidence now before us.

· The increasing prevalence of infectious disease will increase human mortality and morbidity, resulting in gradual erosion of state capacity and in increasing poverty. Because of this relationship, pathogen-induced economic decline will increase the demands of the population on the state for the provision of basic services, even as the ability of the state to provide those goods and to govern effectively declines. This combination of declining state capacity and increasing deprivation may contribute to increasing governance problems and development problems in affected states, and may in extreme cases contribute to political destabilization. This confluence of negative trends may compromise the ability of transitional states (e.g., Russia and South Africa) to consolidate democratic and effective systems of governance.

• Since increasing disease prevalence destroys or debilitates national populations and compromises both productivity and governance, infectious disease may be correctly seen as both a direct and an indirect threat to the national security of seriously affected states.

• The balance of the evidence suggests that increasing human-induced degradation of the planet's ecological systems may accelerate the emergence of pathogens, promote recrudescence, alter the spatial distribution of pathogens, and make pathogens more virulent.

Empirical Findings

As I have demonstrated throughout this volume, indicators measuring disease-induced population mortality show a significant negative association with indicators of state capacity. Thus, these mortality indicators would seem to be excellent predictors of both current and downstream state capacity. In addition, infectious disease prevalence levels show a significant negative empirical association with measures of state capacity. Owing to the large effect that the proliferation of infectious disease will have on population mortality and morbidity, the increasing proliferation, lethality, and transmissibility of pathogens may compromise state capacity in significantly affected states. Furthermore, the observed negative empirical association between disease and state capacity holds at the state, regional, and global levels and over time. This is important in that the negative association between the two variables is generalizable across societies and state structures, across geographic areas, and across historical periods.

Perhaps of greatest significance, this study demonstrates the existence of an asymmetric feedback loop between population health and state capacity. Fifteen-year lagging of the variables shows that disease levels tend to drive state capacity down over the entire period of the lag, whereas state capacity drives disease prevalence only within a 9-year lag period. The symmetry of the lags demonstrates that public health affects state capacity more than vice versa. Thus, increasing prevalence of pathogens within a state's population is likely to undercut that state's capacity over the long term. This diminished capacity, in turn, will lead to increasing proliferation of infectious disease within that society in a negative and self-reinforcing feedback loop. The proliferation of disease will probably intensify poverty and general human misery in seriously affected states, which will logically contribute to greater relative or absolute deprivation.

I have also articulated the probabilistic linkages between increasing disease prevalence and declining state economic productivity (at the micro and macro levels). The analysis in chapter 3 empirically confirms the hypothesis that the continuing global proliferation of infectious disease poses an increasingly significant obstacle to the economic, political, and social development of societies throughout the world. The negative empirical association of infectious disease with indices of economic and social development within the aggregate state capacity variable suggests that disease will stunt the development of seriously affected societies. This may provide some explanation as to why sub-Saharan Africa (the historical cradle of many human pathogenic agents) has continually found itself at the bottom of the Human Development Index rankings, despite a wealth of natural resources in the region and the constant infusion of capital and of social and technical ingenuity from exogenous sources such as the World Bank, the International Monetary Fund, individual donor countries, and development initiatives sponsored by non-governmental organizations. Perhaps the findings of this book will help to inform the theoretical debate on the determinants of international development.

Theoretical Ramifications

This volume reconceptualizes the theoretical linkages between infectious disease and security, demonstrates that there is an empirical association between disease and state capacity, and provides preliminary evidence supporting the argument that infectious disease may promote poverty and, in certain cases, political instability. It also clearly maps out the probabilistic relationships among the independent, intervening, and dependent variables and the probable direction and polarity of associations between these variables, and then demonstrates the statistical strength of these associations.

Having examined the interaction of complex human and natural systems, we may logically conclude that changes in the natural world can and often do affect social and economic phenomena, and that these effects may by extension contribute to political instability. This means that the natural world does have significant (though difficult-to-observe) effects on human social structures. This provides additional ammunition for the theories of Sir Francis Bacon, William Whewell, Edward O. Wilson, and William McNeill, who have consistently argued that great truths may be found when we investigate the possibility of consilient knowledge between the great branches of scientific endeavor. Conversely, the continued fragmentation and compartmentalization of knowledge in the sciences as a general trend may lead us to bypass certain avenues of consilient scientific investigation, which may in turn induce a greater ignorance of the perils that may await us as we continue to alter the world's ecology.

Because of the significance and the scale of the correlations between health indicators and state capacity, we may be able to employ population health data to predict downstream state capacity in a country with some success. This may in turn help social scientists devise increasingly accurate models to predict state stability over the long term. However, further empirical analysis with a greater sample size and increased number of data points will be necessary before we can draw any hard and fast conclusions concerning the exact predictive value of health data in its relationship with state capacity.

The discovery that population health seems to drive state capacity in a reciprocal spiral over a broad span of time is not only theoretically novel and intriguing in and of itself; it also provides significant evidence to buttress the claims of Loren King, Bruce Moon, and William Dixon that poverty is not the principal determinant of population health and that pathogen emergence and proliferation is occasionally quite independent of the socio-economic status of a society. This allows us to reject the simplistic and common assumption that disease is simply a product of the maldistribution of scarce economic resources; indeed, there is in fact widespread evidence to the contrary. One only has to look at the fact that HIV spread throughout Europe and North America before it spread throughout Eastern Europe and South Asia to comprehend that poverty alone does not account for the proliferation of disease. One case in point is that the

Spanish Influenza pandemic of 1918 began in the United States, spread throughout Europe, and only later reached the developing countries. The finding that disease-induced mortality tends to have a greater long-term effect on state capacity over the 15-year lag period than the obverse may be of significant theoretical interest to those involved in development studies. This finding may help to explain the rapid development of northern states (in which fewer endemic diseases have historically afflicted the population) relative to tropical countries. Of course this idea remains speculative, but it may partially explain why tropical countries have industrialized at a slower pace than countries in temperate climates, why they started from a lower initial base of state capacity during the process of industrialization, and why they continue to experience underdevelopment and often lack effective governance.

This examination of the feedback loop leads to the conclusion that countries with lower initial state capacity are in greater danger of pathogen-induced destabilization and poverty than states that currently exhibit high state capacity, owing to the reciprocal nature of the Population Health/State Capacity spiral. Thus, disease represents a greater threat to developing countries and to regions in transition (e.g., South Africa, Colombia, Russia) than to developed states with relatively high initial state capacity (e.g., Canada, Germany, Japan).

Insofar as disease will act as a stressor on state capacity and will reverse development gains in seriously affected states, the resultant disease-induced poverty and general human misery may exacerbate relative and absolute deprivation. Disease may thus increase relative and/or absolute deprivation, simultaneously increasing the demands of the populace on the state for the provision of basic needs and services. All this occurs as the state's capacity to respond to these demands diminishes correspondingly. Thus, if the deprivation hypothesis or the state weakness hypothesis is correct (or if both are correct), the worldwide proliferation of infectious disease may accelerate and/or exacerbate pre-existing societal tensions, and may in some cases contribute to increased criminal activity, to low-intensity intra-state violence, and (in certain extreme cases) to the collapse of effective governance.

Finally, I have attempted to develop a new theoretical framework that examines the probabilistic relationship among diseases, state capacity, and societal deprivation and that may assist to some extent in the prediction of state failure and intra-state violence in the future. This book does not explain all civil and intra-state conflict, nor does it seek to do so; rather, it seeks to shed some light on the increasing economic instability and problems of effective governance that we are currently observing throughout the developing countries, and to warn the peoples of the developed countries that they remain potentially vulnerable to the various negative macro effects of infectious disease.

Policy Ramifications

Drawing on the evidence provided in this book, one can reasonably conclude that the proliferation of disease will result in the increasing destruction and debilitation of the population base of seriously affected countries. Disease will also simultaneously increase poverty and misery throughout these societies, erode and/or prevent the consolidation of endogenous human capital, and (through the erosion of state capacity) increase the probability of social unrest, governance problems, and political violence within states with high infection rates.

The resurgence of infectious disease may have significant implications for the survival, stability, and prosperity of a state, and it may also have ramifications for inter-state relations. The premature death and debilitation of a significant proportion of a state's population erodes worker productivity, undermines the state's prosperity, erodes human capital within the society over the long term, threatens the state's ability to defend itself and to project force, generates institutional fragility, and generally impedes the state's ability to govern effectively.[1]

Plagues have contributed to the collapse of governance over the broad span of history. They hampered the Athenian war effort during the Peloponnesian war, contributed to the demise of Byzantine Rome and to the destruction of the feudal order in Europe, and were the primary force in the annihilation of the pre-Colombian societies in the Americas.[2] This dynamic is not relegated to the annals of history; it continues to affect state capacity. Because of the negative association between infectious disease and state capacity, the global proliferation of emerging and re-emerging diseases (particularly HIV, tuberculosis, and malaria) is a threat to international economic development and to effective governance at the state level. This allows several preliminary policy conclusions:

• The growing destabilization of sub-Saharan Africa may be due in part to the exceptionally high levels of various diseases in the region, particularly HIV/AIDS, tuberculosis, and malaria. Indeed, the extreme and persistent governance problems in the Great Lakes region of central Africa may be related to increasing disease-induced stresses on state capacity.

• The balance of the evidence demonstrates that humanity's increasing negative effect on the biosphere will only serve to accelerate the emergence of pathogens into the human ecology, simultaneously altering the distribution of current pathogenic organisms known to the human species. Continuing global change may also alter the infectivity and the lethality of known and emerging microorganisms, and it may affect the basal health and immunoresponse capacity of potential human hosts. Global phenomena such as infectious diseases often act in concert with other global collective action problems, such as environmental degradation and resource scarcity, to strain state capacity. This synergy between stressors of state capacity will increasingly destabilize seriously affected states and in some cases entire regions (such as sub-Saharan Africa). We must foster increased communication and cooperation between the global policy and medical communities and provide increased resources for surveillance, containment, and cooperative policy measures to check the global proliferation of emerging and re-emerging diseases. Above all, we must bring the gravity of these issues to the attention of the heads of all governments, as the greatest requirements for stemming the global tide of infection are political will in concert with timely and adequate amounts of social and technical ingenuity.

• Tangible actions that governments should take include the establishment of a global disease surveillance system incorporating elements of the successful civil-society model of the ProMED network that currently monitors disease outbreaks. Governments should also undertake the collection of "health intelligence" so as to monitor the progression of diseases through the populations of states that either cannot provide accurate statistics on disease prevalence or refuse to do so for political reasons. Policy makers must also take action to reduce the pace of global environmental degradation, curb the abuse of anti-microbial medications within their societies, and provide increased funding for research to develop vaccines and other anti-microbial agents. To date, the World Health Organization has been the principal actor engaged in tracking disease emergence and proliferation, but it faces several problems in dealing with these issues. Although funding is increasingly diverted within the WHO to surveillance, treatment, and control of infectious diseases, these programs are generally underfunded and understaffed, and they have proved generally less than effective in fighting the simultaneous re-emergence of many infectious diseases on many fronts. Thus, greater resources must be given to the WHO, and those funds should be specifically targeted to deal with the greatest current disease threats: HIV, tuberculosis, and malaria. The United States and Japan are currently developing a policy framework for greater cooperation in checking the spread of disease within and between their own territories. Furthermore, the Group of Seven (G-7) states are exploring the means by which they might collaborate to reduce the threat of emerging diseases to their populations. Although these efforts have not yet produced any concrete results in the form of multilateral anti-contagion regimes, they are a step in the right direction.

The following policy recommendations can be made at this time:

• Infectious disease poses a direct threat to stability and prosperity throughout the developing countries. The region currently experiencing the greatest amount of disease-induced poverty and instability is sub-Saharan Africa. Rising disease levels in South Asia, Southeast Asia, and Eastern Europe demand increased surveillance. Vulnerable "key states" that are experiencing rapid increase in disease prevalence include South Africa, Russia, Ukraine, India, China, and Brazil. Since our resources to mitigate the growing crisis in public health are finite, we shall have to pick our spots and allocate funds to disease prevention with discretion in order to maximize the stability of key states and promote regional stability. Examples of such possible interventions might include massive campaigns against the proliferation of HIV in Russia, Ukraine, Brazil, India, China, and South Africa.[3]

• Disease-induced mortality is climbing throughout the developed countries, and at some point disease may constitute a direct threat to political and economic stability in these countries. However, short of the re-appearance of a rapid and lethal pandemic, disease does not present an immediate threat to the stability of states with high initial state capacity. Therefore, the globalization of disease is not a direct threat to the security of industrialized nations at the present time, at least not on the magnitude that it presents to states in the developing countries. However, infectious disease will continue to undermine stability throughout the developing countries, compromising key foreign policy concerns of the developed states (such as global political and economic stability), and it may contribute to the development of indirect threats to the security of the developed countries.

• In view of the nature of the global threat to public health, the policy community must acknowledge the infectious disease problem and must marshal significant political will to deal with the situation before it deteriorates much further. In Uganda and Thailand, campaigns to limit the spread of HIV were successful only because political elites used their leadership skills to mobilize both the resources of the governments and aid from external donors. In the absence of informed and committed political leadership, disease continues to spread inexorably. Given the will, policy makers can enact the required redistribution of fiscal resources, ingenuity, and technology to stem the rising tide of disease and to promote global prosperity and stability.

• In addition to the mobilization of political will and capital, nascent global disease-surveillance regimes must be strengthened and enlarged. Systems already in place, such as ProMED and GEIS, can be geographically enlarged, and their information-processing capacity can be augmented. Furthermore, a global disease-containment regime should be designed and built, with active cooperation by all states and leadership by the G-7 nations. The G-7 has the economic and technological capacity to take on such a role, and at their last several summits G-7 leaders have expressed growing concern about the proliferation of infectious disease. Such a containment regime would require significant cooperation between the majority of states in issue areas as diverse as increasing the availability of public health data, strengthening local public health capacity, augmenting national and international communication structures, limiting humanitarian disasters and war, and stemming the misuse of antibiotic agents.

• Global environmental degradation and overpopulation must be addressed and slowed, as these two processes affect viral traffic in their roles as disease amplifiers and probabilistically increase the chance that lethal new zoonoses will take hold within the human ecology.

An Agenda for Future Research

The findings presented in this book are based primarily on the analysis of quantitative data from a random sample of twenty countries. These preliminary findings suggest that increasing pathogen-induced mortality and morbidity within a country's population will have a negative long-term effect on its state capacity. However, it behooves us to explore this research in greater depth, and to refine our understanding of the hypothesized relationships. Future studies should try to increase the sample size, refine the indicators employed, and, as appropriate, employ alternative statistical metrics. More research can be done on modeling and quantifying state capacity by substituting or adding different logical index measures, and perhaps by weighting some of the individual measures of state capacity differently to reflect their logically greater importance within the equation.

It may be too early to tell which indicators (if any) are most prominent in the determination of state capacity, and thus greater research in the form of case studies should precede any attempts at differential weighting. Regarding the independent variable, data on infectious disease prevalence and incidence within populations are becoming increasingly available at the national and sub-national levels for many states. This is particularly true of HIV/AIDS. As the data become available, it will be possible to perform in-depth case studies of the relationship between infectious disease and state capacity within selected countries. This increasing amount of specific data per pathogen and per country may permit deeper analysis of the association between the prevalence of various pathogens and state capacity at the sub-national, national, and regional levels. This will allow us to distinguish pathogens that generate great mortality and/or morbidity in a population and significantly affect state capacity (e.g., HIV and the malaria and tuberculosis pathogens) from relatively innocuous or rare pathogens (e.g., rhinovirus and legionella). By determining which pathogens have the greatest negative effect on state capacity, we can target policy to be increasingly effective in mitigating the effects of disease on states and societies.

Systematic exploration of these relationships through detailed case studies will increase the availability of data on pathogen prevalence and incidence in a country and will allow the development of a comprehensive diachronic data base of country-specific indicators of state capacity. The case studies will also allow us to see how pathogens interact with differentiated societal and political structures across states. This may provide answers as to why certain societies (e.g., Thailand) seem to adapt more effectively to the pathogen threat than others (e.g., the former Zaire), as certain structures of governance may prove more resilient in the face of disease. These case studies should be carried out on a global basis, drawing on cases from Africa, South Asia, East Asia, Eastern Europe, Latin America and the Caribbean, North America, and Europe. Case studies will also allow us to observe and document the varying strategies that states employ to counter the proliferation of disease within their populations. It is worthwhile to analyze the policy responses of certain countries (e.g., Thailand and Uganda) that have had some success in curtailing the rise in HIV incidence within their populations, and to compare these adaptive strategies with those of countries that have decisively failed to adapt to the HIV crisis (e.g., Zimbabwe, South Africa). Such a comparative policy analysis would undoubtedly provide significant value in terms of informing policy prescriptions for countries that are currently experiencing rapid disease proliferation (Russia, Ukraine, India). The study also suggests that the linkages between state capacity and political stability must be explored in greater depth, and this inquiry may in turn contribute to the nascent literature on state failure.[4] This project may lead to deeper inquiries into the nature of state survival, power, and stability. Under what conditions does effective governance collapse, and how can we explain and predict the phenomena of state failure and intra-state violence?

Within environmental policy circles, there is also great interest in the increasingly clear relationship among environmental change, disease prevalence, and social violence at the sub-state level. For example, global climate change may affect variability in rainfall, which in turn will affect the levels of vector-borne diseases within certain regions. Following the deprivation hypothesis, increasing human misery and poverty resulting from increased disease levels will generate increased levels of grievance in society, which may manifest itself in random social violence (e.g., theft, assault, homicide) or in organized violence and resistance against the state. The reciprocal effects of natural and human systems must be explored in greater depth, particularly with respect to their influence on political outcomes.

In view of the strong empirical association between population health and state capacity, it would seem logical to explore how other factors that induce human morbidity and mortality might also induce governance and deprivation problems. Given that global warming, ozone depletion, and environmental toxicity all compromise population health to a certain degree, one might explore the possible relationship among global environmental change, deteriorating human health, declining state capacity, increasing deprivation, and social violence. One might also explore non-environmental phenomena such as alcoholism and narcotics addiction, which may also have long-term effects on human mortality. Such dynamics are obviously at work in present-day Russia and Ukraine, where falling state capacity, substance abuse, and infectious disease are feeding off one another in a negative feedback loop.

Furthermore, we must quantify other theoretical stressors of state capacity (such as environmental degradation/scarcity and demographic growth) in order to evaluate the strength of their correlations with state capacity. Given an empirical examination of the effects of these stressors on state capacity, we can evaluate the relative importance of these factors to the health component and thus determine which of these variables poses the greatest future threat to state capacity (and, by extension, state stability). This will allow us to set accurately targeted research priorities and inform the policy-making process as to where we should concentrate scarce resources to meet the most significant threats. Social scientists must also gather empirical evidence on the relative importance of intervening variables (disease amplifiers) in determining the spread and intensity of epidemics and pandemics. By determining which of these amplifiers have the greatest effects in maximizing the global distribution and/or lethality of diseases, we can then target policy in order to minimize amplifiers such as the misuse of antibiotics. Of course, reducing the frequency of war, famine, and environmental degradation will inevitably prove a more elusive goal. Finally, a significant amount of work needs to be done concerning the implications of infectious disease for economic productivity and international developmental. This is one of the most important aspects of this research, and tragically the influence of public health on economic and political development has been almost entirely ignored until very recently.

Microbial threats to human health do not respect international borders and are extremely difficult to monitor and contain. Infectious disease constitutes a truly global challenge, and such it must be met with international cooperation. The implication here is that Realist policy prescriptions (which emphasize self-help strategies) will not protect states from the negative consequences of disease resurgence. Unilateral efforts that focus on limiting the spread of disease within one's own state are bound to fail over the long term, as disease is a trans-boundary phenomenon.[5] Liberal theory, which emphasizes cooperation between states, holds an optimistic view of human nature, sees international organizations as significant actors, and argues that states seek prosperity and stability in addition to survival and power, is likely to provide a better theoretical foundation than Realism for tackling the problems posed by the resurgence of infectious disease and other global issues. Liberal solutions to disease proliferation would take the form of a global multilateral health regime that would seek to prevent, monitor, and control the spread of disease. Of course, certain regimes already exist to deal with the spread of pathogens between sovereign states,[6] and the nascent global surveillance system (ProMED) has proved highly effective in monitoring pathogen outbreak events.

Despite the technological advances made in the past 100 years, the human species now faces a truly daunting and persistent challenge in the global pandemics of tuberculosis, malaria, and (in particular) HIV/AIDS. When I embarked on this study, in the mid 1990s, many optimistic colleagues scoffed at the notion that infectious disease would continue to proliferate on a global scale and threaten the prosperity and stability of many nations. Humanity was constantly reassured by the scientific community that a vaccine for HIV would soon be forthcoming, and that the pandemic would soon be brought to a halt by the combined efforts of international organizations, non-governmental organizations, and national governments and by the combined technological and social ingenuity of the human species. Yet such solutions have failed to materialize, and the HIV/AIDS pandemic continues its inexorable spread through developing and transitional societies. Where did we go wrong? Aside from technological failures (notably the inability to develop a vaccine to prevent HIV infection or a cure for those now infected), perhaps we must accept the fact that technological ingenuity, in and of itself, cannot stop the HIV/AIDS pandemic. It is increasingly evident that we need more social ingenuity in order to tackle pandemics—social ingenuity that can be used to devise increasingly effective policy and resilient structures of governance and to increase education on these issues with the object of breaking down the obstacles of denial, intolerance and ignorance.

Perhaps we have, as a species, overestimated our capacities to master the natural world and bend it to our will. It is, of course, prudent to recognize that we remain inextricably linked to the rest of the biosphere as but one species within the web of life, albeit the most powerful. As we continue to alter the global ecology and to play with biological mechanisms that we do not completely understand, we increase the probability that other nasty surprises (such as emergent pathogens) will find niches to exploit in our rapidly changing world. It is now evident that the HIV/AIDS pandemic represents a significant and novel challenge to the well-being of the entire human species, and a great deal of international cooperation and ingenuity will be needed to contain it let alone eradicate it. As a species, we must discard the veil of denial and complacency so that we may address this pandemic before it surpasses our capacity to do so effectively. It is my greatest hope that humanity will rise to this enormous challenge in collective fashion. It is my fear that we will continue to bicker among ourselves, or to languish in apathy, as the pandemics of HIV/AIDS, tuberculosis, malaria, and cholera continue to spread, and that many of the possibilities documented herein (destruction of populations, erosion of prosperity, collapse of order) will increasingly become reality for many of the societies on this planet. Let us not permit that to happen.

Notes

Introduction

1. See T. Homer-Dixon, "On the threshold: Environmental changes as causes of acute conflict" and "Environmental scarcities and violent conflict: Evidence from cases," M. Weiner, "Security, stability, and international migration," and P. Gleick, "Water and conflict: Fresh water resources and international security," all in *Global Dangers*, ed. S. Lynn-Jones and S. Miller (MIT Press, 1995).

2. This project examines the effects of the most destructive emerging and re-emerging infectious diseases. The disease agents central to this project are HIV/AIDS, malaria, tuberculosis, hepatitis, cholera, dengue fever, diarrheal rotaviruses and adenoviruses, plague, the bovine spongiform encephalopathy prion, and synctatial respiratory viruses. Different societies will be at risk from different pathogens, varying with differences in climate, wealth, and geographical position.

3. Until very recently the concept of microbial threats to human security had not been explored. Two of the works that initiated preliminary explorations of the disease threat are Laurie Garret's article "The return of infectious disease" (*Foreign Affairs* 75 (1996), no. 1: 66–79) and Dennis Pirages's paper Ecological Security: Micro-Threats to Human Well-Being (presented at Annual Meeting of International Studies Association, San Diego, 1996).

4. *World Health Report 1996: Fighting Disease Fostering Development* (World Health Organization, 1996), p. 15.

5. See W. McNeill, *Plagues and Peoples* (Doubleday, 1976).

6. This incorporates statistics from both inter-state and intra-state warfare.

7. "Mortality" represents deaths that result from infectious disease; "morbidity" denotes serious physical debilitation of an individual as a result of prior or current exposure to infectious pathogens. These statistics on the causes of death around the world in 1990 are derived from pp. 224–225 of the World Bank's *World Development Report 1993: Investing in Health* (Oxford University Press, 1993).

8. See p. 21 of UNAIDS, Waking Up to Devastation (Epidemic Update, June 2000) (www. unaids.org/epidemic_update/report/index. html).

9. All statistics in this sentence are from p. 18 of *World Health Report 1995: Bridging the Gaps* (WHO, 1995).

10. Centers for Disease Control and Prevention, "Addressing emerging infectious disease threats: A prevention strategy for the United States, executive summary," *Morbidity and Mortality Weekly Report* 43 (RR-5), p. 1.

11. J. Lederberg, R. Shope, and S. Oaks Jr., *Emerging Infections* (National Academy Press, 1992), p. 15.

12. BSE is a prion-induced condition in cattle that results in massive deterioration of the brain, ultimately causing death. These prions (infective proteins) may be transmitted via contact with infected meat to humans, causing Creutzfeldt-Jacob disease (usually fatal) in the human host.

13. The evolutionary capability of viruses was discovered by Joshua Lederberg in 1952. For a current discussion of how microbial evolution imperils human health, see Joshua Lederberg, "Viruses and humankind: Intracellular symbiosis and evolutionary competition," in *Emerging Viruses*, ed. S. Morse (Oxford University Press, 1993).

14. J. Paul, *A History of Poliomyelitis* (Yale University Press, 1971).

15. F. Fenner and D. Henderson, *Smallpox and Its Eradication* (WHO, 1988).

16. Vector-borne pathogens are disease agents that are transmitted to humans through an intermediary animal or insect host. The malaria plasmodium, a classic example of a vector-borne pathogen, uses the mosquito to jump from one human host to another.

17. A zoonosis is a pathogenic agent that has crossed over from its original animal or insect host into human populations. Recent crossover pathogens (e.g., HIV and *Falciparum malaria*) tend to exhibit exceptional lethality in human populations, but this lethality tends to decline over millennia as the pathogen and the host adjust to each other.

18. M. Drohan, "Disease goes global," *Globe and Mail*, March 30, 1996; W. Thorsell, "The tuberculosis emergency," *Globe and Mail*, April 1, 1996. (The *Globe and Mail* is a well-known Toronto daily.)

19. On occasion, emergent illnesses may shift their effect on a given population distribution, from one region of the distribution to another. The classic case is that of Spanish Influenza, which killed otherwise healthy adults in the prime of their lives. Normally influenza is only fatal to the extremely young and very old, who possess weakened immune systems.

20. D. McNeil Jr., "AIDS in Africa: The silent stalker," *New York Times*, December 27, 1998.

21. An epidemic is an outbreak of disease that exhibits both geographical and temporal boundaries. One example is the brief outbreak of Plague in Surat, India during the autumn of 1994. A pandemic is a outbreak of disease that is not geographically restricted (e.g. HIV), nor is it necessarily confined within a set time frame (e.g. malaria, tuberculosis).

22. See pp. 2–3 of UNAIDS, AIDS Epidemic Update: December 1998 (http://www.unaids.org/highband/document/epidemio/wadr98e.pdf).

23. See Global Summary of the HIV/AIDS epidemic, 1999 (http://www.unaids.org/epidemic_update/report/Epi_report_chap_glo_estim.htm).

24. Ibid.

25. Seroprevalence is an estimation of the rate of pathogen-infected individuals in a given population set. For example, if country X shows 20% HIV seroprevalence, then 20% of that country's population is HIV positive.

26. Namibia and Swaziland currently report HIV seroprevalence levels in excess of 20%, and Zimbabwe and Botswana have infection levels of more than 25% of the total population. For individual countries' annual seroprevalence statistics, see http://www.unaids.org/highband.

27. See http://www.unaids.org/epidemic_update/report/Table_E.htm. See also "A turning point for AIDS?" *The Economist* (US edition), July 15, 2000, p. 2.

28. S. Daly, "A post-apartheid agony: AIDS on the march," *New York Times*, July 23, 1998.

29. D. McNeil Jr., "AIDS stalking Africa's struggling economies," *New York Times*, November 15, 1998.

30. Ibid.

31. A. Picard, "UN warns of alarming gap in prevention of AIDS," *Globe and Mail*, June 24, 1998.

32. M. Feschbach, "Dead souls," *Atlantic Monthly*, January 1999, p. 26.

33. See UNAIDS data (http://www.unaids.org/epidemic_update/report/table_E.htm). See also "HIV rising in CIS countries," *Globe and Mail*, April 22, 1998.

34. See http://www.unaids.org/epidemic_update/report/table_E.htm). See also L. Altman, "Dismaying experts, HIV infections soar," *New York Times*, November 24, 1998.

35. J. Stackhouse, "Nagaland choking in grip of AIDS," *Globe and Mail*, December 1, 1997.

36. *World Health Report 1996*, p. 27.

37. Ibid.

38. Ibid., p. 28.

39. M. Specter, "Doctors powerless as AIDS rakes Africa," *New York Times*, August 6, 1998. (N.B.: Studies of the kind cited in this volume are done quite sporadically. In general, if it is stated here that something was predicted to happen by a date that presumably had already passed by the time of writing, the reader may assume that a later prediction was not available at that time.)

40. Feschbach, "Dead souls," p. 27.

41. Endemic diseases are those that are geographically but not temporally bounded. In other words, malaria has always been present in northwestern Brazil

(endemic), but it has not always been present in Patagonia (non-endemic). Human actions had pushed malaria out of certain regions where the disease had been endemic prior to the 1960s, but vector-resistance to pesticides and new strains of malaria have seen the pathogen re-conquering its former territory.

42. Specter, "Doctors powerless."

43. E. Ruppel Shell, "Resurgence of a deadly disease," *Atlantic Monthly*, August 1997, p. 47.

44. Ibid., p. 48.

45. Ibid., p. 45. Malaria's re-emergence as an endemically transmitted disease in Toronto has been verified by Kevin Kain of the Toronto General Hospital's Tropical Disease Unit (personal communication, October 30, 1998).

46. *World Health Report 1996*, p. 2.

47. On the evidence compiled by Paul Ewald, see J. Hooper, "A new germ theory," *Atlantic Monthly*, February 1999, pp. 41–53.

48. A detailed technical definition of state capacity is given in chapter 1.

49. For data see http://cdc.gov/nchswww/fastats.

50. L. Garret, *The Coming Plague* (Farrar, Straus and Giroux, 1994).

51. Garrett, "The return of infectious disease," pp. 66–79.

52. D. Pirages, Microsecurity: Disease Organisms and Human Well-Being, report issued by Woodrow Wilson Center Environmental Change and Security Project, 1996, p. 13.

53. Thucydides, *History of the Peloponnesian War* (Penguin, 1980), p. 155.

54. On the gradual collapse of the Roman Empire and the Han Dynasty, see McNeill, *Plagues and Peoples*, pp. 101–106.

55. Gibbon, quoted in H. Zinsser, *Rats, Lice, and History* (Little, Brown, 1934), pp. 147–148.

56. For further details see Zinsser, *Rats, Lice, and History*, pp. 132–175.

57. On the conquest of the American peoples by smaller European forces through infectious disease, see W. Denevan, *The Native Population of the Americas in 1492* (University of Wisconsin Press, 1992). McNeill also provides a valuable account of this demographic disaster in *Plagues and Peoples*. See also A. Crosby, *The Colombian Exchange* (Greenwood, 1972) and *Ecological Imperialism* (Cambridge University Press, 1994).

58. McNeill, *Plagues and Peoples*, pp. 180–181.

59. M. Oldstone, *Viruses, Plagues and History* (Oxford University Press, 1998), p. 5.

60. Ibid., p. 34. See also H. Thursfield, "Smallpox in the American War of Independence," *Annals of Medical History* 2 (1940), p. 312; C. Ward, *The War of the Revolution* (Macmillan, 1952).

61. Oldstone, *Viruses, Plagues and History*, pp. 47–48.

62. McNeill makes this argument, occasionally verging on biological determinism, in *Plagues and Peoples*.

63. A. Shaw, "Under the shadow of the big kill," *Globe and Mail,* June 1, 1996.

64. H. Labelle, speech to International Health Program, University of Toronto, February 26, 1999.

65. G. Mutizwa, "African leaders break ground over Congo war," *Globe and Mail,* December 14, 1998.

66. These are my terms.

67. "The old enemy," *Economist,* October 1, 1994.

68. H. MacDonald, "Surat's revenge: India counts the mounting costs of poverty," *Far Eastern Economic Review,* October 13, 1994, p. 76.

69. "Were ultras responsible for Surat plague?" *Hindustan Times,* July 9, 1995.

70. "Was it the plague?" *Economist,* November 19, 1994.

71. For an analysis of human reaction to, and aversion of risk, with the attendant irrational behavior that results, see R. Kasperson et al., The Social Amplification of Risk: A Conceptual Framework (Center for Technology, Environment, and Development, Clark University, 1989).

72. See J. Darnton, "France and Belgium ban British beef over cow disease," *New York Times,* March 22, 1996; D. Wallen, "European partners ban UK beef," *Globe and Mail,* March 22, 1996.

Chapter 1

1. See the following works by R. Fogel: Economic Growth, Population Theory, and Physiology: The Bearing of Long-Term Processes in the Making of Economic Policy (Working Paper 4638, National Bureau of Economic Research, April 1994); "The conquest of high mortality and hunger in Europe and America: Timing and mechanisms," in *Favorites of Fortune,* ed. D. Landes et al. (Harvard University Press, 1991); "Nutrition and the decline in mortality since 1700: Some preliminary findings in long-term factors in American economic growth," in *Conference on Research in Income and Wealth,* volume 41 (University of Chicago Press, 1986).

2. See T. Homer-Dixon, "On the threshold: Environmental changes as causes of acute conflict" and "Environmental scarcities and violent conflict: Evidence from cases," in *Global Dangers,* ed. S. Lynn-Jones and S. Miller (MIT Press, 1995); J. Goldstone, *Revolution and Rebellion in the Early Modern World* (University of California Press, 1991); A. Westing, ed., *Global Resources and International Conflict* (Oxford University Press, 1986).

3. Edward O. Wilson, "Back from chaos," *Atlantic Monthly,* March 1998, p. 41. The term "consilience" was originally coined by William Whewell in his 1840 book *The Philosophy of the Inductive Sciences.* Whewell wrote: "The Consilience of Inductions takes place when an Induction, obtained from one class of facts,

coincides with an Induction, obtained from another different class. This Consilience is a test of the truth of the Theory in which it occurs."

4. For Bacon's recognition of the need for consilience between the disciplines of scientific thought, and the deficiencies wrought by the specialization and fragmentation of knowledge, see *The Advancement of Learning* (1605), *Novum Organum* (1620), and *The Sylva Sylvanum* (1626).

5. Seminal works on this relationship include the following: S. Morse, ed., *Emerging Viruses* (Oxford University Press, 1993); T. McKeown, *The Modern Rise of Population* (Edward Arnold, 1976); S. Preston, *Mortality Patterns in National Population* (Academic Press, 1976); H. Zinsser, *Rats, Lice, and History* (Little, Brown, 1934); W. McNeill, *Plagues and Peoples* (Doubleday, 1989); L. Garrett, *The Coming Plague* (Farrar, Straus and Giroux, 1994); World Health Organization, *World Health Report 1996: Fighting Disease Fostering Development* (WHO, 1996).

6. There is still much work to be done on each of these issues. Although significant amounts of academic print have been devoted to the question of the effects of environmental scarcity and degradation on state stability and development, there is still a question as to whether this relationship can be demonstrated empirically. Therefore, I shall leave this to those scholars who specialize in the environmental subfield.

7. See these occasional papers prepared for the Project on Environmental Scarcities, State Capacity, and Civil Violence of the American Academy of Arts and Sciences and the University of Toronto (1997): C. Barber, The Case Study of Indonesia E. Economy, The Case Study of China—Reforms and Resources: The Implications for State Capacity in the PRC; T. Homer-Dixon and V. Percival, The Case Study of Bihar, India. All are available at http://utl1.library.utoronto.ca/www/pcs/state.htm.

8. During the Dynamics of Human Well-Being Project of the Canadian Institute for Advanced Research, Thomas Homer-Dixon, Jack Goldstone, and I stressed the need to move away from static concepts of state capacity.

9. This ranking reflects my ordering of state needs, which ranks survival as most important and ideological projection as least important.

10. Goldstone makes this argument in *Revolution and Rebellion in the Early Modern World*.

11. The year 1973 may be viewed as a turning point in the "health transition." Until the early 1970s, advances in public health had contributed to the dramatic worldwide decrease in infectious-disease-induced morbidity and mortality. Thus the prevalence of infectious disease had reached its nadir circa 1973. This year also saw the recognition of a new pathogen "rotavirus," the first of many new pathogenic agents to emerge in the coming decades. Essentially, 1973 is the turning point in the health transition where the curve of infectious disease incidence stops declining and begins its ascension. See Report of the NSTC Committee on International Science, Engineering, and Technology (CISET) Working Group on

Emerging and Re-Emerging Infectious Diseases: Global Microbial Threats in the 1990s (White House, September 1995).

12. Zoonoses are microbial or parasitic agents that cross over from the vast reservoir of disease agents that exist in animal reservoirs in a natural state. As these agents cross over from this exogenous reservoir (the zoonotic pool) and enter the human ecology, they may become pathogenic to humanity.

13. Murray and Lopez's study measures the burden of disease for the year 1990 on an aggregate basis for eight demographic regions of the world. Murray and Lopez employ the concept of disability-adjusted life years (DALYs) to quantify the burden of morbidity and mortality on given demographical regions. Unfortunately, while this study is very useful on many levels it does not provide us with *national* prevalence data per specific diseases. See C. Murray and A. Lopez, eds., *The Global Burden of Disease* (Harvard University Press, 1996). The GBD study follows on Preston's seminal work on global causes of mortality. See, e.g., S. Preston, N. Keyfitz, and R. Schoen, *Causes of Death* (Seminar Press, 1972).

14. Disease prevalence measurement problems are pervasive throughout the public health sciences literature and constitute a significant hurdle to the formation of effective global health policies. For one example of the problem see J. Kaufman et al., "The absence of adult mortality data for sub-Saharan Africa: A practical solution," *Bulletin of the World Health Organization* 75 (1997), no. 5: 389–395. See also C. Murray and A. Lopez, "Mortality by cause for eight regions of the world: Global burden of disease study," *Lancet* 349 (1997), p. 1269; J. Vallin "Theories of Mortality Decline," in *Mortality and Society in Sub-Saharan Africa,* ed. E. van de Walle et al. (Clarendon, 1992).

15. There is a significant differential in IM between developed countries and the rest of the world, as industrialized states have far lower infant mortality rates than the global average. Nonetheless, the greatest proportion of mortality is present within this cohort of the demographic distribution and thus IM is extremely sensitive to changing prevalence and lethality of the spectrum of infectious diseases within the human ecology. See Murray and Lopez, *Global Burden of Disease,* pp. 1128–1133. The notion of IM as a good proxy measure for ERID was reinforced through the author's numerous conversations with Stephen S. Morse.

16. Thanks in particular to Stephen Morse of the Columbia School of Public health for his support on this issue.

17. Murray and Lopez, "Global mortality, disability, and the contribution of risk factors: Global burden of disease study" (http://www.healthnet.org/programs/procor/gbd3.htm).

18. These infections account for 25% of the total global DALYs lost for all populations including all age groups (ibid., p. 1441).

19. Additionally, IM data are useful because they are usually unavailable during years of warfare or extreme conflict. Thus, IM data are generally resistant to statistical distortion that may be induced by the skewing effects of war or intense internal conflict. During years of intense conflict within a given state, the data for

that dyadic statistical year will either be unavailable—or will be adjusted to mirror a standard using statistical models based on data from previous years. Life expectancy data are frequently available during years of conflict and thus logically more sensitive to the skewing effect of war. See A. Hill, "Trends in childhood mortality in sub-Saharan mainland Africa," in *Mortality and Society in Sub-Saharan Africa*, ed. E. van de Walle et al. (Clarendon, 1992), p. 11.

20. C. Madavo, speech: AIDS, Development, and the Vital Role of Government (http://worldbank.org/aids-econ/madavo.htm).

21. See Preston et al., *Causes of Death*.

22. See Preston, *Mortality Patterns in National Population*.

23. See J. Vallin and F. Mesle, Les Causes des Deces en France de 1925 a 1978, Travaux et documents 115, INED-PUF, Paris, 1988; J. Vallin "Theories of mortality decline," in *Mortality and Society in Sub-Saharan Africa*, ed. E. van de Walle et al. (Clarendon, 1992), pp. 410–412. See also S. Johansson and K. Mosk, "Exposure, resistance, and life expectancy: Disease and death during the economic development of Japan, 1900–1960," *Population Studies* 41, no. 2 (1987): 207–235.

24. *World Health Report 1996: Fighting Disease, Fostering Development* (WHO, 1996), p. 59.

25. Ibid., pp. 59–62.

26. These data are available or 1997 at http://www.unaids.org under the epidemiological country fact sheet listings. The annual number of HIV diagnoses are generally available per country per year; however, WHO advises that these incidence rankings are fraught with significant error. The best available data are the national seroprevalence levels for 1997, which are based on new surveillance mechanisms and methodologies.

27. Zinsser, *Rats, Lice, and History*, p. 105.

28. I refer here to comments made by PRIO researchers during a seminar I gave in November 1996 at the International Peace Research Institute in Oslo.

29. The dynamics of chaos seem to govern the likelihood of pathogenic agents swapping genetic information through a process called "antigenic shift," which frequently alters the genetic code of the receiving microorganism and may change its lethality and/or transmissibility. For an excellent discourse on chaos, see J. Gleick, *Chaos* (Penguin, 1988).

30. S. Morse, "Origins of emerging viruses," in *Emerging Viruses*, ed. S. Morse (Oxford University Press, 1993), p. 10.

31. Ibid., p. 16.

32. Ibid., p. 12.

33. Ibid., p. 15.

34. On the need to integrate advanced concepts of complexity when examining natural and social phenomena, see R. Jervis, *System Effects* (Princeton University Press, 1997).

35. Morse, "Origins of emerging viruses," pp. 19–20.

36. Ibid., p. 19.

37. See C. Anderson, "Cholera epidemic traced to risk miscalculation," *Nature* 354 (1991), November 28, p. 255.

38. W. McNeill, "Patterns of disease emergence in history," in *Emerging Viruses,* ed. Morse, pp. 33–34. See also Lederberg et al., *Emerging Infections,* p. 48.

39. *World Health Report 1996,* p. 18.

40. Morse, "Origins of emerging viruses," p. 10.

41. A. Karlen, *Man and Microbes* (Touchstone, 1995), pp. 118–121.

42. See http://www.cdc.gov, http://who.org, and http://cdc.gov/ncidod/eid.

43. The global set of HIV national seroprevalence levels for 2000 was recently published on the Web and represents an opportunity for scientists to correlate HIV prevalence with State Capacity. These prevalence statistics permit some preliminary evaluation of the effect of AIDS on human development.

Chapter 2

1. http://worldbank.org/aids-econ/madavo.htm.

2. In the text, a double asterisk emphasizes that a correlation is significant to <0.010; a single asterisk emphasizes that a correlation is significant to <0.050.

3. Recall that for a correlation to be seen as strong and significant it must exhibit a correlation that is significant to <0.050.

4. Keep in mind that this is standardized to constant US dollars.

5. This idea was derived from conversations with David Welch.

Chapter 3

1. http://www.us.unaids.org/highband/speeches/mandela.html.

2. The geographical distribution of industrialized and developing nations and its possible relation to disease prevalence were discussed with Daniel Deudney in Toronto on November 18, 1997.

3. See R. Fogel, "The conquest of high mortality and hunger in Europe and America: Timing and mechanisms" in *Favorites of Fortune,* ed. D. Landes et al. (Harvard University Press, 1991). See also Fogel, "Nutrition and the decline in mortality since 1700: Some preliminary findings in long-term factors in American economic growth," in *Conference on Research in Income and Wealth,* volume 41 (University of Chicago Press, 1986); Economic Growth, Population Theory, and Physiology: The Bearing of Long-Term Processes in the Making of Economic Policy (Working Paper 4638, National Bureau of Economic Research, 1994).

4. McNeill, *Plagues and Peoples,* p. 162.

5. S. Watts, *Epidemics and History* (Yale University Press, 1997), pp. 20–21.

6. See Zinsser, *Rats, Lice, and History.* See also Crosby, McNeill, and Watts.

7. See S. Szreter, "Economic growth, disruption, deprivation, disease, and death: On the importance of public health for development," *Population and Development Review* 23, no. 4 (1997): 693–728. See also S. Johansson and C. Mosk, "Exposure, resistance and life expectancy: Disease and death during the economic development of Japan, 1900–60," *Population Studies* 41 (1987), no. 2: 207–235; S. Twarog, "Heights and living standards in Germany, 1850–1939: The case of Wurttemberg," in *Health and Welfare during Industrialization,* ed. R. Steckel and R. Floud (University of Chicago Press, 1997); D. Weir, "Economic welfare and physical well-being in France 1750–1990," ibid.

8. Szreter, "Economic growth"; S. Szreter and G. Mooney, "Urbanization, mortality and the standard of living debate: New estimates of the expectation of life at birth in nineteenth-century British cities," *Economic History Review* 51 (1998), no. 1: 84–112. See also L. King, "Economic growth and basic human needs," *International Studies Quarterly* 42 (1998), no. 2: 385–400; W. Coleman, *Death Is a Social Disease* (Wisconsin Publications in the History of Science and Medicine, 1982); E. Chadwick, *Report on the Sanitary Condition of the Labouring Population of Great Britain* (reprint: Edinburgh University Press, 1965); C. Hamlin, *Public Health and Social Justice in the Age of Chadwick* (Cambridge University Press, 1997); C. Harley, "British industrialization before 1841: Evidence of slower growth during the industrial revolution," *Journal of Economic History* 42 (1982): 267–289.

9. See P. Dasgupta, *An Inquiry into Well Being and Destitution* (Oxford University Press, 1993), pp. 97–103, 402–445, 539–545; B. Moon, *The Political Economy of Basic Human Needs* (Cornell University Press, 1991), pp. 64–69; B. Moon and W. Dixon "Basic needs and growth-welfare trade-offs," *International Studies Quarterly* 36 (1992): 191–212; N. Hicks, "Growth vs. basic needs: Is there a trade-off?" *World Development* 7 (1979): 985–994; D. Wheeler, "Basic needs fulfillment and economic growth: A simultaneous model," *Journal of Development Economics* 7 (1980): 435–451.

10. Cited in King, "Economic growth and basic human needs," p. 387.

11. King, "Economic growth and basic human needs," p. 394.

12. Ibid., p. 394.

13. Based on evidence presented by Laurie Garrett at the CIS/Medicine Conference on Social and Political Impact of Emerging Infectious Diseases, University of Toronto, October 30, 1998.

14. See Watts, *Epidemics and History,* pp. 1–38; D. Herlihy and C. Klapisch-Zuber, *Tuscans and Their Families* (Yale University Press, 1985), pp. 73–78; P. Slack, *The Impact of Plague in Tudor and Stuart England* (Routledge and Kegan Paul, 1985); R. Rapp, *Industry and Economic Decline in Seventeenth-Century Venice* (Harvard University Press, 1976); A. Carmichael, *Plague and the Poor in Renaissance Florence* (Cambridge University Press, 1986); J. Bean, "The Black

Death: The crisis and its social and economic consequences," in *The Black Death*, ed. D. Williman (Center for Medieval and Early Renaissance Studies, 1982); M. Flinn, "Plague in Europe and the Mediterranean countries," in *Journal of European Economic History* 8 (1979), no. 1: 134–148.

15. This is likely to have been due to greater population density in the large urban centers of the developed countries in 1918, wherein the transmission of influenza was enhanced. See A. Crosby, *America's Forgotten Pandemic* (Cambridge University Press, 1989).

16. See D. Cohen, Socio-Economic Causes and Consequences of the HIV Epidemic in Southern Africa: A Case Study of Namibia (Issues Paper 31, UNDP HIV and Development Programme) (http://www.undp.org:80/hiv/issues/English/issue31.htm).

17. M. Ainsworth and A. Mead Over, "The economic impact of AIDS on Africa," in *AIDS in Africa*, ed. M. Essex et al. (Raven, 1994), p. 564.

18. See J. Cuddington, "Modeling the macroeconomic effects of AIDS, with an application to Tanzania," *World Bank Economic Review* 7 (1993), no. 2, p. 175.

19. Ainsworth and Over, "The economic impact of AIDS on Africa," p. 565.

20. C. Myers, S. Obremsky, and M. Viravaidya, The Economic Impact of AIDS on Thailand (Working Paper 4, Harvard School of Public Health, 1992), p. 9.

21. Ibid., p. 8.

22. World Bank, The Macroeconomic Effects of AIDS, Development Brief 17, July 1993 (http://www.worldbank.org/html/dec/Publications/Briefs/DB17.html).

23. See S. Poonawala and R. Cantor, Children Orphaned by AIDS: A Call for Action for NGOs and Donors, National Council for International Health, 1991.

24. AIDS and the Demography of Africa, UN Department for Economic and Social Information and Policy Analysis, 1994, p. 3.

25. For an excellent discussion of pecuniary and non-pecuniary costs associated with ERIDs, see D. Bloom and G. Carliner, "The Economic impact of AIDS in the United States," *Science* 239 (1988), p. 604.

26. Ainsworth and Over, "The economic impact of AIDS on Africa," p. 565.

27. K. Hamilton, Global HIV/AIDS: A Strategy for US Leadership, Center for Strategic and International Studies, 1994, p. 5.

28. AIDS and the Demography of Africa, p. 4.

29. *World Development Report 1993: Investing in Health* (Oxford University Press, 1993), p. 18.

30. For additional information on these re-adjustment processes, see Ainsworth and Over, "The economic impact of AIDS on Africa," p. 564.

31. *World Health Report 1996: Fighting Disease Fostering Development* (WHO, 1996), p. 7.

32. With the obvious exception of the highly lethal falciparum malaria.

33. See D. Shepard, M. Ettling, U. Brinkmann, and R. Sauerborn, "The economic cost of malaria in Africa," *Tropical Medicine and Parasitology* 42 (1991), p. 199.

34. F. Konradsen, W. van der Hoek,P. Amerasinghe, and F. Amerasinghe, "Measuring the economic cost of malaria to households in Sri Lanka," *American Journal of Tropical Medicine and Hygiene* 56 (1997), no. 6, p. 656.

35. D. Ettling, D. McFarland, L. Schultz., and L. Chitsulo, "Economic impact of malaria in Malawian households," *Tropical Medicine and Parasitology* 45 (1994), no. 1, p. 74.

36. See R. Barlow, *The Economic Effects of Malaria Eradication* (University of Michigan, 1967); M. Gomes, "Economic and demographic research on malaria: A review of the evidence," *Social Science and Medicine* 37 (1993), no. 9: 1093–1108; R. Sauerborn et al., "Estimating the direct and indirect costs of malaria in a rural district of Burkina Faso," *Tropical Medicine and Parasitology* 42 (1991): 219–223; R. Castilla and D. Sawyer, "Malaria rates and fate: A socioeconomic study of malaria in Brazil," *Social Science and Medicine* 37 (1993), no. 9: 1137–1145; D. Sawyer, "Economic and social consequences of malaria in new colonization projects in Brazil," *Social Science and Medicine* 37 (1993), no. 9: 1131–1136; E. Nur, "The impact of malaria on labor use and efficiency in the Sudan," *Social Science and Medicine* 37 (1993), no. 9: 1115–1119; N. Kere et al., "The economic impact of plasmodium falciparum malaria on education investment: A Pacific island case study," *Southeast Asian Journal of Tropical Medicine and Public Health* 24 (1993), no. 4: 659–63; A. Mills, "The household costs of malaria in Nepal," *Tropical Medicine and Parasitology* 44 (1993), no. 1: 9–13; W. Asenso-Okyere, "Socioeconomic factors in malaria control," *World Health Forum* 15 (1994), no. 3: 265–268; B. Popkin, "A household framework for examining the social and economic consequences of tropical diseases," *Social Sciences and Medicine* 16 (1982), no. 5: 533–543.

37. *World Development Report 1993: Investing in Health,* p. 17.

38. T. Wirth, foreword to Global HIV/AIDS: A Strategy for US Leadership, Center for Strategic and International Studies, 1994, p. vii.

39. J. Atwood, speech at USAID Conference on Infectious Disease, Washington, December 17, 1997 (http://www.info.usaid.gov/press/spe_test/speeches/spch560.htm).

40. J. Atwood, speech, December 1, 1997 (http://www.info.usaid.gov/press/spe_test/speeches/spch561.htm).

41. Ainsworth and Over, "The economic impact of AIDS on Africa," p. 566.

42. *Better Health in Africa* (World Bank, 1994), p. 27.

43. See T. Schultz, "Investment in human capital," *American Economic Review* 51 (1961): 1–17; T. Schultz, *Investing in People* (University of California Press, 1981); G. Becker, K. Murphy, and R. Tamura, "Human capital, fertility, and economic growth," *Journal of Political Economy* 98 (1990): S12–S37; N. Stokey, "Human

capital, product quality, and growth," *Quarterly Journal of Economics* 105 (1991): 587–616; Dasgupta, *An Inquiry into Well Being and Destitution,* chapter 16.

44. World Bank. The Macroeconomic Effects of AIDS: Development Brief 17, 1993 (http://www.worldbank.org/html/dec/Publications/Briefs/DB17.html).

45. R. Sykes, Private and Public Partnerships in the Fight against HIV/AIDS (address to World Economic Forum, Davos, 1997) (http://www.us.unaids.org/highband/speeches/sykes).

46. *AIDS in Uganda* (World Bank, 1994), p. 3.

47. C. Madavo, speech: AIDS, Development, and the Vital Role of Government (http://worldbank.org/aids-econ/madavo.htm).

48. Piot is currently the head of UNAIDS in Geneva.

49. *World Development Report 1993: Investing in Health* (Oxford University Press, 1993), p. 20.

50. P. Piot, Business in a World of HIV/AIDS (statement at World Economic Forum, February 3, 1997, Davos) (http://www.us.unaids.org/highband/speeches/davspc.html).

51. J. Cuddington, and J. Hancock, "Assessing the impact of AIDS on the growth path of the Malawian economy," *Journal of Development Economics* 43 (1994), p. 364.

52. Ainsworth and Over, "The economic impact of AIDS on Africa," p. 567.

53. *World Development Report 1993: Investing in Health,* p. 18.

54. D. Cohen, The Economic Impact of the HIV Epidemic (Issues Paper 2, UNDP HIV and Development Programme, 1998) (http://www.undp.org:80/hiv/issues2e.htm).

55. *AIDS in Uganda* (World Bank, 1994), p. 4.

56. Myers et al., The Economic Impact of AIDS on Thailand, p. 15.

57. Ainsworth and Over, "The economic impact of AIDS on Africa," p. 568.

58. Sykes, Private and Public Partnerships in the Fight against HIV/AIDS, p. 3.

59. Lederberg et al., *Emerging Infections,* p. 58.

60. See *World Health Report 1996: Fighting Disease Fostering Development* (WHO, 1996) p. 7; Ainsworth and Over, "The economic impact of AIDS on Africa," p. 569.

61. AIDS and the Demography of Africa, p. 3.

62. Fortunately, there finally seems to be some movement on this issue now that certain pharmaceutical companies have indicated their willingness to lower the prices of some drugs so that they are affordable in the developing countries.

63. J. Chin, "The epidemiology and projected mortality of AIDS," in *Diseases and Mortality in Sub-Saharan Africa,* ed. R. Feacham and D. Jamison (Oxford University Press, 1994). See also AIDS and the Demography of Africa, p. 4.

64. See M. Viravaidya, S. Obremsky, and C. Myers, "The economic impact of AIDS on Thailand," in *Economic Implications of AIDS in Asia*, ed. D. Bloom and E. Lyons (New Delhi: UNDP, 1993); K. Hamilton, *Global HIV/AIDS* (Center for Strategic and International Studies, 1994), p. 20.

65. L. Squire, "Confronting AIDS," *Finance and Development*, March 1988, p. 17.

66. Mandela, AIDS: Facing up to the Global Threat, p. 3.

67. See The Implications of HIV/AIDS for Rural Development Policy and Programming: Focus on Sub-Saharan Africa (Study Paper 6, UNDP HIV and Development Programme) (http://www/undp.org:80/hiv/Study/SP6/sp6chap1&2. htm).

68. See J. Sender and S. Smith, *Poverty, Class and Gender in Rural Africa* (Routledge, 1990); S. Devereux and G. Eele, Monitoring the Social and Economic Impact of AIDS in East and Central Africa (Food Studies Group, Oxford University, Report Commissioned for UNDP, September 1991).

69. AIDS and the Demography of Africa, p. 4.

70. Southern Africa may be understood in this case to incorporate Botswana, Zambia, Zimbabwe, Namibia, and South Africa.

71. Ainsworth and Over, "The economic impact of AIDS on Africa," p. 570.

72. T. Barnett, and P. Blaikie, "The impact of AIDS on farming systems," in *AIDS in Africa* (Guilford, 1992), p. 151.

73. AIDS and the Demography of Africa, p. 4.

74. J. Armstrong, *Uganda's AIDS Crisis* (World Bank, 1994), p. 4.

75. The Socio-Economic Impact of HIV and AIDS on Rural families in Uganda: An Emphasis on Youth (Study Paper, UNDP HIV and Development Programme) (http://www/undp.org:80/hiv/Study/sp2Echap2.htm).

76. For example, aerial vector-borne diseases such as malaria, dengue fever, yellow fever, and various strains of encephalitis have significant negative effects on agricultural productivity throughout the tropical regions of the planet.

77. *World Development Report 1993: Investing in Health*, p. 18. Such crops include maize, wheat, and potatoes.

78. Ibid., p. 18.

79. Ibid., p. 19.

80. *Better Health in Africa* (World Bank, 1994), p. 25.

81. *World Health Report 1996: Fighting Disease Fostering Development* (WHO, 1996), p. 45.

82. Ainsworth and Over, "The economic impact of AIDS on Africa," p. 561.

83. Gerald Helleiner (personal communication, December 18, 1998) noted that 10 of the 20 agro-economists that his group had recently trained in Africa had died of HIV/AIDS within the past year.

84. Cuddington, "Modeling the macroeconomic effects of AIDS," p. 176.

85. Ibid., p. 175.

86. For an extensive review of this argument, see Dasgupta, *An Inquiry into Well Being and Destitution.*

87. *World Development Report 1993: Investing in Health*, p. 18.

88. Cuddington, "Modeling the macroeconomic effects of AIDS," p. 175.

89. See http://www.info.usaid.gov/press/spe_test/speeches/spch560.htm.

90. Ainsworth and Over, "The economic impact of AIDS on Africa," p. 571.

91. Tanzania: AIDS Assessment and Planning Study (Report 9825-TA, Population and Human Resources Division, Southern Africa Department, World Bank, 1992).

92. Cohen, The Economic Impact of the HIV Epidemic (http://www.undp.org:80/hiv/issues2e.htm).

93. See B. Nkowane, "The direct and indirect cost of HIV infection in developing countries: The cases of Zaire and Tanzania," in *The Global Impact of AIDS*, ed. A. Fleming et al. (Alan Liss, 1988); Cohen, The Economic Impact of the HIV Epidemic, p. 11.

94. AIDS and the Demography of Africa, p. 4.

95. Cohen, Case Study of Namibia, p. 16.

96. See Cohen, The Economic Impact of the HIV Epidemic (http://www.undp.org:80/hiv/issues2e.htm).

97. Myers, Obremsky, and Viravaidya, The Economic Impact of AIDS on Thailand, p. 15.

98. See A.-M. Kimball and R. Davis, "The economics of emerging infections in the Asia Pacific: What do we know and what do we need to know?" (paper presented at CIS/CIH Conference on the Social and Economic Impact of Emerging and Re-emerging Infectious Diseases, University of Toronto) (http://www.utoronto.ca/cis/pgha.html).

99. Ibid., p. 578.

100. See G. Kambou, S. Devarajan, and M. Over, "The economic impact of the AIDS crisis in Sub-Saharan Africa: Simulations with a computable general equilibrium model," *Journal of African Economies* 1, no. 1 (1992).

101. Of course, investors exhibit bounded rationality (as do policy makers) in that they do not have perfect information and in that they are subject to a host of perceptual and cognitive factors that impair perfect rationality. For an interesting discussion on the limits of rationality, see R. Jervis, *Perception and Misperception in International Politics* (Princeton University Press, 1976).

102. Cuddington, "Modeling the macroeconomic effects of AIDS, with an application to Tanzania," p. 175.

103. See Cohen, The Economic Impact of the HIV Epidemic, p. 4.

104. Ibid., p. 4.

105. Madelaine Drohan, "Major thwarts EU to protest beef ban," *Globe and Mail,* May 23, 1996.

106. "Mad cows and Englishmen," *Economist,* March 30, 1996.

107. See Kimball and Davis, "The economics of emerging infections in the Asia Pacific," p. 7.

108. Ibid., p. 8.

109. *World Health Report 1996: Fighting Disease Fostering Development,* p. 7.

110. Ibid., p. 22.

111. H. Sawert et al., "Costs and benefits of improving tuberculosis control: The case of Thailand," *Social Science and Medicine* 44, no. 12 (1997), p. 1810.

112. See USAID Factsheets (http://www.info.usaid.gov/pop_health/child_sur/malaria.htm).

113. J. Atwood, speech: Combatting Malaria (http://www.info.usaid.gov/press/spe_test/speeches/spch556.htm).

114. D. Shepard et al., "The economic cost of malaria in Africa," *Tropical Medicine and Parasitology* 42 (1991): 119–203.

115. M. Ettling and D. Shepard, "Economic cost of malaria in Rwanda," *Tropical Medicine and Parasitology* 42 (1991), p. 214.

116. *A Global Strategy for Malaria Control* (WHO, 1994), pp. 1–7.

117. U. Brinkmann and A. Brinkmann, "Malaria and health in Africa: The present situation and epidemiological trends," *Tropical Medicine and Parasitology* 42 (1991), p. 204.

118. V. Sharma, "Malaria: Cost to India and future trends," *Southeast Asian Journal of Tropical Medicine and Public Health* 27, no. 1: 4–14.

119. http://www.us.unaids.org/highband/speeches/davspc.html

120. Disaggregated, the estimated cost of individual care from HIV infection until the development of AIDS is $50,000; the estimated cost from AIDS development until death is approximately $69,000 (F. Hellinger, "The lifetime cost of treating a person with HIV, *JAMA* 270 (1993), no. 4, p. 74).

121. R. Hanvelt et al., "Indirect costs of HIV/AIDS mortality in Canada," *AIDS* 8 (1994), no. 10: F7–F11.

122. D. Lambert, "Prospects of the cost of AIDS-related death in France: 1970–2020," *Cahiers de Sociologie et de Demographie Medicales* 33 (1993), no. 3: 249–287.

123. E. Newton et al., "Modeling the HIV/AIDS epidemic in the English-speaking Caribbean, *Bulletin of the Pan American Health Organization,* 28 (1994), no. 3: 239–249.

124. D. Bloom et al., 1996, cited in Cohen, Case Study of Namibia, p. 12.

125. "Kenya faces 10% drop in GDP as result of AIDS, US study finds," *Independent Online*, July 25, 1997 (http://www.inc.co.za/online/news/politics/africa/afdigest.html).

126. World Bank, The Macroeconomic Effects of AIDS (Development Brief 17, 1993) (http://www.worldbank.org/html/dec/Publications/Briefs/DB17.html).

127. J. Dayton, World Bank HIV/AIDS Interventions: Ex-Ante and Ex-Post Evaluation (World Bank Discussion Paper 389), p. 30.

128. Cohen, Case Study of Namibia, p. 13.

129. UNAIDS Director Calls upon Business Leaders to Initiate Aggressive Efforts against AIDS (UNAIDS news release, February 3, 1997), p. 2.

130. Myers, Obremsky and Viravaidya, The Economic Impact of AIDS on Thailand, p. 8.

131. "AIDS Leading Threat to Public Health" (http://www.webpage.com/hindu/950916/18/1516c.html).

132. Piot, *Business in a World of HIV/AIDS*, p. 3.

133. UN Development Programme, *Human Development Report 1994* (Oxford University Press, 1994), p. 28.

134. Ainsworth and Over, "The economic impact of AIDS on Africa," pp. 581–583.

135. D. Cohen, The Economic Impact of the HIV Epidemic, p. 6.

136. As with many natural systems, the level of inputs into a system may cross boundaries at which the entire system suddenly and chaotically shifts, gradually establishing a new equilibrium that may be irreversible. This argument follows on Homer-Dixon's concept of "threshold" dynamics (T. Homer-Dixon, "On the threshold," pp. 43–83).

137. See Fogel, "The conquest of high mortality and hunger in Europe and America."

138. UNAIDS Director Delivers Opening Plenary at US AIDS Research Conference (press release, January 22, 1997) (http://www.us.unaids.org/highband/press/retpren.html).

139. See also N. Rosenberg, "How the developed countries became rich," *Daedalus* 123 (1994), no. 4: 127–140; N. Rosenberg and L. Birdzell, *How the West Grew Rich* (Basic Books, 1986); A. Sen, "The economics of life and death," *Scientific American,* May 1993, p. 18; World Economic Forum, *World Competitiveness Report 1992,* twelfth edition (World Economic Forum, 1992)

140. In this instance I use the term "human capital" to denote the level of education, training, literacy, knowledge, and ingenuity of an individual or a group of individuals within a society.

141. This conclusion is based on the notion that relative deprivation may lead to increasing intra-state low-intensity violence. See T. Gurr, *Why Men Rebel* (Princeton University Press, 1970); J. Goldstone, *Revolution and Rebellion in the Early*

Modern World (University of California Press, 1992); various works of T. Homer-Dixon.

Chapter 4

1. See the various works of McNeill, Oldstone, Crosby, and Watts.

2. Thucydides, *History of the Peloponnesian War* (Penguin, 1980), pp. 151–155.

3. The recent emergence of legionella, HIV, Lyme disease, and hepatitis are classic examples of disease agents whose emergence is due to changes in the human and non-human ecologies.

4. Though the topic of biological weaponry is intrinsically related to the subject at hand, I will not deal with it in this work except to note that the purposive development of pathogenic biological agents is increasingly feasible. The release of such agents into the human ecology could, of course, have catastrophic consequences for the human species over the long term.

5. See Hobbes's *Leviathan* and Rousseau's *Social Contract*.

6. R. Ullman, "Redefining security," *International Security* 8 (1983), no. 1, p. 129.

7. Ibid., p. 133.

8. This concept of disease-induced destabilization is also voiced in a recent report by the US National Intelligence Council, which echoes the argument that pathogen proliferation may impede governance and threaten state survival. See D. Gordon, The Global Infectious Disease Threat and Its Implications for the United States (National Intelligence Council document NIE 99-17D, 2000) (http://www.odci.gov/cia/publications/nie/report/nie99-17d.html).

9. See T. Gurr, *Why Men Rebel* (Princeton University Press, 1970); J. Davies, "Toward a theory of revolution," *American Sociological Review* 27 (1962), no. 1: 5–19; T. Homer-Dixon, "On the threshold: Environmental changes as causes of acute conflict," *International Security* 16 (1991), no. 2: 76–116.

10. See also P. Ehrlich and A. Ehrlich, *The Population Explosion* (Simon & Schuster, 1990); N. Myers, *Ultimate Security* (Norton, 1993); J. Matthews, "Redefining security" *Foreign Affairs* 68, no. 2 (1989): 162–177.

11. H. Eckstein, "On the etiology of internal wars," in *Why Revolution?* ed. C. Paynton and R. Blackey (Schenkman Books, 1971), pp. 128–129.

12. On the synergy between the deprivation and state failure hypotheses, see C. Kahl, "Population growth, environmental degradation, and state-sponsored violence: The case of Kenya, 1991–93," *International Security* 23 (1998), no. 2: 80–119.

13. See T. Homer-Dixon, *Environment, Scarcity, and Violence* (Princeton University Press, 1999), pp. 99–103; J. Goldstone, *Revolution and Rebellion in the Early Modern World* (University of California Press, 1991); J. Goldstone, "Population

growth and revolutionary crises," in *Theorizing Revolutions*, ed. J. Foran (Routledge, 1997).

14. K. Holsti (*The State, War, and the State of War*, Cambridge University Press, 1996, p. 23) argues that "there have been on average only 0.005 inter-state wars and armed interventions per state per year since the end of World War II. This figure contrasts to the 0.019 wars per state annually in the European states system of the eighteenth century, 0.014 in the nineteenth century, and 0.036 in the 1919–39 period." See also E. Rice, *Wars of the Third Kind* (University of California Press, 1988).

15. Holsti, *The State, War, and the State of War*, pp. 15–16.

16. See Holsti, *The State, War, and the State of War*. See also M. Ayoob, "State making, state breaking, and state failure," in *Managing Global Chaos*, ed. C. Crocker and F. Hampson (US Institute of Peace Press, 1996), p. 37.

17. At this point it is interesting to raise the prospect of a threshold effect whereby the burden of disease may reach a certain level that may "tip the scale" and accelerate processes of state failure. Greater research is needed in the form of meticulous case studies that combine both empirical analysis and process-tracing techniques to analyze precisely when these thresholds are likely to be crossed. It is likely that threshold levels will be influenced by pre-existing levels of state capacity, but they may also be affected by local socio-cultural variations.

18. See NIC report, p. 2.

19. White House, A National Security Strategy of Engagement and Enlargement, February 1996, p. 30.

20. Global Microbial Threats in the 1990s (http://www.whitehouse.gov/WH/EOP/OSTP/CISET/html/ciset.htm).

21. T. Wirth, foreword to K. Hamilton, *Global HIV/AIDS* (Center for Strategic and International Studies, 1994), p. vii.

22. Office of the Vice-President, remarks prepared for delivery by Vice-President Gore at UN Security Council Session on AIDS in Africa, January 10, 2000 (http://www.state.gov/www/global/oes/health/000110_gore_hiv-aids.html).

23. A. Price-Smith, "Ghosts of Kigali: Infectious disease and global stability in the coming century," *International Journal* 54 (1999), no. 3: 426–442.

24. D. Gordon, The Global Infectious Disease Threat and Its Implications for the United States (Report NIE 99-17D, National Intelligence Council, January 2000) (http://www.odci.gov/cia/publications/nie/report/nie99-17d.html).

25. Ibid., p. 31.

26. Ibid.

27. See W. Perry, "A pragmatic US-Russian partnership," *Defense Issues* 11 (1996), p. 97.

28. P. Kelley, "Transnational contagion and global security," *Military Review*, May-June 2000 (http://wwwcgsc.army.mil/milrev/English/MayJun00/kelley.htm).

29. D. Shalala, US Secretary of Health and Human Services, comments at Council on Foreign Relations panel "AIDS: A New Priority for International Security," New York, June 5, 2000.

30. Senator Trent Lott, comments cited in PBS radio feature "National Security Threat" (www.pbs.org/newshour/bb/health/jan-june00/aids_threat_5-2.html).

31. US National Security Advisor Samuel Berger, comments cited in "National Security Threat."

32. Kelley, "Transnational contagion and global security," p. 1.

33. Ibid, p. 2; B. Smoak et al., "Plasmodium vivax infections in US Army troops: Failure of primaquine to prevent relapses in studies from Somalia," *American Journal of Tropical Medicine and Hygiene* 56 (1997): 231–234.

34. Kelley, "Transnational contagion and global security," p. 5.

35. See A. Crosby, *Epidemic and Peace, 1918* (Greenwood, 1976); R. Collier, *The Plague of the Spanish Lady* (Allison and Busby, 1974)

36. Kelley, "Transnational contagion and global security," p. 2.

37. Karlen, *Man and Microbes,* p. 3.

38. Garret, *The Coming Plague,* pp. 537–539. For example, an Asian hantavirus variant is currently endemic in the rat population of Baltimore, and the presence of the pathogen is theoretically associated with the exceptionally high levels of terminal liver disease exhibited by the citizens of that city (source: Stephen Morse, personal communication based on work of Greg Gurri Glass, June 2000).

39. Kelley, "Transnational contagion and global security," p. 6.

40. Holbrooke, comments at comments at Council on Foreign Relations panel "AIDS: A New Priority for International Security," New York, June 5, 2000.

41. P. Ewald, *Evolution of Infectious Disease* (Oxford University Press, 1994), pp. 112–113.

42. D. Bloom and D. Canning, "The health and wealth of nations," *Science* 287 (2000), p. 1207.

43. See M. Zacher and S. Carvalho, "International Health Regulations in Historical Perspective," and D. Fidler, "Public health and international law: The impact of infectious diseases on the formation of international legal regimes, 1800–2000," both in *Plagues and Politics,* ed. A. Price-Smith (Palgrave/St. Martin's, 2001). See also M. Zacher, "Epidemiological Surveillance: International Cooperation to Monitor Infectious Diseases," in *Global Public Goods,* ed. I. Kaul et al. (Oxford University Press, 1999).

44. Stephen Morse, personal communication, February 9, 1999.

45. Lt. Col. Patrick Kelley, personal communications, 1998–99.

46. European Union Joint EU-US Action Plan (http://wwweurunion.org/partner/actplan.htm).

47. Note the extreme underestimation of the actual rate of HIV/AIDS infection, and its potential for global expansion in the Harvard/WHO study The Global Bur-

den of Disease. The spread of the pathogen has markedly outstripped even the worst-case scenario presented in that study. Similarly, the predicted decline of other infectious disease prevalence rates (with respect to non-communicable diseases) has also failed to materialize.

48. NIC estimate, p. 19.

49. Ibid.

50. K. Waltz, *Theory of International Politics* (McGraw-Hill, 1979), p. 96.

51. Holbrooke, comments at "AIDS: A New Priority for International Security."

52. M. Levy, "Is the environment a national security issue?" *International Security* 20 (1995), no. 2, p. 46.

53. Ibid.

54. In chapter 5 I discuss the relationship between environmental change and patterns of disease and vector distribution.

55. Holbrooke, comments at "AIDS: A New Priority for International Security."

Chapter 5

1. David Welch notes that, despite humanity's ever-increasing pressures on the environment during the past century, human life expectancies have risen to higher levels than ever previously recorded. This is true, but there is increasing evidence that the pendulum is reversing, particularly in areas such as sub-Saharan Africa where the burden of disease is acute. In many of these societies life expectancy is in fact falling rapidly, primarily due to HIV/AIDS and co-infection with other pathogens such as tuberculosis. (Based on author's conversation with Welch, May 23, 2000.)

2. It is important to recognize the growing volume of evidence in the medical sciences that links cancer to the presence of pathogenic organisms. The global proliferation of infectious disease has been linked to both the development of cancers and other major health problems such as heart disease and multiple sclerosis.

3. A. McMichael, *Planetary Overload: Global Environmental Change and the Health of the Human Species,* (Cambridge University Press, 1993), p. 73.

4. Intergovernmental Panel on Climate Change, *The Regional Impacts of Climate Change: An Assessment of Vulnerability* (Cambridge University Press for UNEP, 1998), p. 7.

5. *Potential Health Effects of Climatic Change* (WHO, 1990).

6. P. Reiter, Weather, Vector Biology, and Arboviral Recrudescence (http://www.ciesin.org/docs/001-387/001-378.html).

7. See M. White, Characterization of Information Requirements for Studies of CO_2 Effects: Water Resources, Agriculture, Fisheries, Forests and Human Health (http://www.ciesin.org/docs/001-235/001-235.html).

8. J. Mitchell et al., "Equilibrium climate change," in *Climate Change,* ed. J. Houghton et al. (Cambridge University Press, 1990).

9. See http://www.who.org/peh/climate/climate_%20change.html.

10. A. Haines, P. Epstein, and A. McMichael, "Global health watch: Monitoring impacts of environmental change," *Lancet* 342 (1993): 1464–1469.

11. Humidity may in fact exert differential effects on the spectrum of pathogens with various microorganisms thriving at different humidity levels.

12. See S. Tromp, *Biometeorology: The Impact of Weather and Climate on Humans and their Environment* (Heyden and Son, 1980); C. Armstrong, "Poliomyelitis and the weather," *Proceedings of the National Academy of Science* 38 (1952): 613–618.

13. See M. White, Characterization of Information Requirements for Studies of CO_2 Effects: Water Resources, Agriculture, Fisheries, Forests and Human Health (http://www.ciesin.org/docs/001-235/001-235.html).

14. J. Ford, *The Role of the Typansomiases in African Ecology: A Study of the Tsetse Fly Problem* (Clarendon, 1971).

15. White, Characterization of Information Requirements for Studies of CO_2 Effects, p. 23.

16. R. Shope, "Impacts of global climate change on human health: Spread of infectious disease," in *Global Climate Change,* ed. S. Majumdar et al. (Pennsylvania Academy of Science).

17. J. Patz, P. Epstein, T. Burke, and J. Balbus-Kornfeld, "Global climate change and emerging infectious diseases," *JAMA* 275 (1996), no. 3, p. 218.

18. M. Craig et al., "A climate-based distribution model of malaria transmission in sub-Saharan Africa," *Parasitology Today* 15 (1999): 105–111.

19. White, Characterization of Information Requirements for Studies of CO_2 Effects, p. 24.

20. Patz et al., "Global climate change and emerging infectious diseases," p. 219.

21. T. Scott et al., "Blood-feeding patterns of *Aedes Aegypti* (Diptera: Culicides) collected in a rural Thai village," *Journal of Medical Entomology* 30 (1993): 922–927.

22. D. Watts et al., "Effect of temperature on the vector efficiency of *Aedes Aegypti* for dengue 2 virus," *American Journal of Tropical Medicine and Hygiene* 86 (1987): 143–152.

23. Patz et al., "Global climate change and emerging infectious diseases," p. 217; R. Shope, "Infectious diseases and atmospheric change," in *Global Atmospheric Change and Public Health,* ed. J. White (Elsevier, 1990); J. Longstreth and J. Wiseman, "The potential impact of climate change on patterns of infectious disease in the United States," in *The Potential Effects of Global Climate Change in the United States,* ed. J. Smith and D. Tirpak (US Environmental Protection Agency, 1989), appendix G.

24. M. Loevinsohn, "Climatic warming and increased malaria incidence in Rwanda," *Lancet* 343 (1994), p. 714.

25. J. Koopman et al., "Determinants and predictors of dengue infection in Mexico," *American Journal of Epidemiology* 133 (1991): 1168–1178.

26. National Health and Medical Research Council, *Health Implications of Long Term Climatic Change* (Australian Government Printing Service, 1991).

27. McMichael, *Planetary Overload*, p. 158.

28. Conversely, in areas where water scarcity is an acute problem increased precipitation levels may improve the hygienic quality of local water supplies.

29. White, Characterization of Information Requirements, p. 23.

30. McMichael, *Planetary Overload*, p. 159.

31. R. Shope, "Global climate change and infectious diseases," *Environmental Health Perspectives* 96 (1992): 171–174.

32. J. Gillett, "Direct and indirect influences of temperature on the transmission of parasites from insects to man," in *The Effects of Meteorological Factors upon Parasites*, ed. A. Taylor and R. Muller (Blackwell, 1974).

33. See A. McMichael et al., eds., *Climate Change and Human Health* (WHO, 1996), p. 220.

34. Shope, "Global climate change and infectious diseases," p. 367.

35. P. Liehne, Climatic Influences on Mosquito-Borne Diseases in Australia (http://www.ciesin.org/docs/001-485/001-485.html).

36. P. Whetton, "Implications of climate change due to the enhanced greenhouse effect on floods and droughts in Australia," *Climatic Change,* 25 (1993): 289–317; T. Karl et al., "Trends in US climate during the 20th century," *Consequences* 1 (1995), no. 3: 8–12.

37. Based on interview with Paul Epstein of Harvard Medical School, September 26, 1999.

38. R. Wenzel, "A new hantavirus infection in North America," *New England Journal of Medicine* 330, no. 14: 1004–1005; R. Stone, "The mouse–pinon nut connection," *Science* 262 (1993), p. 833.

39. National Health and Medical Research Council, *Health Implications of Long Term Climatic Change* (Australian Government Printing Service, 1991).

40. See http://www.jhu.edu/~climate/health.html.

41. W. Stevens, "Warmer, wetter, sicker: Linking climate to health," *New York Times,* August 10, 1998 (late edition).

42. L. Mearns, "Implications of global warming for climate variability and the occurrence of extreme climate events," in *Drought Assessment, Management, and Planning*, ed. D. Wilhite (Kluwer, 1998).

43. Patz et al., "Global climate change and emerging infectious diseases," p. 221.

44. P. Epstein, *Extreme Weather Events: The Health and Economic Consequences of the 1997/98 El Niño and La Niña* (Center for Health and the Global Environment, Harvard Medical School, 1999), p. 5.

45. See http://www.who.org/inf-fs/en/fact192.html.

46. M. Bouma et al., "Climate change and periodic epidemic malaria," *Lancet* 343 (1994), p. 1440; A. McMichael et al., eds., *Climate Change and Human Health* (WHO/WMO/UNEP, 1996); P. Epstein et al., "Climate and cisease in Colombia," *Lancet* 46 (1995): 1243–1244.

47. This is due to the fact that certain vector species thrive under differential precipitation levels. See http://www.who.org/inf-fs/en/fact192.html.

48. Patz et al., "Global climate change and emerging infectious diseases," p. 221.

49. N. Nicholls, "El Niño-southern oscillation and vector-borne disease," *Lancet* 342 (1993): 1284–1285.

50. M. Glants, R. Katz, and R. Nicholls, eds., *Teleconnections Linking Worldwide Climate Anomalies* (Cambridge University Press, 1991).

51. G. MacDonald, "The analysis of malaria epidemics," *Tropical Disease Bulletin*, 50 (1954): 871–892.

52. J. Zulueta, "Malaria control and long-term periodicity of the disease in Pakistan," *Transactions of the Royal Society of Tropical Medicine and Hygiene* 74 (1980): 624–632.

53. Glants et al., *Teleconnections Linking Worldwide Climate Anomalies*, p. 55

54. *Weekly Epidemiological Record*, no. 20, May 15, 1998, p. 148.

55. Source: EPA Web site (URL now obsolete).

56. Source: EPA Web site (URL now obsolete).

57. E. Ross, "Scientists again link El Niño to health problem," Associated Press, February 4, 2000 (http://phillynews.com/inquirer/2000/Feb/04/national/NINO04.htm).

58. M. Macan-Makar, "Health: Diarrheal diseases linked to El Niño," Inter Press Service, February 7, 2000.

59. P. Epstein, Saving Scarce Public Health Resources and Saving Lives: Health Sector Applications of Climate Forecasting (http://www.noaa.gov/ogp/Ensoarcl2.html).

60. See htttp://www.who.org/inf-fs/en/fact192.html.

61. Ibid.

62. Ibid.

63. P. Epstein et al., Global Change and Human Health: The 1997–98 ENSO and its Impacts on Disease and Fire Occurrences (Region 4: Asia) (http://chge32.med.harvard. du/emso/asiaprt.html).

64. D. Engelthaler et al., "Climatic and environmental patterns associated with hantavirus pulmonary syndrome, Four Corners region, United States," *Emerging Infectious Diseases* 5 (1999), no. 1, p. 3.

65. See S. Nichol et al., "Genetic identification of a novel hantavirus associated with an outbreak of acute respiratory illness in the southwestern United States," *Science* 262 (1993): 615–618 ; J. Childs et al., "A household-based, case-control study of environmental factors associated with hantavirus pulmonary syndrome in the southwestern United States," *American Journal of Tropical Medicine and Hygiene* 52 (1995): 393–397; R. Parmenter et al., The hantavirus epidemic in the southwest: Rodent population dynamics and the implications for transmission of hantavirus-associated adult respiratory distress syndrome (HARDS) in the Four Corners region (Publication 41, Sevilleta Long-Term Ecological Research Program, Department of Biology, University of New Mexico, Albuquerque, 1993).

66. WHO, *World Health Report 1996*, p. 39.

67. Patz et al., "Global climate change and emerging infectious diseases," p. 220.

68. McMichael, *Planetary Overload*, p. 155. See also Gillett, "Direct and indirect influences of temperature on the transmission of parasites from insects to man" and WHO, Potential Health Effects of Climate Change: Report of a WHO Task Group (Document WHO/PEP/90/10, WHO, Geneva, 1990).

69. See M. El Alamy and B. Cline, "Prevalence and intensity of *Schistosoma haematobium* and *S. mansoni* infection in Qalyub, Egypt," *American Journal of Tropical Medicine and Hygiene* 26 (1997): 470–472; M. Abdel-Wahab, *Schistosomiasis in Egypt* (CRC Press, 1982).

70. D. Thompson et al., "Bancroftian filariasis distribution and diurnal temperature differences in the southern Nile delta," *Emerging Infectious Diseases* 2 (1996), no. 3 (http://www.cdc.gov/ncidod/eid/vol2no3/thompson.htm).

71. B. Gryseels et al., "Epidemiology, immunology and chemotherapy of *Schistoma mansoni* infections in a recently exposed community in Senegal," *Tropical Geographic Medicine* 46 (1994): 209–219.

72. See W. Cort et al., *Researches on Hookworm in China* (Johns Hopkins University Press, 1926); E. Faust and H. Meleney, *Studies on* Schistosomiasis Japonica (Johns Hopkins University Press, 1924).

73. P. Hotez et al., "Emerging and reemerging helminthiases and the public health of China" *Emerging Infectious Diseases* 3 (1997), no. 3, p. 1. See also S. Yu, "Control of parasitic diseases in China, current status and prospects," *Chinese Medical Journal*, 109, 1996; pp. 259–65.

74. Ibid., p. 7.

75. B. Lilley et al., "An increase in hookworm infection temporally associated with ecologic change," *Emerging Infectious Diseases* 3 (1997), no. 3 (http://www.cdc.gov/ncidod/eid/vol3no3/lilley.htm).

76. Ewald, *Evolution of Infectious Disease*, p. 205.

77. A. Mobarak, "The schistosomiasis problem in Egypt," *American Journal of Tropical Medicine and Hygiene* 31 (1982) 87–91; D. Bradley "Environmental and health problems of developing countries," in *Environmental Change and Human Health*, ed. J. Lake et al. (Wiley, 1993).

78. H. Van der Schalie, "Aswan Dam revisited," *Environment* 16 (1974): 237–242.

79. Patz et al., "Global climate change and emerging infectious diseases," p. 220.

80. G. Daily and P. Ehrlich, Development, Global Change, and the Epidemiological Environment (http://dieff.com/page108.htm).

81. Ewald, *Evolution of Infectious Disease,* p. 206.

82. D. Sawyer, "Economic and social consequences of malaria in new colonization projects in Brazil," *Social Science and Medicine* 37 (1993): 1131–1136; P. McGreevy et al., "Effects of immigration on the prevalence of malaria in rural areas of the Amazon basin of Brazil," *Memorial Instituto Oswaldo Cruz* 84 (1989): 485–491.

83. R. Sutherst, "Arthropods as disease vectors in a changing environment," in *Environmental Change and Human Health,* ed. J. Lake et al. (Wiley, 1993).

84. S. Morse, ed., *Emerging Viruses* (Oxford University Press, 1993).

85. M. Wilson et al., eds., *Disease in Evolution: Global Changes and the Emergence of Infectious Disease* (New York Academy of Sciences, 1994), p. 7.

86. F. Black, "Measles endemicity in insular populations: Critical community size and its implications," *Journal of Theoretical Biology* 11 (1966): 207–211.

87. G. Daily and P. Ehrlich, Development, Global Change, and the Epidemiological Environment (http://dieoff.com/page108.htm).

88. G. MacDonald, "The analysis of equilibrium in Malaria," *Tropical Diseases Bulletin* 47 (1952): 907–915; R. May and R. Anderson, "The population biology of infectious diseases, part II," *Nature* 280 (1979): 455–461.

89. M. Bartlett, "The critical community size for measles in the United States," *Journal of the Royal Statistical Society* 123 (1960): 37–44.

90. I. Humphry-Smith et al., "Evaluation of mechanical transmission of HIV by the African soft tick," *Ornithodorous moubata, AIDS* 7, no. 1: 341–347.

91. Ewald, *Evolution of Infectious Disease.*

92. Wilson et al., *Disease in Evolution,* p. 4.

93. A. Azad et al., "Flea-borne Richettsioses: Ecologic considerations," *Emerging Infectious Diseases* 3 (1997), no. 3, p. 1.

94. Ibid., p. 1.

95. J. Mackenzie, "Emerging viral diseases: An Australian perspective," *Emerging Infectious Diseases* 5 (1999), no. 1, p. 2.

96. D. Gubler, "Resurgent vector-borne diseases as a global public health problem," *Emerging Infectious Diseases* 4 (1998), no. 3, p. 7.

97. M. Molina and F. Rowland, "Stratospheric sink for choro-fluoro-methanes: Chlorine atom catalyzed destruction of ozone," *Nature* 249 (1974): 810–814.

98. J. Kerr and C. McElroy, "Evidence for large upward trends of ultraviolet-B radiation linked to ozone depletion," *Science* 262 (1998) 1032–1034.

99. H. Taylor et al., "Effects of ultraviolet radiation on cataract formation," *New England Journal of Medicine* 319 (1988): 1429–1433; *Solar and Ultraviolet Radiation* (International Agency for Research on Cancer, 1992).

100. *Solar and Ultraviolet Radiation;* K. Cooper et al., "UV exposure reduces immunization rates and promotes tolerance to epicutaneous antigens in humans," *Proceedings of the National Academy of Sciences* 89 (1992): 8497–8501; W. Morison, "Effects of ultraviolet radiation on the immune system in humans," *Photochemical Photobiology* 50 (1989): 515–524; J. Van der Luen et al., eds., Environmental Effects of Ozone Depletion: 1991 Update (UN Environment Programme, 1991).

101. McMichael, *Planetary Overload*, p. 192.

102. Van der Luen et al., Environmental Effects of Ozone Depletion.

103. J. Lederberg, "Infectious disease as an evolutionary paradigm," *Emerging Infectious Diseases* 3 (1997), no. 4, p. 6.

104. Ewald, *Evolution of Infectious Disease;* Wilson et al., *Disease in Evolution;* S. Levy, "The challenge of antibiotic resistance," *Scientific American* 278 (1998): 46–55; S. Olshansky et al., "Infectious diseases-New and ancient threats to world health," *Population Bulletin* 52, no. 2: 1–52.

105. I. Okeke et al., "Socioeconomic and behavioural factors leading to acquired bacterial resistance to antibiotics in developing countries," *Emerging Infectious Diseases* 5 (1999), no. 1: 1–14.

106. J. Lederberg, "Emerging infections: An evolutionary perspective," *Emerging Infectious Diseases* 4 (1998), no. 3.

107. Daily and Ehrlich, Development, Global Change, and the Epidemiological Environment, p. 8.

108. S. Levy, *The Antibiotic Paradox* (Plenum, 1992); S. Holmberg et al., "Drug-resistant *Salmonella* from animals fed antimicrobials," *New England Journal of Medicine* 311 (1984): 617–622.

109. F. Meslin, "Global aspects of emerging and potential zoonoses: A WHO perspective," *Emerging Infectious Diseases* 3 (1997), no. 2, p. 6.

110. See F. Cartwright, *Disease and History* (Hart-Davis, 1972).

111. "Rediscovering wormwood: Qinghaosu for malaria" (editorial), *Lancet* 339 (1992): 649–650.

112. P. Principe, *The Economic Value of Biological Diversity among Medicinal Plants* (Organization for Economic Cooperation and Development, 1988).

113. See http://www.ran.org/ran/info_center/factsheets/05f.html. See also M. Plotkin, "The outlook for new agricultural and industrial products from the tropics," in *Biodiversity*, ed. E. Wilson (National Academy Press, 1988); C. Caufield, *In the Rainforest* (University of Chicago Press, 1984); N. Farnsworth, "Screening plants for new medicines," in *Biodiversity*, ed. Wilson.

114. P. Raven and J. McNeely, "Biological extinction: Its scope and meaning for us," in *Protection of Global Biodiversity*, ed. L. Guruswamy and J. McNeely (Duke University Press, 1998), p. 22.

115. See J. Lederberg, R. Shope, and S. Oaks, eds., *Emerging Infections: Microbial Threats to Health in the United States* (National Academy Press, 1992).

116. W. Darrow et al., "The social origins of AIDS: Social change, sexual behavior, and disease trends," in *The Social Dimensions of AIDS*, ed. D. Feldman and T. Johnson (Praeger, 1993).

117. For a detailed account of airline-based travel's role in the emergence of HIV/ AIDS, see R. Shilts, *And the Band Played On: Politics, People and the AIDS Epidemic* (St. Martin's, 1987).

118. Mackenzie, "Emerging viral diseases," pp. 3–4.

119. G. Aviles et al., "Dengue reemergence in Argentina," *Emerging Infectious Diseases 5* (2000), no. 4: 1–7.

120. See World Health Organization, "Smallpox: Yugoslavia," *Weekly Epidemiological Record* 47 (1972): 161–162.

121. P. Moore et al., "Intercontinental spread of an epidemic group A *Neisseria meningitidis* strain," *Lancet* 338 (1991): 260–263.

122. M. Wilson, "Travel and the Emergence of Infectious Diseases," *Emerging Infectious Diseases* 1 (1995), no. 2, p. 1.

123. See the works of William McNeill, Alfred Crosby, Michael Oldstone, and Sheldon Watts.

124. A. Grubler and N. Nakicenovic, *Evolution of Transport Systems* (ILASA, 1991).

125. Goma Epidemiology Group, "Public health impact of Rwandan refugee crisis: what happened in Goma, Zaire in July 1994?" *Lancet* 345 (1995): 339–344.

126. W. McNeill, *Plagues and People* (Doubleday, 1989), pp. 102–105.

127. R. Taylor, "Epidemiology," in *Yellow Fever*, ed. G. Strode (McGraw-Hill, 1971), p. 442.

128. L. Garrett, *The Coming Plague* (Farrar, Strauss and Giroux, 1994), p. 67.

129. See S. Morse, *Emerging Viruses* (Oxford University Press, 1991); P. Reiter and D. Sprenger, "The used tire trade: A mechanism for the worldwide dispersal of container breeding mosquitoes," *Journal of the American Mosquito Control Association* 33 (1987): 494–501.

130. See A. Matson, "The history of malaria in Nandi," *East African Medical Journal* 34 (1957): 431–441.

131. P. Garnham, "The incidence of malaria at high altitudes," *Journal of the National Malaria Society* 7 (1948): 275–284.

132. M. Malakooti, "Reemergence of epidemic malaria in the highlands of western Kenya," *Emerging Infectious Diseases* 4 (1998), no. 4, p. 2.

133. McMichael, *Planetary Overload*, p. 7.

134. See E. Hargrove, *Foundations of Environmental Ethics* (Prentice-Hall, 1989)

135. McMichael, *Planetary Overload*, p. 48.

136. J. Lederburg, "Infectious disease as an evolutionary paradigm," *Emerging Infectious Diseases* 3 (1997), no. 4, p. 6.

137. Interview with Paul Ewald, March 28, 2000. For a deeper understanding of Ewald's persuasive arguments, see P. Ewald, *Evolution of Infectious Disease* (Oxford University Press), 1994.

138. Ewald, *Evolution of Infectious Disease*

139. IPCC Regional Impacts of Climate Change: An Assessment of Vulnerability Summary for Policymakers (http://www.usgcrp.gov/ipcc/html/RISPM.html).

Conclusion

1. Of course, this assumes that states seek more than just survival and power. Liberalism argues, correctly, that states seek prosperity and stability in addition to survival and security.

2. This conclusion is based on the aforementioned negative empirical association between infectious disease and SC. The statistical evidence shows that the arguments of historians such as McNeill, Crosby, Zinsser, Watts, and Oldstone (linking plagues with the collapse of empires and societies) are likely accurate. See Oldstone, *Viruses, Plagues and History.*

3. In view of South Africa's soaring HIV and tuberculosis prevalence rates, it may in fact be too late for a successful anti-HIV intervention in that country.

4. See Holsti, *The State, War, and the State of War.* See also Migdal's *Strong Societies and Weak States* and the various works of Goldstone and Homer-Dixon.

5. The construction of a global ERID surveillance and containment regime requires significant investments to be made, and maintained, in the health infrastructure of all states to permit the diagnosis and treatment of disease on a global scale. This is no mean feat when one considers that the only facility in the world with a 100% rate of pathogen diagnosis is the CDC. The central diagnostic laboratories in other developed countries like Canada, France, and Britain only succeeded in correctly identifying 50% of the pathogens sent to them in a recent test by the CDC. See Garret, *The Coming Plague,* p. 606.

6. See D. Fidler, "Microbialpolitik: Infectious diseases and international relations," *American University International Law Review* 14 (1998), no. 1: 1–53; "The future of the World Health Organization: What role for international law?" *Vanderbilt Journal of Transnational Law* 31 (1998), no. 5: 43–86.

Index